The Curriculum of the Future

For
Alice
and
Elinor

The Curriculum of the Future
From the 'New Sociology of Education' to a Critical Theory of Learning

Michael F.D. Young

RoutledgeFalmer
Taylor & Francis Group

LONDON AND NEW YORK

First published in 1998
By Falmer Press.
Reprinted 2003
By RoutledgeFalmer
11 New Fetter Lane, London, EC4P 4EE

Transferred to Digital Printing 2003

A catalogue record for this book is available from the British Library

ISBN 0 7507 0789 5 cased
ISBN 0 7507 0788 7 paper

Library of Congress Cataloging-in-Publication Data are available on request

Jacket design by Caroline Archer

Typeset in 10/12 pt Garamond by
Graphicraft Limited, Hong Kong
Printed and bound by Antony Rowe Ltd, Eastbourne

Contents

Acknowledgments

Writing a book is both an isolating and a deeply social experience. This has been especially true of this book as it covers such a large part of my academic life. Full acknowledgment to all the many people who have influenced me is therefore impossible. However, if I go back to the 1960s, when I began studying sociology, certain people stand out as having been particularly important in the development of my ideas. Among these were Stephen Cotgrove, then Head of Sociology at Regent Street Polytechnic (where I was a part-time student) and later Professor of Sociology at the University of Bath, and Geoffrey Hawthorn, Roland Robertson and Dorothy Smith at the University of Essex, where I studied for an MA. At Essex and later at the Institute of Education, I learned much of lasting value from Basil Bernstein and, in particular, that there could (and should) be a sociology of the curriculum. Despite the later divergence of our intellectual paths, I find myself returning to the issues which he raised in the early 1970s and is still exploring today.

Knowledge and Control, the book which I edited in 1971, was very much a collaborative effort. The idea for it grew out of discussions with Basil Bernstein and Pierre Bourdieu following the 1970 British Sociological Association Annual Conference and was developed during the MA course in Sociology of Education at the Institute of Education. The book would have been impossible without Geoff Esland's vision and Nell Keddie's (1971) remarkable study, *Classroom Knowledge*, which became the most widely read chapter in the book. The 1970s were a special time to be teaching the sociology of education to practising teachers and I owe a special debt to my first group of students, especially Ian Hextall and Ralph Williams and to Geoff Whitty, John Beck, Richard Winter, Denis Gleeson and many others who were excited by the possibilities opened up by the sociology of knowledge and who shared their experience of trying to find a way beyond its relativist pitfalls. I learned much in collaborating with Geoff Whitty in the late 1970s on two books which significantly extended the scope of sociological approaches to the curriculum.

I am deeply grateful for the inspiration and support which I have received from David Layton, now Emeritus Professor of Science Education at the University of Leeds. It was his study of the beginnings of school science in England, *Science for the People* (Layton, 1973), which helped me to link the sociology of the curriculum to my previous experience as a science teacher (Young, 1973; 1976). More than anyone, he saw and argued for the relevance of a sociological approach to those working in science and technology education.

As has often been said, the 1980s were not easy years for the sociology of education and certainly that was my experience. It was attacked by the Conservative governments of the time on the grounds that it made young teachers too critical, and it was undermined from within by its own disputes and divisions. By the mid 1980s, however, I had the opportunity to think about the curriculum from a quite new and more practical perspective — through my role as Chair of Governors of Kingsway College of Further Education in central London. I was most fortunate that the Principal of Kingsway College at the time was Fred Flower. An outstanding educationist, he saw that the educational possibilities of relating the curriculum to the world of work could be taken far beyond the narrow confines of vocational education.

For the opportunity to establish the Post-16 Education Centre at the Institute of Education in 1985 and to launch a whole new area of research and teaching at the Institute, I have much to thank Denis Lawton. As Deputy Director of the Institute of Education, he not only asked me to be responsible for the Centre and later, as Director, gave it his full support, but he introduced me to Tom Dodd, then an Adviser for the Employment Department, who supported the Centre unstintingly from 1987 to 1991 and made possible the appointment of Ken Spours and later Annette Hayton and Andy Green. All have been a continuing source of intellectual support to me. The joint work on the 14–19 curriculum that I have undertaken with Ken Spours, which began in 1988, has been of particular importance and led to our involvement in writing the IPPR Report, *A British Baccalaureate* (Finegold et al., 1990), which continues to set the terms for much of the debate on the post compulsory curriculum.

During the last decade, I have also had the opportunity to develop links with researchers in other countries. These links have given me valuable opportunities to share ideas with Adrienne Bird, Linda Chisholm, Jean Gamble, Judy Harris, Peter Kallaway, André Kraak, Joe Muller and others in South Africa, with Teresinha Froes Burnham, Menge Ludke and Flavio Moreira in Brazil, with Ari Antikainen, Anya Heikkinnen and Johanna Lasonen in Finland and with Amparo Tome in Spain.

I have many debts to colleagues at the Institute of Education. Members of the Post 16 Education Centre include not only those already mentioned, who joined the Centre in its early days, but also Louise Baines, Bryan Cunningham, David Guile, Mary Hill, Ann Hodgson, Vicky James, Tom Leney, Norman Lucas, Jeremy McDonald, Andrew Morris (now with FEDA) and Alan Shaffer. From other parts of the Institute of Education, I would like to thank Bob Cowen, Michael Barnett, Gerald Grace, Gunther Kress, Diana Leonard, Ingrid Lunt, Brahm Norwich, Margaret Spencer, Elaine Unterhalter, Geoff Whitty and Alison Wolf. Peter Mortimore, the present Director, has always been supportive, especially in the last year when this book finally took shape. The Institute remains a remarkable place where something exciting is always going on. We constantly complain about it but most of us love it and would be reluctant to work anywhere else.

I would also like to thank colleagues from other universities in the UK: David Raffe and Cathy Howieson of the Centre for Educational Sociology at the University of Edinburgh, with whom I have worked on the ESRC-funded Unified Learning Project, Inge Bates at Leeds, Phil Hodgkinson at Manchester Metropolitan, Sally Inman at Goldsmiths College, Ian Jamieson at Bath, Ewart Keep at Warwick, Anne Sassoon at Kingston, Helen Rainbird at Nene College, Harold Silver at Plymouth and Lorna Unwin and William Richardson at Sheffield.

Books are not only a product of *working* with colleagues when, as has so often, they are also friends. They also depend on the *support* of friends who, although not directly involved, are no less important. For being such good friends over many years, I would particularly like to thank Charmian and Cyril Cannon, Ian Hextall, Jack Mallinson and Barbara and John Marshall.

It has required hope and optimism to bring this book to completion and the main source of that optimism has been my two daughters, Alice and Elinor. Being a parent has taught me more about education than I could have imagined. However, hope and optimism are not enough. To write a book one also needs self belief. For believing in me, and for much else, I owe more than words to Toni Griffiths; without her, there would be no book.

Michael Young
London
January 1998

Introduction

This book is first and foremost a study in critical curriculum theory. It is based on papers published over a period of 25 years, although all but two were in fact written in the last decade. They were originally presented to very different audiences in countries as far removed as Finland, Australia, the United States and Chile as well as this country. They have therefore been extensively revised for this book. Readers will find that a number of themes recur but I hope they will find this justified as a way of ensuring that the concreteness of the arguments in the different chapters is retained and the overall argument of the book strengthened. The sections of the book reflect three distinct foci of my work over the period as whole and, in the case of Section 1, a distinct period of my professional life.

At the core of the chapters in Section 1 is the question of knowledge in the secondary school curriculum, in teacher education and in society. The assertion by sociologists that all knowledge is socially produced for particular purposes in particular contexts is by now relatively uncontentious. However, does this mean that what counts as knowledge in society or what is selected to be included in the curriculum at a particular time is no more than what those in positions of power decide to be knowledge? Chapter 1 puts the case for this argument and Chapters 2 and 3 outline some of the problems to which it gave rise in what became known as the 'new sociology of education' of the early 1970s.

The chapters in Section 2 begin with changes in the organization of work and the role of qualifications and how since the early 1980s both have shaped debates about the post-compulsory curriculum. The period was one when in the UK economic changes were forcing a whole new section of each cohort of 16 year olds into full-time education and when educational policy was increasingly driven by economic pressures to make more and more of them obtain qualifications. The assumption has been that, whereas the curriculum for the minority (although now a much larger minority) which goes on to university could stay relatively unchanged, for the rest the curriculum must be linked as closely as possible to their future employability, regardless of whether or not this is related to actual jobs. Section 2 begins with a chapter based on a paper first written in 1988 when academic subject teachers in secondary schools were beginning to feel that their role was being undermined by the wave of new pre-vocational programmes. The remaining chapters in Section 2 represent a sustained attempt to develop a model of the post-compulsory curriculum of the future in response to the massive economic changes being experienced by all western countries. The educational context was dominated since the early 1980s by the attempts by successive Conservative governments to maintain divisions between academic and vocational learning and siphon off as many young people as possible into vocational education and training programmes, thus excluding them in effect from access to the understandings they would need in the future as adults in an increasingly complex and uncertain society.

The chapters in Section 3 are based on papers which, when originally published, overlapped in time with those which form the basis of many of the chapters in Section 2. However, they represent a more recent development in my own thinking and interests as I have tried to locate the knowledge and curriculum issues in current debates about the possibility of a learning society. The section begins in Chapter 10 with a critical review of the idea of a learning society and its curriculum implications. Three related arguments that are implicit in ideas such as the learning society run through each of the chapters. First, there are real social changes underlying the recent interest in ideas such as lifelong learning and a learning society despite the frequently ideological and rhetorical character that they have taken (Strain and Field, 1997). Second, this means, that although more importance must be given to learning at work, learning outside school and in adult life generally, the crucial implication of this shift in emphasis for educational policy and theory is the new relationships between school and non-school learning which need to be developed. The third argument is that learning is too important to be left to those learning theorists whose mistaken assumption is that learning is an individual phenomenon that must be abstracted from the contexts in which it takes place so that it can be a topic for specialized psychological study. The chapters in Section 3 begin to explore the implications of the alternative view that learning is a socially situated process which takes place in the context of organizational and broader social changes.

Although there is a continuity in the aims of the chapters of this book, there are quite explicit changes in their theoretical basis. These changes are a result of the lessons of reflecting critically on the early work and of developing some understanding of the real social changes that have taken place in industrial societies since the beginning of the 1970s. The chapters in Section 1 draw on the ideas that informed what became known as the 'new sociology of education'. As I point out in Chapter 3, these developments were influenced by an eclectic set of ideas, although this only became apparent with hindsight. They are best described as several varieties of social constructivism which at the time included social phenomenology, symbolic interactionism and Deweyian sociology of knowledge but which now also include both Vygotskian psychology and cognitive anthropology. What is striking in retrospect, and what is perhaps most noticeable to the reader, is that beyond a radical though somewhat over-generalized critique of the inequalities of western capitalist society, this tradition in the sociology of education had no clear theory of society or social change. It may well be that this was why the Marxist sociologies of education of the late 1970s and early 1980s had a longer life, although they were to be even more fundamentally undermined when the Soviet system in Eastern Europe collapsed at the end of the 1980s.

The focus on knowledge and the curriculum continues in Section 2 but the chapters reflect two fundamental changes in emphasis. First, the papers on which the chapters are based were written primarily as an intervention in the policy debates of the late 1980s and early 1990s. They were not, as was the case with the 'new sociology of education' discussed in Section 1, initially part of a dialogue with other academic colleagues. This partly reflected a shift in my own priorities and partly the fact that, with notable exceptions (Whitty, 1986), knowledge and the curriculum issues were no longer at the centre of debates in the sociology of education. The chapters in Section 2 are, therefore, critical analyses of aspects of curriculum policy and practice rather than challenges to other theories, at least not explicitly. Second, unlike the early chapters, those in Section 2 *are* dependent on a theory of society or, rather, of social change. This claim may appear contradictory, given the less narrowly academic and disciplinary context in which they were written. However, the aim of the papers was to influence policy and without at least some theory of the forces underlying changes in society and the different policy options they point to, it is difficult to see how a plausible case for alternative policies could be made.

The theory of social change which informs the chapters in Section 2 and which is outlined explicitly in Chapter 5 is that associated with the concepts of post-Fordism and flexible specialization and found in the socio-economic ideas of Piore and Sabel (1984), Murray (1988) and Mathews (1989). All these writers argue that western capitalist societies are not collapsing but are at the end of an era when mass production dominated most aspects of economic life. They do not suggest that the emerging forms of capitalism are necessarily more benign but that the new era needs new analyses and creates new opportunities for debates about policy and practice. The significance of these ideas for those working in the field of post-compulsory education was that the core issue identified by these researchers was changes in the organization of work under the dual impact of global competition and the opportunities offered by the new information technology. The outcome, it was argued, was a gradual shift from material to human resource-based production and services (Brown and Lauder, 1991). As with any ideas that point to a future emerging from the present, these theories tended to over-emphasize the new forms of production and work when, in practice, older forms were still dominant. However, if new concepts of work and production are emerging, albeit under specific conditions, and they do represent possibilities for the future (and there is at least some evidence for this), then such seemingly commonplace and uncontentious notions as qualification, skill and knowledge and the traditional division between academic and vocational learning, can never be the same again. It is the curriculum implications of these possibilities as well as resistances to them that are explored in the chapters in Section 2.

As implied earlier, the chapters in Section 3 reflect a further change in theoretical emphasis. Post-Fordism and flexible specialization are 'powerful ideas but are limited in their application to education by being primarily economic in origin. They deal in only a partial way with questions about knowledge, learning and the changing role of educational organizations, such as schools and universities. The chapters in Section 3, and more explicitly in the case of Chapters 11 and 12, draw upon the 'reflexive modernization' thesis (Beck, Giddens and Lash, 1994) as one way of conceptualizing current changes in industrial societies and demonstrate why learning needs to have a central place in responding to them. These authors argue that the premises and contours of traditional industrial society and its associated organizational forms are breaking up and 'pathways' or opportunities for new forms of organization are emerging. They argue that a shift from 'wealth' to 'risk' production is taking place and that, once modern societies and organizations begin to understand the risks they produce, opportunities are created for them to reflect upon themselves which begin to point to new kinds of learning relationships between organizations and new ways of conceptualizing their roles. The chapters in Section 3 begin to explore the educational implications of these ideas. The remainder of this introduction outlines what this might mean for a critical curriculum theory that is relevant to the curriculum of the future.

Referring to this book as a study in **critical** curriculum theory is not primarily a way of asserting a set of political priorities nor of identifying myself with a specific theoretical perspective. Critical theories, although usually showing some acknowledgment of the Frankfurt School and the writing of Horkheimer, Adorno and Habermas take on increasingly diverse forms; furthermore, a critical theory is not necessarily a good theory. Like any other theories, critical theories can be successful or not in what they set out to do. What distinguishes **critical** curriculum theories from other types of curriculum theory is, as I argue at the beginning of Chapter 12, that they are theories about curriculum policies and practice which recognize that their aim is both understanding *and* change. In other words, critical theories involve purposes because their point of origin is education as a form of purposeful action and any purposeful activity such as education cannot simply be the subject of understanding alone. However, understanding the post-compulsory curriculum becomes meaningful if that understanding has a role in changing it in a way that extends the quality and quantity of learning opportunities. Such a view of a critical curriculum theory and its relation to policy and practice involves a dialogue with policy makers and practitioners as well as other researchers. It involves establishing some shared purposes between researchers in the universities whose role it is to develop theories and those in government, state agencies and the schools who have the power to implement policy, and others, such as employers, parents and trades unionists, who have a role in shaping the climate of educational debate.

A lack of awareness of the context of implementation of alternatives was one of the weaknesses of the 'new sociology of education' discussed in Section 1. It developed an analysis and a critique, it challenged what policy makers and practitioners took for granted and it offered explanations for why the dominant form of the curriculum was 'as it was'. However, although it argued for a curriculum based on a less stratified view of knowledge which valued more types of learning, it offered no realistic alternatives and had no ideas about how any changes might be implemented; in other words, it had no model of a curriculum of the future. The result was that many people rejected the whole approach and an important truth was lost, namely that curriculum knowledge is socially and historically produced and changeable and what individual teachers do and, even more, the assumptions they make about knowledge, do matter in terms of the learning they encourage in the class-room. What teachers can achieve is not just determined either by the givenness of knowledge structures or by the vast, impersonal forces of history; that givenness is shaped, at least in part, by what teachers do in their classrooms and in their wider professional roles — although not, of course, by them alone.

The idea that knowledge is socially stratified in society and in school that is introduced in Chapter 1 is powerful — unless it is seen as a total description of the origins and structure of the curriculum, when it becomes naive and misleading. The argument which I hope comes through the first three chapters is simple and in some sense obvious, even if often forgotten. It is that, whereas the curriculum is always partly designed to enable students to acquire concepts and forms of understanding and learn how to apply them in different contexts, it is also always organized to preserve vested interests and maintain the status quo. Developing the curriculum of the future depends on building on this insight. It involves being willing consistently to question the extent to which any curriculum is based more on the preservation of 'interests' than on promoting learning. It also involves asking whether a particular form of curriculum organization, such as that based on school subjects, provides reliable frameworks for young people to make sense of the world they face or the extent to which it is primarily a leftover of past traditions which have come to be seen as the only way of organizing knowledge. What, then, should be the principles of the curriculum of the future?

The curriculum principle that has emerged most clearly for me in preparing this book for publication is best expressed as a form of dialectic. I do not use this term in any deep philosophical sense but as a recognition that critique is only the starting point of analysis and not itself a theory. I mean this in two senses. First, any critique of the prevailing curriculum has to recognize that it will always embody conflicting purposes. These invariably take the form of regressions to the past and possibilities for the future. On the other hand, it is equally important not to fall into the trap that radicals can set for themselves of equating the past with what is bad and the future with what is good; this can easily become little more than the mirror image of a conservative position and even less defensible. The second sense in which critique can only be a starting point is based on rejecting what I see as an irresponsible view that intellectuals can only remind everyone else that the social world is produced by human beings and 'things could, at least in principle, always be otherwise'.

The logic of this position is that any kind of planned social change is imposs-ible as various contingent factors, such as inertia and interest will inevitably get in the way. It is difficult to see what rationale for theory or even for the university might follow from such a view, except the contradictory position, at least for radical critics that 'it was ever thus'. Going beyond critiques is not to dismiss them, as the more prescriptive and policy-oriented forms of educa-tional research often do. It is to argue that any critique must make explicit the alternatives it implies. Here I am not referring to specific policies or practices, for university based researchers are in no position to develop them in any detail. I mean making explicit alternative principles which can inform changes in policy and practice.

The principle that lies at the heart of the proposals for a curriculum of the future is not primarily an emphasis on new knowledge contents, although these will be developed. It is for new forms of knowledge relationships. This idea is discussed in relation to a number of themes that recur throughout the book. They are concerned with new relationships between subjects and dis-ciplines and between subject and non-subject knowledge, with new forms of specialization and the links between the specialization of knowledge and spe-cialization in the division of labour in society, with new relationships between theoretical understanding and their application as alternatives to separating academic from vocational education, and new relationships between school and non-school learning. In each case, the analysis begins as critique, of the stratification of knowledge in existing curricula, of the insularity of subjects, of the divisions between academic/vocational learning and of the separation of school from non-school learning. However, the concept of a curriculum of the future does not rely on critique alone, for that would be no basis for systematic knowledge and learning at all. It involves a concept of a future society, the kinds of skills, knowledge and attitudes that will be needed to create and sus-tain it, and the relationships between types of knowledge, between academic and vocational learning, between theory and practice and between subjects that will make such a society a real possibility. It proposes that the principle of connectivity should define relationships between subjects and the world of work and between forms of specialist and expert knowledge and everyday and common sense knowledge. In each case, the principle of connectivity poses the question of educational purpose in defining the relationships. The curriculum debate thus becomes a debate about different purposes and about different views of the kind of society we want to see in the next century and how they are embedded in different curriculum concepts. The role of a critical curriculum theory is to make explicit those different purposes which are often hidden in specific curriculum proposals and ground them in the realities facing teachers in schools and colleges and the social and political demands facing all countries in an increasingly interdependent world.

Section 1

Constructing and Reconstructing a Sociology of the Curriculum

Chapter 1

The Curriculum as Socially Organized Knowledge

Introduction

The history, the social divisions and the many competing interests and value systems found in a modern society are expressed in the school curriculum as much as they are in its system of government or its occupational structure. Likewise, curriculum debates, implicitly or explicitly, are always debates about alternative views of society and its future. These links between the curriculum and society provide both the topic and the rationale for the sociological approach to the curriculum set out in this chapter.

The chapter is based on a paper first published in 1971 (Young, 1971) and the analysis which it presents inevitably reflects the time and context. The specific examples, which are taken largely from the secondary curriculum in England and Wales, will be of primary interest to the educational historian. However, the intractable character of academic/vocational divisions (Finegold et al., 1990) and the international concern with the issue of parity of esteem between academic and vocational learning (Lasonen, 1996; Lasonen and Young, 1998) suggest that the idea of exploring the links between the stratification of knowledge in the curriculum and wider social divisions is as relevant now as it was nearly thirty years ago. In order to enable the reader to separate those elements of the analysis specific to the earlier context from those of current relevance, the first two parts of this chapter are concerned with that earlier context. Part 1 considers a number of educational policy issues in the period 1950–1970 and Part 2 considers the intellectual context of the time through an analysis of developments in the sociology of education in the UK up to 1971. Part 3 develops the theoretical framework which links social change and the curriculum through the concept of the **stratification of knowledge**.

The Secondary Curriculum in Context:
Educational Policy Themes 1950–1970

It is possible to trace three stages in the public debates on education in England and Wales between 1950 and 1970 through three interrelated themes: (i) *equality of opportunity*: (ii) *the organization and selection of pupils for secondary education,* and (iii) *the curriculum.* In the first stage, the facts of educational 'wastage' were documented by the Early Leaving Report (HMSO, 1953) and the Crowther Report (MOE, 1959) and the social class basis of differences in educational opportunities was demonstrated by sociologists such as Glass (1954) and Floud, Halsey and Martin (1957). The research complemented the public reports and both were used by successive governments as a justification for expanding secondary and higher education. However, the research also threw up a set of questions concerning the basis of selection at 11+ and the fact that it was as much a social as an educational process. This exposure of 'wastage of talent', especially of able working class children, led to the second phase of public debate which began in the mid 1960s and focused on critiques of the 11+ test for entry to grammar school. It leads to demands for the *comprehensive reorganization* of what was then a tripartite system of secondary education. Public debate in the second phase became increasingly political, an indication that the policies involved, such as the abolition of selective schools, threatened significant and powerful interests in society. However, the manifest inefficiency and less well-publicized injustice of the 11+ test made its abolition a realistic political commitment for reformist politicians of the time.

It was only towards the end of the 1960s that the focus of the debate moved from questions of the *organization* of secondary schooling to the content of education and therefore to the *curriculum* itself. The likely reasons for this shift are worth referring to briefly as they set the context for what was later to become a more explicit focus on the curriculum from the 1970s onwards by both policy makers and researchers. Three reasons can be distinguished as follows:

Government pressure for more and better technologists and scientists

The origins and implications of the concern to increase the numbers of pupils studying science were widely discussed at the time, although some cast doubts on whether pupils in secondary schools were 'swinging from science' (McPherson (1969), Blaug and Gannicott (1969) and Gorbutt (1970)). However, the 'swing' became an 'official' problem with the publication of the Dainton Report (DES, 1968) and the various solutions that it proposed. In retrospect, the most interesting recommendation of the Dainton Report that was little noticed at the time was that the 'swing from science' was unlikely to be reversed without some change in the narrow form of subject specialization that was forced on pupils by A-Levels (see Chapter 9).

The commitment to raising the school leaving age

Throughout the 1960s there were proposals, not in fact implemented until 1973, that the school leaving age should be raised to 16. The reasoning behind the proposals arose from the obvious if neglected fact that the length of a student's school career is probably the single most important determinant of the level of attainment he or she is likely to reach. However, a compulsory additional year for all pupils posed quite new curriculum problems since a significant section of the cohort already wanted to leave school at 14 or 15. Various alternatives for 'more meaningful curricula' were introduced including a new teacher assessed national examination, the Certificate of Secondary Education, which gave teachers a new flexibility in planning a curriculum that still would lead to a public examination. Curriculum alternatives for those making up the new Vth and VIth Forms were to become a major pre-occupation of the Schools Council after it was launched in 1964 and were to provide the policy context for more fundamental questions to be raised about relations between the curriculum and other social priorities (Young, 1972).

Comprehensive reorganization of secondary education

Following the government Circular on secondary reorganization 10/65, many local education authorities merged grammar schools and secondary modern schools to create comprehensive schools. This meant that many grammar school teachers were obliged, for the first time, to receive a non-selective pupil intake. Thus, teachers who for years had successfully produced good A-Level results from highly selective groups of pupils were faced with pupils who appeared neither to know how to learn academic subjects nor to want to. This inevitably generated new curriculum problems that had not arisen when pupils were separated into secondary modern, technical and grammar schools.

Educational and Political Debates about the Curriculum in the 1960s

In the UK, the public debate about the curriculum in the 1960s and afterwards took place on two levels, the 'political' and the 'educational'. At the political level, the main protagonists were the Marxist 'Left' (Anderson, 1969) and the conservative or Black Paper 'Right' (Cox and Dyson, 1969a, 1969b). The 'Left' criticized contemporary curricula for 'mystifying the students' and 'fragmenting knowledge into compartments'. They also claimed that typical higher education curricula denied students the opportunity to understand society as a 'totality' and therefore acted as little more than a mechanism of social control. The conservative 'Right' criticized progressive teaching methods, mixed ability teaching and the various curricular innovations designed to broaden the teaching of English and history, as well as the expansion of what they saw as the 'soft' social sciences. However the 'politics of the curriculum' at the time remained firmly outside party politics. Furthermore, apart from the requirement for compulsory religious instruction, the formal autonomy of the headteacher over the school curriculum was not questioned. This autonomy was in practice limited, especially in the upper forms of secondary schools, by the control of curricula by the universities, both through their entrance requirements and their domination of all but one of the school examination boards.

Three features of the educational debates about the curriculum at the time should also be mentioned. They are the emphasis on secondary curricula, the important role of philosophers of education and the marginal role of sociologists. Virtually all the curriculum debates in the 1960s focused on the phase which had in practice undergone least change, the secondary school curriculum. The absence of debate over changes in the primary curriculum appeared to point to the much greater autonomy of that part of the educational system with the lowest status. However, as has since become apparent, this relative autonomy of the primary curriculum at the time depended not only on the low status of primary school teachers but on a 'hands off' view of the curriculum on the part of politicians which was taken for granted at the time but which was to change dramatically two decades later.

By the end of the 1960s the approach to the philosophy of education associated with Peters and Hirst had established a dominant role in educational studies and in the curriculum of teacher education. It was to have a profound influence on debates about the curriculum. Starting from a view of knowledge which they traced back to Kant (Hirst, 1969), they criticized the new topic-based and integrated syllabi which they saw as neglecting the fundamental 'forms of knowledge' which everyone needed to make sense of the world. It was not **subjects**, which Hirst recognized were the socially constructed ways that teachers organize knowledge, but **forms of understanding**, which he claimed were not open to debate or change. However, in the debates that followed, the distinction between school subjects and forms of understanding easily got lost and the philosophy of education became associated with opposition to a socio-historical view of the curriculum (Pring, 1972; White and Young, 1974; 1975) and at the time served to limit more fundamental debates.

Despite their significant role in debates about educational inequality and secondary re-organization, sociologists played little role in the curriculum debates of the 1960s. In order to understand why, and to provide the basis for the sociological approach to the curriculum developed later in this chapter, it is necessary to look in more detail at the sociology of education of the time.

Sociology of Education and the Curriculum 1950–1970

Education is always, as Raymond Williams (1961) so evocatively pointed out, a set of cultural choices, some conscious and some unconscious. It follows that the curriculum is always a selection and organization of the knowledge available at a particular time. However, at least until the 1970s, sociologists of education did not see their task as trying to relate the principles of selection and organization of knowledge in curricula to the wider social structure. I want to suggest that this may be explained by examining the ideological and methodological assumptions of sociology of education at the time and the institutional context within which it developed.

British sociology in the late 1950s drew its political priorities from Fabian socialism and its methodology from the political arithmetic tradition of research associated with Booth and Rowntree. Sociologists such as Halsey and Floud broadened the definition of poverty from lack of income to lack of education and identified lack of educational opportunities as a significant way in which working class life chances were limited. However, in their concern to promote greater equality of opportunity, these early studies pointed not only to the need to expand educational opportunities but also to identifying the characteristics of those who failed, the early leavers and the drop-outs. Partly because they wanted evidence to justify educational expansion, their explanations of school failure focused on the educability of those who failed rather than on features of the education system that failed them. A characteristic but taken for granted feature of the curriculum of that system was the way grammar schools obliged pupils from about 14 to take up to 10 different subjects which had very little relation either to each other or to the rest of their lives and then at 16 to drop all but three, usually selected from a narrowly specialized group.

The sociological studies of the time set out to show how the distribution of life chances through education could be seen as an aspect of the class structure. Inevitably, this led to an over-mechanistic conception of social class which isolated the social class characteristics of individuals from the social class content of their educational experience. It may clarify this point to represent the model of explanation of school failure of such studies diagrammatically:

Assumptions	Independent variables	Dependent variables
Criteria of educational success — curricula, teaching methods and assessment. What counts as 'knowledge and knowing' in school	Social characteristics of the groups who succeed and fail	Distribution of success and failure at various stages in terms of participation and attainment

Though presenting a somewhat over-simplified picture, the diagram does show that, in terms of the model, the curriculum and content of education is taken as a 'given' and not as a possible variable to be investigated; furthermore, the model inevitably represents successes as normal and educational failures as a form of 'deviance' from the norm. What such a model cannot consider is how differential rates of educational success and failure may be explained in terms of the criteria and definitions of success that are used (Keddie, 1971). To ask such questions is to consider how definitions of success arise and are legitimized through methods of assessment, selection and organization of knowledge.

However, to treat such definitions as objects of study raises not just theoretical and methodological questions; it also raises political questions about the distribution of power and the ability of some to define what counts as educational success. Furthermore, bearing in mind the reformist mission of the sociologists of education of the time, it is difficult to see to what policies a refocusing of the model of educational failure might have pointed. This is a point that will be returned to in Chapter 3.

Turning to the institutional context, teaching and research in the sociology of education expanded in the 1960s in teacher training colleges and university departments of education, where previously it had hardly existed. The new specialists had to legitimize their contribution to the education of teachers and justify their particular field of expertise — particularly when the philosophers had defined the curriculum and knowledge as 'their area'. They mapped out areas previously unexplored in educational studies. They started from the social context of education with an emphasis on social class, relationships between education and the economy, the occupational structure and the family, and moved to the consideration of schools as organizations and pupil subcultures. It is perhaps not surprising that a tacit consensus emerged, at least for a time, among sociologists and non-sociologists alike, that the curriculum was not a field for sociological research.

Although this discussion has focused on British sociology of education, the general points are more widely applicable. Structural-functionalism, which was the perspective of the majority of sociologists in the USA, presupposes an agreed set of societal values or goals which define, among other things, the selection and organization of knowledge in curricula. Thus, sociology of education in the USA was primarily concerned with socialization, seen as the 'organization' and 'processing' of people, and with notable exceptions, for example the pioneering early work of Apple (1979) and Wexler (1983), continued to take the organization of knowledge in the curriculum for granted.

Towards a Framework for Analysing the Curriculum as Socially Organized Knowledge

The previous section has suggested that it was the taken for granted assumptions of the sociology of education of the 1960s that accounted for its neglect of the curriculum. The next section of this chapter turns this critique into a positive programme for raising sociological questions about the curriculum. It does so by starting from the assumption that those in positions of power will attempt to define what is to be taken as knowledge in society, how accessible to different groups any knowledge is and what are the accepted relationships between different knowledge areas and between those who have access to them and make them available. It is the exploration of these issues that is the basis to the approach to the curriculum as *socially organized knowledge* that follows. Drawing on Bernstein (1973), the approach gives rise to three interrelated questions about curricula concerning the stratification of knowledge, the extension of the scope of knowledge (or degree of specialization) and the relations between knowledge areas.

1 The power of some to define what is 'valued' knowledge leads to the question of accounting for how knowledge is **stratified** and by what criteria. The idea of knowledge being stratified has two aspects — what might be referred to as its 'prestige' and 'property' components. Differences in prestige refer to the different ways that different kinds of knowledge are valued — for example, pure and applied, academic and vocational, and general and specialist knowledge. The property aspect of the stratification of knowledge refers to how access to knowledge is controlled, in modern societies, largely by professionals and other experts. Thus the 'property' aspect of stratification points to the distribution of knowledge in use and its associated reward structure. It suggests that in different societies the dominant conception of knowledge is likely to be associated with dominant ideas about property in general — whether this is private, state or communal.

2 The restriction of the access of some knowledge areas to specific groups is also a question of power. It poses the question in relation to curricula as to what is the scope of curricula provided for different groups and to the factors that may influence what is seen as the degree and kind of specialization appropriate to different groups of learners at different ages.

3 The third question points to relations between knowledge areas and between those with access to them. Relations between knowledge areas are also expressions of power; in this case the power of some to maintain or break down knowledge boundaries. Relations between knowledge areas can be seen as on a continuum between being *insulated* and being *connective*.

We can therefore conceptualize options for organizing the curriculum in terms of three dimensions which can, for simplicity, be seen as a continua between (i) high and low stratification, (ii) broad and narrow degrees of specialization and (iii) insulated and connective relations between knowledge areas.

There is a more fundamental question, only hinted at in this chapter, as to whether, as knowledge expands, it necessarily becomes more stratified. The growth of knowledge and the access to it have undoubtedly been paralleled by an increasing differentiation and specialization of knowledge. It is also likely that increasing differentiation is a condition which allows for some groups to legitimize 'their knowledge' as superior — in other words, the growth of knowledge is a condition for its greater stratification. The high value of some knowledge is institutionalized by the creation of schools, colleges and universities to transmit it as the curriculum and to produce it as research. Although the differential social evaluation of knowledge often follows from its increasing differentiation, there is no necessary relationship between the two processes. It is possible that greater differentiation could be associated with reduced stratification in a society where the fragmenting tendencies of differentiation are balanced by the integrative trend of less stratification. Chapter 5 explores these possibilities in relation to recent changes in the occupational structure of modern societies. My argument is that patterns of social evaluation must be explained, independently of the process of differentiation, in terms of the power that certain groups have to restrict access to certain kinds of knowledge, the opportunity for those who have access to knowledge to legitimize its status and the beliefs they have about the relations between knowledge and society.

The general hypothesis underlying the analysis, which is explored in later chapters of this book, is of a shift from 'curricula of the past', which were insulated, narrowly specialized and highly stratified to 'curricula of the future', which I predict will need to be connective, broader and with low degrees of stratification. However, as will be indicated, this does not imply any straightforward or smooth process of evolutionary change. Later chapters will explore the many barriers to such changes and the contradictions which they involve.

The framework presented focuses on the principles of the organization and selection of knowledge and only implicitly suggests how these might be related to changes in the social structure. The assumption here is that the most explicit relation between the organization of knowledge and the wider society will be on the dimension of stratification. Moves to 'destratify' or give equal value to different kinds of knowledge, or 'restratify' (or legitimize other criteria of evaluation), by posing a threat to the existing power structure, are likely to be resisted. However, a qualification needs to be made to these general propositions. Power is not distributed in a monolithic way in most modern societies; there is unlikely to be a consensus about definitions of knowledge among the different economic, political, bureaucratic, cultural and educational interest groups, except at a very general level. One would imagine, for example, that business and academic elites would not, except if faced with a common threat, share many assumptions in their definitions of knowledge. Another aspect of the relations between knowledge and power will be apparent in any attempt to reduce the degree of specialization in the curriculum and to make the relations between knowledge areas more connective. Such attempts are likely to pose threats to the patterns of social relations implicit in the more specialized and insulated forms and likewise will be resisted. A good example is in the long history of attempts to broaden the A-Level curriculum (see Chapter 8).

The Academic Curriculum and the Stratification of Knowledge

In the remaining part of this chapter, I want to focus primarily on the academic curriculum associated with the upper forms of secondary schools, both private and state, as a test of the theoretical framework I have outlined. It is undoubtedly an area of the curriculum which has been highly resistant to change and should therefore provide evidence of relations between patterns of dominant values, the distribution of rewards and power and the organization of knowledge as well as the explanatory potential of the concept of the stratification of knowledge.

All curricula involve assumptions that some kinds and areas of knowledge are more 'worthwhile' than others. In England and Wales, the academic curriculum is based on the assumption that learning should become highly specialized as early as possible and give minimum emphasis to relations between the different subjects. Changes in the academic curriculum can be conceptualized as involving changing valuations of a less stratified, less specialized and more connective organization of knowledge. Furthermore, as we assume some pattern of social relations is associated with any curriculum, these changes will be resisted in so far as they are perceived to undermine the values, relative power and privileges of the dominant groups involved.

Before looking in more detail at the stratification of knowledge, I should like to make brief reference to the dimensions of specialization and connectedness referred to earlier. By referring to the degree of specialization, we are by implication concerned with the distribution of resources (pupil and teacher time, books and materials)[1]. This suggests why, in spite of many rhetorical statements about the importance of curriculum breadth that have been made over the years by politicians and others and which have culminated in the manifesto commitments of the New Labour government (DfEE, 1997), existing patterns of specialization remain firmly entrenched.

The issue of the *connectedness of knowledge areas* raises basic questions about how knowledge areas are defined and about the interests involved in keeping them separate. It also raises more fundamental questions about the categories a society uses to make sense of itself and the physical world. Subjects or even broad fields like 'arts' and 'sciences' cannot be treated as if they continued independently of any social changes (Gibbons et al., 1994).

The key issue for this chapter to which I now return is the idea of the *stratification of knowledge* in the academic curriculum. It is through the concept of stratification, I suggest, that we are led to consider the social basis of different kinds of knowledge and that we can begin to raise questions about relations between the power structure of society and curricula, the access to knowledge and the opportunities to legitimize it as 'superior' and the relation between knowledge and its functions in different kinds of society.

If knowledge is highly stratified, there will be clear definitions of what is taken to count as knowledge which will provide the criteria for deciding what knowledge to include and exclude in curricula. It would follow that highly stratified curricular models are likely to presuppose and legitimate a rigid hierarchy between teacher and taught. The implications of changes in a highly stratified model have recently been explored in relation to the academic curriculum of higher education by Gibbons et al. (1994). They argue that external pressures on the university to produce more useful knowledge more quickly is undermining the traditional forms of academic hierarchy and in particular relations between the producers and consumers of knowledge.

So taken for granted by most people, in education and outside, is the idea that knowledge is stratified that it is difficult to conceive of the possibility of a curriculum based on knowledge which is differentiated but not stratified. That it is a radical idea is apparent when one considers whether the terms 'teacher', 'pupil' and 'examination' in the sense normally used would have any meaning at all within such a curriculum. This argument suggests that the stratification of knowledge is not only deeply implicit in our ideas of what education 'is' and what teachers 'are' but that some stratification of knowledge is in principle a feature of any curriculum and any teaching. However, acceptance of such a principle does not deny the possibility that the degree of stratification of knowledge is a social and historical product that can change.

As previously suggested, the contemporary British educational system remains dominated by an academic curriculum with a rigid stratification of knowledge. It is not surprising, therefore, that high status and rewards are associated with areas of the curriculum associated with formal assessment and the 'ablest' children.

Two contradictory implications follow from this argument. If curricula are designed on the basis of criteria other than those associated with high status knowledge, they will only be taken up in programmes for low ability pupils. An example, referred to earlier in this chapter, was the early work of the Schools Council on a curriculum for the 'young school leaver'. The Council accepted the existing stratification of knowledge but produced most of its early recommendations for reform in low-status knowledge areas (Young, 1972). Proposals such as *Mathematics for the Majority* which were designed for less able pupils only, and therefore did not challenge any of the criteria of high status knowledge, came up against the stratification of knowledge in another form. Despite the fact that they had achieved little in the conventional mathematics curriculum, low ability pupils tended to accept the 'academic' definitions of what counted as mathematics and rejected the curricular and pedagogic innovations which involved alternative definitions of mathematical knowledge; they wanted 'real mathematics' like fractions (Spradberry, 1976).

The idea of knowledge being stratified in the curriculum can be extended by asking two further questions. First, by what criteria are different areas of, kinds of and approaches to knowledge associated with high status? No criteria will be universal to all academic curricula: they will inevitably have developed in particular social and historical contexts. However, if identified, they may be related to forms of social, political and economic organization, and be the basis for explaining changes and resistance to change in the academic curriculum. Second, can we relate the *extent* to which knowledge is stratified in society as well as the kinds of criteria on which such stratification may be based[2] to features of social organization?

The first question requires an attempt to identify some of the social characteristics of academic curricula and to show how over time they have become legitimized as high status by those in positions of power. A number of sources suggest what these might be. First, there are comparative perspectives on pre-literate and literate societies. For example, Mead (1938) discusses the way in which the emphasis on formal education in literate societies has moved from 'learning to teaching'. She links the idea of groups holding some kinds of knowledge as superior to the notion of a 'hierarchical arrangement of cultural views of experience' and the increasing emphasis on the importance of changing the beliefs, habits, knowledge, ideas and allegiances that children bring with them to school. Second, in studies of the consequences of literacy for contemporary culture, Goody and Watt (1962) argue that so great is the discontinuity between the private, oral traditions of family and home and the public literate tradition of the school that 'literate skills form one of the major axes of differentiation in industrial societies'. They go on to suggest that reading and writing, the activities which occupy most of the time of young people when they are at school, are inevitably solitary and so a literate culture brings with it an increasing individualization. This curricular individualization is brought out most clearly in the dominance of written modes of assessment in school. In comparing literate and non-literate cultures, Goody and Watt (1962) suggest that the peculiar characteristic of the former is the priority that they give to

> an abstraction which disregards an individual's social experience . . . and a compartmentalisation of knowledge which restricts the kind of connections which the individual can establish and ratify with the natural and social world.

The third source of criteria for high status knowledge is the evidence of the link in modern education systems between formal education, examinations and specialist knowledge (Weber, 1952). Weber discussed the process of what he called the 'bureaucratic domination of the nature of education'. He suggested that the major constraint on what counts as knowledge in modern societies and therefore in curricula was whether something could be objectively and, in practice, quantitatively assessed. As the Scottish physicist, Lord Kelvin, once said of science 'when you cannot express it in numbers, your knowledge is of a meagre and unsatisfactory kind'. This is not so far from the assumption that appears to underlie much modern educational policy that if you cannot examine or test for something, it is not worth knowing.

We can draw together the main ideas of the previous paragraphs to suggest the dominant characteristics of high-status knowledge and how they represent the organizing principles underlying academic curricula. These are **literacy** — an emphasis on writing as opposed to oral communication; **individualism** — an avoidance of group work or co-operation in how academic learning is assessed; **abstractness** of knowledge and its structuring and compartmentalizing independently of the knowledge of the learner[3]. Finally, and linked to abstractness, is what can be described as the **unrelatedness** of academic curricula; this refers to the extent to which academic curricula are frequently 'at odds' with daily life and common experience.

If high status is accorded to knowledge in terms of these criteria, we would expect academic curricula to be organized on such principles. In other words academic curricula will tend to be abstract, literate, individualistic and unrelated to non-school knowledge. Curricula can therefore be ranked on these characteristics which then become four dimensions in terms of which knowledge is stratified. Low status curricula will be characterized by the extent to which they are organized in terms of oral presentation, group activities and assessment, concreteness of the knowledge involved and its relatedness to non-school knowledge. These criteria are typical, in varying degrees, of many secondary vocational curricula. The academic/vocational divide, therefore, can be seen as an almost paradigmatic example of how the stratification of knowledge has the effect of maintaining wider social divisions and inequalities.

One way of viewing these characteristics of the academic curriculum is to see them as the historical outcome of how mass education was established on a model of bookish learning for priests which was extended first to lawyers and doctors but which increasingly has come to dominate the curricula of all older age groups in industrial societies (Goodman, 1969). If such curricular characteristics persist, it may not be because they are the most pedagogically effective but because they are the conscious or unconscious cultural choices which accord with the values, beliefs and interests of dominant groups at a particular time. It is in terms of these choices that educational success and failure are defined. Why, then, do such characteristics of curricula persist? The conventional explanation of the persistence of an academic curriculum with such characteristics is that it transmits the specialist knowledge needed by key occupations in a modern society. An alternative view that arises from the approach to the curriculum developed in this chapter is that any very different cultural choices, or the granting of equal status to sets of cultural choices that reflected variations in terms of the suggested characteristics, would involve a politically unacceptable redistribution of rewards in terms of wealth, prestige and power and the labels of educational success and failure.

Three important limitations of this latter approach must be mentioned. *First*, there is a danger in contrasting conventional and sociological explanations of the curriculum in a way which equates the former uncritically with common sense and therefore by definition as inferior. In reality academic criteria are not **just** social or just an expression of dominant views of the world; they are also ways of making knowledge available that do work in the real world as well as in the classroom. It is this epistemological reality, together with what may be judged as politically feasible at a particular time, that will limit the extent to which curricula reorganization is possible. *Second*, the categories identified for describing academic curricula are formal and do not relate directly to issues of curriculum content. In any analysis of texts, syllabi, school reports, examination questions or 'marking' criteria that make up the curriculum, it is not the 'abstractness' of the student's work that is judged but the particular **subject** forms of abstractness. This may be a scientific law or a historical explanation. *Third*, by its primary emphasis of the social organization of knowledge and not its social functions, this approach does not make explicit that access to certain kinds of knowledge is also potential access to the possibility of creating new knowledge. However, creating new knowledge is a practical activity and inevitably *concrete, collective* and *related* as well as abstract and as likely to involve oral as well as written communication. It may be that it is through the devaluing of practical activity and in elevating the value of 'knowledge for its own sake' through the separation of knowledge from practical action that the academic curriculum serves its most significant social function. It may be that 'Really useful knowledge', as the Chartists referred to it (Johnson, 1980), involves combining theory and practice, something rarely experienced through the academic curriculum.

Finally, let us return to how we might account for the criteria implicit in the different ways educational knowledge is stratified in academic curricula. At least in the case of Europe, it is possible to trace schematically a set of stages from non-literate societies where there were no separate educational institutions to feudal societies where formal education in separate institutions was largely restricted to a priestly caste and where schools remained largely independent of the economic and political forces of the time. Gradually, as schools and colleges became differentiated and increasingly dependent on the economies of their societies, the new economic and political classes began to play a major role in determining the stratification of knowledge, in how knowledge areas are kept separate and in defining degrees of specialization for different groups. Comparative studies might shed light on these relationships and why, for example, they shaped such a narrow form of curricular specialization and such a high degree of insulation of knowledge areas in the secondary schools of England and Wales.

To sum up, this chapter has presented a framework for a sociological approach to the organization of knowledge in curricula. It is inevitably schematic and reflects the concerns and context of its time. However, though the social and economic context has changed out of all recognition since 1971, when the paper on which this chapter is based was first published, many of the features of academic curricula which it identifies are still with us and still largely unquestioned. Part of the difficulty of conceiving real curriculum alternatives is that many curricular assumptions are so much part of our take-for-granted world. Approaching the curriculum as socially organized knowledge is a tool for analysis and a way of conceptualizing alternatives and their implications; it is not, of itself, a basis for prescribing a new curriculum. What the chapter has tried to do is to show that academic curricula are as much the products of people's actions in history as any other form of social organization. They are not given, nor, in today's language, do they represent an unchanging *gold standard.* They can therefore be transformed. The issue is one of purposes and the extent to which the existing curriculum represents a future society that we can endorse or a past society that we want to change. Later chapters will explore both the potential and the limitations of this form of analysis.

Chapter 2

Curriculum Change:
Limits and Possibilities

Introduction

This chapter is concerned with the problem of curriculum change and with developing a theory that might assist teachers in changing and improving the curriculum at school level. It is based on a paper written over a decade before the National Curriculum was introduced, when in theory, individual secondary schools had much freedom to devise their own curricula. It was written as a kind of cautionary warning about over-simplified interpretations of the idea that educational reality was 'socially constructed'. The relevance of the argument to teachers and others in 1998, a decade after the National Curriculum became law, is likely to be very different. Its focus, like that of Chapter 1, is on the conceptions of knowledge that underlie different views of the curriculum rather than on the specifics of curriculum content. However, in developing what I would call a modified social constructivist view of knowledge, it stresses how even an external structure such as the National Curriculum has to be interpreted by teachers to become a reality in schools and that it is in that process of interpretation that the scope and need for teachers' professional autonomy can be found. It is therefore more about interpreting than constructing the curriculum and about what it means to assert the importance of teachers *interpreting* National Curriculum guidelines. The argument implies that, if, following the 1998 Review of the National Curriculum, the prescriptions on schools, at least in Key Stage 4, are to be reduced, teachers will need a more sophisticated theory of knowledge and the curriculum than is made available to them in many teacher training courses which concentrate largely on the specifics of content. The analysis recognizes that the learning experiences of students are shaped as much by the communities where they live as by what is possible in the classroom and that this has implications for schools and for how teachers see their role. It is based on a critical examination of two contrasting conceptions of the curriculum, which are well expressed by the American philosopher Maxine Greene (1971). She describes the dominant view of the curriculum in terms of 'a structure of socially prescribed knowledge, external to the knower, there to be mastered' and goes on to contrast this with her own phenomenological view of the curriculum as 'a possibility for the learner as an existing person mainly concerned with making sense of his own life-world'. This latter view has many affinities with the idea that the curriculum is *socially constructed* that was introduced in Chapter 1; it had a powerful influence, through the writings of Alfred Schutz, George Herbert Mead and Berger and Luckman, on the sociology of education in the 1970s.

For the purposes of this chapter, I shall call these two views, 'curriculum as fact' and 'curriculum as practice'. The view of the 'curriculum as fact' was widely criticized by radical educationalists such as the Brazilian Paulo Freire (Freire, 1971) as dehumanizing and mystifying the process of learning. Freire's educational philosophy started from the intentions and actions of men and women not the structure of knowledge which he saw as produced by human beings but often experienced as external to them. I shall argue that such a view was an over-reaction to the pervasiveness of conceptions of the curriculum associated with subjects, forms of knowledge and learning objectives and itself became a form of mystification. I shall suggest that the curriculum needs to be seen not just as something *imposed on* teachers' and pupils' classroom practice, but as a historically specific social reality which teachers *act on*. and thus transform.

The view of the 'curriculum as fact' is mystifying in a number of ways. It presents the curriculum as having a life of its own and obscures the social contexts in which it is embedded; at the same time, it leaves the curriculum as a given — neither understandable nor changeable. The alternative conception of 'curriculum as practice' can be equally mystifying. In its attempt to put students and teachers back into the curriculum, it denies its external reality and over emphasizes the subjective intentions and actions of teachers and pupils as if they were not always acting on a curriculum that is in part external to and preceding them. If the curriculum is located solely in the classroom practice of teachers and pupils, it becomes impossible to understand the historical emergence and persistence of particular ways of organizing curricula and of how individual teachers and schools can 'make a difference'. In that it limits us from being able to see the curriculum historically, a view of 'curriculum as practice' also limits our capacity to conceive of alternatives other than in terms of some form of utopian rejection of traditional curricula as in the free school and deschooling literature of the 1960s and 1970s (Lister, 1974).

Before exploring these contrasting views in more detail, I should like to take mathematics, the almost paradigmatic school subject, to illustrate the distinction between the ideas underlying 'curriculum as fact' and 'curriculum as practice'. To do this, I shall draw on a paper by Bloor (1973), who quotes G.H. Hardy's view that:

> 317 is a prime, not because we think so or because our minds are shaped in one way rather than another, but because it is so, because mathematical reality is built that way.

Hardy's statement exemplifies a view of knowledge which posits a realm of truth independent of human beings which we all have to adapt to. Such a theory underlies what I have referred to as the view of the 'curriculum as fact'. Bloor contrasts Hardy's view of mathematics with that of Wittgenstèin (1967) who in discussing logical inferences involved in simple number sequences, wrote that:

> with endless practice, with merciless exactitude, that is why it is inexorably insisted that we shall all say '2' after '1' and '3' after '2' and so on.

For Wittgenstein, it is *we* not mathematics who are inexorable. As he says:

> Our children are not only given practice in calculation but are also trained to adopt a particular attitude towards a mistake in calculating

Students have to *learn*, Wittgenstein implies, that calculations have a life of their own, even if they as calculators do not follow. This seems to me a profound insight into how our concepts of knowledge are related to our ideas about teaching and learning. As Bloor points out, Wittgenstein does not deny the reality of mathematics but sees it as as social rarity. He views mathematics as an invention not a discovery, but that, like all inventions, it comes to have a life of its own; in other words, it becomes reified and therefore *experienced as external*. The question for teachers, to which I shall return, is how and why particular forms of curriculum reification emerge and persist and what ways can be found of interpreting them. These issues are not adequately dealt with either by dismissing the problem as Hardy does, or by treating the rules of mathematics as mere conventions as Wittgenstein might be interpreted as doing. With these two contrasting views of mathematics in mind, the next section returns to the first of my two views of curriculum, 'curriculum as fact'.

Curriculum as Fact

Most writing and research concerned with the curriculum unavoidably treats it in some way as a topic, thus affirming its external reality rather than explaining it as socially produced. The curriculum becomes something to be preserved or brought up to date for high achievers, modified or made more relevant for low achievers and broadened or integrated for those who specialize too soon, etc. We can also trace features of school organization and administration that sustain the idea of the curriculum as something to be studied, reorganized and analysed. For example, we find deputy head teachers and vice principals for curriculum, professors, journals, degrees and departments of curriculum studies and, of course, the final academic accolade of all otherwise unrecognized activity, attempts to develop curriculum 'theory'. Parallel to this, we find subfields, like the sociology and psychology of the curriculum, in which the disciplines apply their respective perspectives and methodologies. Typically, sociology addresses issues around the stratification and integration of different knowledge areas, whereas psychology has been concerned with mental development and stages of learning. I want to suggest that because the starting points of such research have been curricula *as products* rather than the production of curricula in teachers' and pupils' practices but set in their wider social context, problems are created, such as the separation and hierarchies between different knowledge areas, which our theories and methods do not enable us to solve. Educational researchers can be far more naive than teachers. The curriculum is presented as a reality and the language of cause and effect, resistance and change is applied to it; we discover articles with titles like, 'How does the curriculum change?' as if the curriculum was a thing which changed like the weather. There are similarities between such views of the curriculum and references by politicians and journalists to the 'National Interest' or the 'Economy'; in each case, a set of social relations is treated as a set of beliefs about the world. In the case of the curriculum, the social relations are those between teachers and taught and between the classroom context and the wider context in which classroom practices are shaped and the assumptions about knowledge and curriculum embedded in them. It is such assumptions and practices which can become masked by the language of curriculum theory.

This conception of 'curriculum as fact', with its underlying view of knowledge as external to knowers, both teachers and students, and embodied in syllabi and text-books, is widely held and has profound implications for our conceptions of teaching and learning. To say 'I teach history or physics' implies a body of knowledge to be transferred from the teacher who has it to the pupil who has not, whether by rote and test or by enquiries and assignments. It is teachers as well as philosophers who see teaching as initiating children into 'worthwhile' activities. So long as the idea of education as initiation, with the associated ideas about knowledge and what is worthwhile, is not questioned, educational theory merely confirms what every teacher and pupil knows. The only possible explanations of pupil failure that it provides are either in terms of 'bad teaching' or in terms of the social or psychological deficits that students bring to school or college. Keddie (1971) describes well what is involved in such a conception of curriculum and teaching. She argues that, in order to succeed in school, students must become initiated into the teacher's forms of knowledge and avoid questioning its grounds. I would like to illustrate the link between a view of 'curriculum as fact' and of teaching as 'knowledge to be transmitted' and how they can shape teacher–pupil interactions with an extract from a transcript of a science class for 12-year olds. The transcript also illustrates how, when such a conception of knowledge prevails, passivity is almost forced on, in this case, a remarkably reluctant pupil.

(The teachers and pupils have a live worm in a dish in front of them)
T: Have you ever seen examples of when it [soil] is produced?
P: No
T: Earth on the grass
P: No I just seen holes on the grass

T: Have you ever seen anything else that might tell you there was a worm on the grass?

P: Yeah, they're what's called again, the holes they make are called

T: Have you seen those little piles?

P: Piles?

T: Have you seen those little heaps of

P: Leaves

T: On the grass, little

P: Holes

T: Em?

P: Dots

T: Have you seen have you ever come

P: I've seen holes

T: Have you heard of something called a cast?

The point of including the transcript here is not just that this could be seen as an example of 'bad teaching' but that it illustrates the consequences of a particular view of teaching, which might be carried out more or less effectively. Assumptions about knowledge as external and 'to be transmitted' can be as much a feature of 'good' teaching than 'bad'; they are integral for both teachers and pupils in creating a sense of pupils as 'not knowing' or at least not knowing until his or her 'knowledge' is confirmed by the teacher.

This conception of 'curriculum as fact' is pervasive, even in sociology. Most sociologists from Durkheim to Parsons treat education as a process of socialization or the acquisition of particular knowledge, skills and values. Thus, the teacher's problem becomes defined as how to devise more effective ways of transmitting these skills and knowledge, whatever they are, to as many pupils as possible. All research from such a perspective can do is to offer a range of explanations, for why schools continue to be unsuccessful with so many pupils. These vary from the cultural inadequacy or the basic lack of ability of pupils to some reference to the 'structure of society'. In each explanation the curriculum remains unquestioned.

The school curriculum is presented as a set of gateways to the adult world, even though the relationships between school and non-school definitions of knowledge and skill are at best tenuous. It is predominantly a subject-ordered world — even when it takes the form of integrated studies. For the learner, there is little to distinguish between integrated science or humanities and physics and chemistry or history. Integration invariably produces an ordering of the world through which the learner has to find his or her way, rather than requiring learners themselves to be involved in the process of integration. Where pupils reject the discontinuity between their knowledge of the world and the way the school orders the world into subjects or themes, they invariably become described as less-able or non-academic. Such descriptions depend for their plausibility on a view of the 'curriculum as fact', which tells us what the terms 'able' and 'academic' refer to. This view of curriculum has not only been an assumption of academic curricula; it is also presupposed in vocational curricula. The difference is that while knowledge is still seen as external to both teacher and pupils, it involves not only ideas about what counts as knowledge but about how knowledge relates to different occupational fields. More generally then, I would suggest that the notions of 'curriculum as fact' expresses particular power relations between teachers and students, and in society, which are designed to reproduce knowledge produced elsewhere by others.

To sum up this section, I have suggested that a view of 'curriculum as fact' expresses many of the prevailing assumptions of educational practitioners, teachers and policy makers. By accepting similar assumptions, curriculum theory does little more than re-describe a world that teachers already know, albeit sometimes in terms they find far from familiar. It also confirms for teachers both the irrelevance of theory for practical change in schools and their own passive role in such changes. Teachers have theories of knowledge, teaching and curriculum that are often remarkably like the ideas of curriculum 'theorists' and which, I shall argue later, play an important, albeit unconscious role in curriculum change or resistance to it. They continue to hold such views because they are congruent with views of the curriculum in the wider society and because, in part, they make some sense of the situation in which teachers find themselves. As a theory, however, 'curriculum as fact', though pervasive amongst academics, administrators and teachers, fails according to the criteria with which I started. It does not enhance the capacity of teachers to become aware of the possibilities of change and of gaining an understanding of the conditions of their own practice. 'Curriculum as fact' presents the curriculum as a thing, hiding the social relations between the teachers, students and curriculum policy makers who have historically and collectively produced it. What then does the 'curriculum as practice', which takes a quite opposite view, have to offer?

Curriculum as Practice

The basic premise of the view of 'curriculum as practice' reverses the assumptions of the 'curriculum as fact'. It does not begin with the structure of knowledge but with how knowledge is produced by people acting collectively. In education, the focus of such a view has been on teachers' and pupils' classroom practices and how educational realities such as school subjects or the distribution of student abilities are not external structures or fixed attributes of pupils, but are products of these practices and the assumptions about knowledge, learning and teaching which are embedded in them. From this view, teachers' practices are crucial in both sustaining or challenging prevailing views of knowledge and curriculum. The curriculum thus ceases to be separate from the activities through which teachers devise assignments, produce marks and grades and differentiate between subjects and identify pupil achievements. The implication of such a view is that if teachers subject the assumptions underlying their practices to critical examination, they will understand how to change the curriculum.

Such a theory, while valuable in challenging the view of 'curriculum as fact' and asserting the active role of both teachers and students in the learning process, is misleading both theoretically and practically in locating the possibilities of curriculum change primarily in the interactions of teachers and their students. The concept of 'curriculum as practice' gives teachers a spurious sense of their power, autonomy and independence from the wider contexts of which their work is a part. It thus provides them with no way of understanding their own failure to make changes, except in terms of their personal inadequacies.

The view of 'curriculum as practice' involves a radically different concept of knowledge to that of the mathematician GH Hardy, referred to at the beginning of this chapter. No longer is knowledge viewed as a kind of private property handed down from the academic 'discoverers' for the teacher to distribute or 'transmit'. Knowledge becomes that which is accomplished in the collaborative work of teachers and pupils. In theory, such a view has profound implications for existing school hierarchies and for the organization of education. What might be involved, for example, in seeing the curriculum as a site for the collaborative production of history or science, when we normally think of teaching as the transmission of historical or scientific knowledge, even if it involves a student project? The problem is not just that such possibilities may seem exciting to some and threatening to others but that they remain possibilities only 'in theory', generated as they are from a view of the curriculum *as* the product of the practice of teachers. Attempts at radical curriculum change based on the idea of 'curriculum as practice' will very quickly face the practical experience that the curriculum is far from being *just* a product of teachers' and pupils' practices. It is also a product of the views about what education should be of parents, employers, administrators and so on. If a group of teachers began to examine critically and reformulate their current practice, there would be two likely outcomes. Either they would immediately come up against external constraints from the Governing Body or Local Authority or, in their attempts to implement alternatives, they would *in practice* be taken outside the context of the classroom and into discussions with local employers and parents. They would be forced, without any theoretical guide, to try and develop a more adequate understanding of their situation than that provided by a view of 'curriculum as practice'.

I would like to illustrate these comments on the view of 'curriculum as practice' by two specific examples, taken from science education. I would argue, however, that the underlying arguments developed from the case of school science are relevant to the question of curriculum change more generally. Innovation in science education in the 1960s and 1970s was virtually synonymous with the Nuffield/Schools Councils Projects. Despite many practical innovations in pedagogy, they tended without exception to sustain rather than challenge existing conceptions of school science and to perpetuate its stratification into 'pure' and 'applied' sciences (Young, 1976). The Nuffield perspective was exemplified in a speech at the British Association in September 1974 by Professor Jevons who claimed that, as science teachers 'we are up against something in the cognitive structure of science itself' and that therefore science was not appropriate 'to meet the more radical ideals of education'. This represents a very clear example of the mode of reasoning underlying the view of 'curriculum as fact' discussed earlier. If, however, we go back a century we can see how our contemporary conceptions of school science as a body of knowledge enshrined in textbooks, syllabuses and laboratories gradually gained ascendancy over quite different possibilities. Layton's (1973) well known study brings this out well by describing the fate of a movement during the early days of school science and called by its founder, Richard Dawes, the 'Science of common things'. In the work of this movement, the everyday experiences of pupils of the natural world in their homes and their daily lives formed the basis for developing the school science curriculum. A particular example cited by Layton was the 'radical curriculum' of Arthur Rigg, Principal of Cheshire Training College, in which a major emphasis was placed on the kind of science and workshop skills relevant to an area where most people were employed in the cotton industry. Rigg's experiment was short lived, Layton suggests, because it undermined the separation of teachers from those they taught; it was feared by the Schools Inspectorate of the time that if students investigated their own work context they might come to see it too critically. Furthermore, it was felt that teachers emerging from such a course might become, as one Inspector put it, 'active emissaries of misrule'. Both Dawes and Rigg can be seen as working with notions of curriculum as *practice*, in which school or college science was viewed as the emergent product of the collaborative activities of teachers and students. However, their proposals were perceived by their opponents as raising uncomfortable political questions of significance far outside the classroom or the school laboratory. The ultimate demise of the 'Science for common things' movement can be seen in part as reflecting the limitations of the ideas of its leaders, who thought they could bring outside experiences into the school and leave both the school laboratory and the world outside unchanged. Although it is not possible to draw any direct parallels with science education today, the examples emphasize both the limitations of a view of curriculum as practice and the *social* and *historical* roots and political character of some of the most basic assumptions of what is now taken to be school science.

My second example also illustrates the limitations of the idea of 'curriculum as practice' and suggests how examinations are involved in sustaining particular notions of school knowledge. The example is from an A-Level science syllabus in which part of the assessment involved a project to be devised and written up by candidates and allocated a proportion of the marks in the final examination. In one case, a student chose to investigate problems of streamlining a boat and in doing so she had to learn a considerable amount about viscosity — a topic in most A-Level physics syllabuses of the time. In the context of the student's project, viscosity became a way of understanding and transforming something that was important to her outside school — building a boat. Viscosity was not an external body of knowledge to be learnt because it was on the syllabus. The teacher's advice and the pupil's activities, both theoretical and practical, became in this instance the reality of the student's education in science. However, this *practice*, as a part of teachers' and pupils' activity on a physical science course, was squeezed into one afternoon a week, while the rest of the timetable was used in the 'real' work of reproducing knowledge for the formal examinations which counted for 85 per cent of the marks. It may be, therefore, that such a limited experience of the science 'curriculum as practice' would sustain rather than challenge both for teachers and pupils a view that knowledge of viscosity, like all *real* knowledge, is something to be learnt and reproduced rather than being part of a way of understanding and transforming the world of which we are part. In other words the marginalization of 'science as practice' sustains a view of 'curriculum as fact'.

To summarize this section, I have argued that a view of the 'curriculum as practice' does not offer an adequate alternative to ideas about the curriculum defined in terms of the structures of knowledge. Its weakness is in the limitations of its concept of practice. It replaces a notion of reality located in the structures of knowledge by one located in teachers' classroom practice. Attempts by teachers to develop strategies for changing the curriculum derived from such a theory will confront with the limits of what they can do in their classroom practice. Teachers will also become aware of the limits of a theory that does not enable them to comprehend the origins of such limits or show them how their classroom practice does in part shape the external reality of the curriculum in meaningful ways for their students.

Conclusions

I should like to conclude this chapter by drawing together my critiques of the two curriculum models in relation to my original problem — developing a theory that could assist teachers in transforming the curriculum and so improve the learning experience of their students. 'Curriculum as fact', with its fixed concepts of teaching, knowledge and ability, takes for granted just that which its task as a theory should be to explain. How did curricula based on such assumptions originate and why do they persist? By failing to address this question, such a theory assumes, at least for advanced industrial societies, not only that the organization of knowledge into subjects is in some sense necessary or inevitable but that teachers do not construct the curriculum in the process of interpreting it. The first outcome of such a view of the curriculum is a kind of end-of-history argument in which the past as a dynamic of action and interest which produced the present is forgotten and future possibilities are viewed as the continuation of some kind of universal present. The second outcome is to deny the constructive role of teachers in shaping the curriculum and to underwrite a highly mechanistic view of the curriculum as something to be delivered and tested which flies in the face of much recent research on learning (Prowat, 1993). The significance of the view of 'curriculum as fact' is that it is not just a theory produced by academics but that it is the basis on which our education system is organized. In other words, it represents part of the circumstances within which anyone concerned with changing educational practice has to work.

However, such a view cannot be treated as mere illusion, the irrelevant product of ivory tower academics or bureaucratic curriculum developers that is imposed on teachers. To do so is the major weakness of the view of 'curriculum as practice'. Though challenging prevailing conceptions of curriculum, it treats them as arbitrarily imposed on the practices of students and teachers and, as a consequence, it misleads teachers as to the possibilities of change. In doing so it directly contradicts the experience of those about whom it theorizes and contributes, paradoxically, to the very division between theory and practice which its critique would seem to question. In emphasizing the conventionality of prevailing hierarchies of knowledge — academic and non-academic, theoretical and practical, abstract and concrete — it provides no basis for understanding how and why particular educational hierarchies originate in social relations both in and beyond education. Viewing curricular organization as a set of conventions implies that they could be otherwise (which is like equating the ordering of academic knowledge with customs). It assumes that school subjects like mathematics only persist through habit or custom or because that is how those in power define what should be taught. What starts as a critique of the separation of knowledge from the knower, ends up by having to invoke the crudest of mechanistic relations between knowledge and social position. In effect, it explains nothing and not surprisingly offers no strategies for change.

A theory that can provide for the possibilities of curriculum change does not emerge either from the dominant view of 'curriculum as fact' or from its opposite, the idea of 'curriculum as practice' that was proposed by radical educational theorists in the 1970s. The first, by starting from a view of knowledge abstracted from people in history and specifically from the teachers and pupils, denies them any roles except as deliverers of what has been decided elsewhere. The second, in its concern to recognize teachers as conscious agents of change and to emphasize the human possibilities in all situations, becomes abstracted, albeit in a different way, from the constraints of teachers' experience, and therefore, ironically, from their capacity to shape student learning. The idea of 'curriculum as practice' may recognize possibilities in *theory* but their practical implementation is experienced by teachers as little more than utopian. A *theoretical* critique of the *necessity* of hierarchies of knowledge and ability may be exciting in a seminar but is of little use to teachers who experience such necessities as real in *practice*. The problem then is not to deny these hierarchies nor accept them uncritically, but to try and reformulate them as the outcomes of collective and historical actions — and thus render them understandable, potentially changeable and interpretable. This leads me to a number of suggestions for transcending the dichotomy of 'curriculum as fact' and 'curriculum as practice':

1   The prescription to *start* from teachers' and pupils' practices and the theories that they evolve in their day to day practices can easily itself remain mere theory. This will be so unless there are changes in the relations between 'theorists' based in the universities and those about whom they theorize. This is not an argument against theory, for this could lead to an uncritical acceptance of any tradition and custom currently found in schools or prescribed by government. It is a recognition that the ideas of 'curriculum as fact' and 'curriculum as practice' have their origins in conservative and radical strands of academic debates that were largely removed from educational practice. Whereas the ideas associated with 'curriculum as fact' appealed to specialist subject teachers who wanted to justify what they were doing, it provided no way for them to see what new roles their subjects might have. On the other hand, although the existentialist ideas associated with 'curriculum as practice' struck a chord with teachers resistant to the bureaucratic forms of schooling, they did little to help them locate their practice.

A genuinely radical concept of the curriculum that would enable teachers to transform their practice and enhance their students' learning cannot be developed in isolation from that practice. Despite the tendency, much evident today in teacher education to dismiss the importance of theory, the new forms of university-school partnership on which teacher education is increasingly based offer the possibility of establishing 'communities of practice' consisting of teachers and academics; they could provide the context for developing more practically informed theories as well as more theoretically informed practice.

2   School learning is often experienced and thought about as if it were either isolated or separate from other types of learning. Furthermore, educational theories rarely challenge this separation and show the interconnections between school and non-school learning. If examining assumptions about the curriculum and its interconnections is to go beyond mere questioning, the broad 'political' problems of the links between different kinds and sites of learning will inevitably be raised for teachers and others involved in education. Prevailing notions about curricula and knowledge, although sustained by the practices and institutional arrangements of formal education, are not sustained by them alone. A more adequate theory of the curriculum would not restrict its concept of practice to that of teachers, nor would it restrict its focus on teachers' practice to their activities in the classroom. If the school curriculum is to become an emancipatory experience for a much larger section of each cohort of students, this is going to require much greater involvement of many people who currently have no direct links with school, including parents and employers, and many activities by teachers and pupils which are not confined to the school nor, in conventional terms, are usually defined as 'educational' at all.

3   Both views of the curriculum to which I have referred in this chapter
    tend to obscure the political and economic character of education.
    This, as I have argued, sets limits on their possibilities as theories of
    change. They also lack, in common with much educational writing, a
    sense of history or, more generally, an understanding of the present in
    terms of the past. One way of reformulating, and so potentially under-
    standing and transcending the limits of specific contexts is to see, as in
    Layton's example in the history of school science, how such limits are
    not given or fixed but produced through the conflicting actions and
    interests of people in history. For example, studies of Trades Councils
    and Local Schools Boards at the turn of the century suggest a very
    different strategy for involving working-class parents in the education
    of their children than the well intentioned paternalism of the Edu-
    cational Priority Areas of the 1970s (Lynch, 1974) or the Education
    Action Zones and Homework Clubs of the late 1990s.

These suggestions are no more than illustrative as to how aspirations
implicit in models of the curriculum might be made real in practice. They argue
for more explicit links between learning at work and in the community and
learning in classrooms. I see this as recognizing that much school and curriculum improvement will not necessarily begin in schools and that those who
work in education need to learn far more about the non-school world that
young people experience, how it differs from the world that they experience
through the curriculum and how we can help them strengthen the connections.

Chapter 3

The Curriculum and the
'New Sociology of Education'

This chapter is based on an invited address to the 1988 Annual Conference of the American Educational Research Association with the title *Lessons from a Critique of the New Sociology of Education*. Since then, there have been a number of related transformations of educational policy and practice in the UK which put some of the questions raised in that paper in quite a new context. The first is the period of systematic central government intervention into the minutiae of educational practice which began with the National Curriculum in 1988 and is culminating in the series of detailed school reforms being implemented by the new Labour Government. The second is the significantly diminished role of local government which has left individual schools, albeit within tighter national regulations, with quite new responsibilities for staffing, staff development, expenditure and admissions. The third is the emergence of a more limited role for universities in the training of teachers and their professional development, as more responsibilities are taken over by individual schools within a framework being developed by the Teacher Training Agency. All these changes need to be set within the context of vastly increased pressure from central government for all parts of the education service to cut costs and raise standards, and of changes in the economy characterized by a growth in the demand for highly qualified employees and the demise of semi-skilled and unskilled jobs. We have also seen the virtual demise of many distinct research and teaching programmes in the main educational disciplines with the exception of psychology and the growth of all kinds of partnerships with schools and colleges as university education departments struggle to survive. Two related questions which are germane to the theme of 'The Curriculum of the Future' that runs through this book arise from these developments. One is specific to the sociology of education and, to some extent, to the other educational disciplines and the other is a more general question about the future role of university-based educational studies.

The first question is whether and in what form there may be a future role for an educational discipline such as sociology of education in the curriculum of teacher education. The more pessimistic view is that sociology of education, as a unique flowering in the UK in the 1960s and 1970s, was very much a product of certain conditions of the time and in particular the relatively free-floating voluntarism that still distinguished the options open to schools in the

UK from those elsewhere in Europe. It would follow that in a new era of far greater state control of the curriculum, the sociology of education will be found, not, as before, in University Departments of Education, but as a small sub-section of mainstream university sociology departments with little direct connection to educational practice. An alternative view, which is consistent with the overall argument of this chapter and the book as a whole, is that the crisis in sociology of education did not just reflect the contingent circumstances of the 1980s and in particular the deeply felt antagonism towards sociology of the government of the time. The origin of the crisis was, at least in part, that sociology of education reflected an out-of-date view of the specialization of knowledge in educational studies. From the 1960s there was an assumption that the peculiarly insular form of specialization that characterized the academic curriculum in England and Wales could be the basis of all kinds of expansion of knowledge, both in research and teaching. Sociology of education and its dedication, at least in the 1970s, to defining itself apart from any other form of educational enquiry was one of the more obvious examples of this process. It was never going to be realistic to build the teacher education curriculum on six or seven different educational disciplines as well as on a student's own specialist teaching subject; furthermore a narrow form of disciplinary specialization was equally problematic as a basis for educational research. An alternative, which follows from analysing the demise of the new sociology of education in the 1970s, is developed in this chapter. The argument is that it is necessary to re-examine our concept of specialization and the possibility of what I shall call *connective* rather than *insular* specialization as the basis for educational studies within which sociology of education could have a new but less insulated and more connected role.

The more general question, which I shall be able to do no more than allude to here, concerns the future of educational studies in general as a university-based discipline. From the late 1960s, sociology of education (and to a lesser extent philosophy and history), defined itself as a form of critical enquiry with the main task of exposing the rhetoric and compromises of government policies and the way they promoted divisions and inequality while frequently claiming to be dedicated to achieving the opposite. Opposition to government, to official agencies and to any reference to business involvement in education was a main criterion of academic freedom and integrity for many university-based educational researchers in the 1970s. The theoretical perspectives that underpinned this intellectual oppositionism ranged widely from forms of liberalism and libertarianism to Marxism and more recently to post-modernism; since the 1980s the latter has been frequently linked to feminist and anti-racist critiques. What each shared and what I shall question in the case of the 'new sociology of education' was a resistance to being involved in implementing policies, or even in many cases in suggesting alternatives. It was as if for university-based educational studies critique was enough and it was the responsibility of others to take up the practical implications of the questions raised by academic research. While making and implementing policy is clearly a distinct activity from research and analysis and no positive purpose is served by trying to conflate them, they are not unrelated. I share the view of Carr (1995) that education is inescapably a practical activity and that therefore there can be no such thing as research geared solely to understanding; ultimately, research can only have meaning if it contributes to changing practice. It follows that critique cannot be entirely separate from policy or practice; research depends on policy and practice for its topic. This view has implications both for the role of disciplinary enquiries in educational studies and the relationship between the university and the sites of policy making and practice which it researches; I shall return to these issues at the end of the chapter.

This chapter can only touch on some aspects of the issues which I have raised and limits its focus by concentrating on the sociology of education as an example of disciplinary study in education. Furthermore, it examines one development within that field which has been the subject of considerable professional and political controversy in a number of countries: the emergence (and demise) of the 'new sociology of education' in the 1970s and 1980s. As I argued in Chapter 1, those working in the sociology of education in the 1970s took advantage of the much wider climate of political and cultural radicalism of the time to bring questions concerning knowledge and the curriculum and their relationship to the distribution of power in society onto the agenda of educational debate for the first time. The sociology of education provided a way of enabling the critique of the curriculum to be seen not just as an educational issue but as a critique of society. Why, then, as an intellectual and, at least in a weak sense, a political movement, did the 'new sociology of education' (NSOE) have such a short life? I begin with two of the basic problems which relate to themes touched upon in the previous chapter.

First, in its concern to demonstrate the arbitrariness and social exclusiveness of the existing academic curriculum, the 'new sociology of education', at least by implication, replaced the givenness of the academic curriculum by equally unexamined notions of popular consciousness or common sense as the basis for a more equitable and democratic curriculum. There is one lesson that can be learnt from the 1980s, and probably ought to have been learned at the time from the writings of the Frankfurt School of Critical Theory; it is that 'popular consciousness' can be no basis for a democratic curriculum. Aided by the tabloid press in the 1980s, forms of populism were appropriated in directions totally at odds with the radical aims espoused by the sociology of education and other forms of cultural radicalism of the 1970s.

In making explicit some of the limitations of the 'new sociology of education' and, in effect, of the position put forward in Chapter 1, this chapter does not seek to justify the existing academic curriculum and its assumptions which have changed little since the beginning of the century; on the contrary, it seeks to provide a more reliable basis for a social theory of the curriculum. School subjects, insulated from each other, are one particular historical form of systematizing knowledge and going beyond experience and common sense. They have a history associated with the emergence of the early forms of mass schooling of the nineteenth century, when the main parameters of our current academic curriculum were laid down and given their institutional basis. Nineteenth century mass schooling was not common schooling for all but divided schooling; school subjects emerged as part of that divided structure. What is needed is not a curriculum based on common sense or a 'curriculum of life', as Stuart Hall (1983) evocatively called it, but an exploration of the different forms systematizing knowledge and how they might represent more or less inclusive ways of relating to and going beyond common sense and popular experience. A curriculum that promotes real understanding will always be at odds with common sense. The question is how this separation of curriculum from common sense knowledge can enable the largest number of learners to see its worth and where it is leading them and how they can be motivated to learn with the kind of commitment and enthusiasm that has in the past been limited to a minority.

The second but closely related theme of this chapter is to suggest that the 'new sociology of education' for all its radicalism, took a highly unreflective view of the role of academic subjects in educational studies. The issues at stake are much wider than the limited concerns of this chapter and touch on questions of the social basis of intellectual work and the role of sociologists and others as intellectuals. They also relate to the different forms that systematically organized knowledge can take to which I referred in connection with school subjects. In examining the demise of one sub-discipline, we need to ask whether the analysis suggests the possibility of a new basis for a more critical educational studies that has the rigour associated with disciplinary study but is not bound by the traditional disciplines and their inter-professional rivalries.

Some researchers are beginning to argue that we are witnessing the emergence of new modes of knowledge production which will replace or at least develop alongside the traditional disciplinary forms (Gibbons et al., 1994). Others have suggested that the transformations of global capitalism are undermining the whole basis and credibility of academic subjects (natural sciences as much as the arts and social sciences) as the main forms of social organization for the production of knowledge. Wexler (1988) for example suggests that in the USA, corporate capitalism, with its demands for technical efficiency and the solution of immediate practical problems, has become disenchanted with the typical university-based organization of knowledge. Within this scenario, new kinds of research institutions are emerging, which are not tied to the conservatism of academic cultures and which attract an increasing proportion of the private funding that used to go to universities. There is some parallel with the emergence, in the 1980s and 1990s, of politically directed 'think tanks' in this country, although on a much smaller scale.

It may be that we are entering a period in which the values and interests of those involved in even quite esoteric research are becoming more and more visible and contested. If so, then it will be necessary to reappraise forms of intellectual work such as the educational disciplines and to ask whether their traditional assumptions about autonomy and objectivity are still appropriate. This chapter argues that academic work in education is inescapably involved in the wider movements and forces for social change and that therefore there is no escape from a clearer and more explicit sense of its political purposes. Furthermore, I would suggest that the implications of accepting the political nature of educational knowledge may be less painful than some fear. First, the emergence of the New Labour Government has cast traditional views of the 'Intellectual as Partisan', to paraphrase Alvin Gouldner's phrase, into doubt and confusion. As Giddens (1994) has argued, the divisions between Right and Left, except at the extremes, are increasingly unclear as are questions of political loyalty. Increasingly some of those who have traditionally seen themselves as 'on the left' can find themselves 'on the right' on some policy issues. Second, a positive outcome of a greater clarity of the political purpose of intellectual work could make the constructive contribution of academic disciplines in educational studies more widely recognized as well as giving a direction and sense of purpose to discipline-based research that is often lacking. This is the context from which I turn to the specific topic of this chapter, the rise and fall of the 'new sociology of education' and its origins in the early 1970s.

Origins of the 'New Sociology of Education'

The term 'new sociology of education' is itself open to various interpretations and often overlaps with the terms 'radical' (Moore, 1988) and 'critical' sociologies of education (Young, 1986; 1987). I begin by locating quite specifically the body of work to which I refer as the new sociology of education by connecting it to two closely related publishing events. First, there was the publication in 1971 of the book *Knowledge and Control* (Young, 1971) subtitled *New Directions for the Sociology of Education*. This was linked to the launch in 1971 of the first Open University course in the sociology of education — **School and Society** — for which *Knowledge and Control* was a set book. That meant that not only were several thousand teachers who registered for the course obliged to purchase the book, but that it was widely available, at least in the UK, at a relatively low price. Both developments undoubtedly played major roles in the early dissemination of the book's ideas.

It was however, in 1973 that the term, 'new sociology of education', was coined and the connection was first made between the sociological analysis of the curriculum and the role of teachers as potential agents of radical educational change (Gorbutt, 1973). *Knowledge and Control* (1971) was less explicit about its political objectives, a point to which I shall return. Rather, it set out to chart a new course for the sociology of education as an academic field. It aimed to define a distinct field of enquiry for the sociology of education and break with the earlier tradition of the sociology of education as being largely derivative of social stratification research. In doing so it asserted that the primary topic of study for the sociology of education must be the curriculum and pedagogy as social processes. In doing this it set itself apart from earlier work in the field both in the US and UK which had concentrated on input/output models of education and paid very little attention to processes. It was this attempt to define the sociology of education as concerned with the problem of school knowledge, its definition and transmission, that held together the diverse and in some cases theoretically contradictory set of papers collected in *Knowledge and Control*.

As soon as the book was published, the theoretical differences amongst its contributors became apparent. On the one hand, it included the Durkheimian structural analyses of Bernstein and Bourdieu and, on the other hand, an anti-positivist sociology of knowledge, much influenced by the early papers of Wright Mills (1939; 1940), was represented in *Knowledge and Control* by the introduction and the chapters by Esland, Keddie and Young. Of course such a distinction is oversimplified but for the purposes of the argument in this chapter, it is useful. The anti-positivist tradition in the sociology of knowledge, with a particular focus on the curriculum informs Chapter 1 of this book, and is what I shall identify as the 'new sociology of education'. The Durkheimian tradition, to which it was certainly indebted, developed quite separately, although some interesting connections have been made more recently (Moore, 1988).

The 'new sociology of education', as a set of ideas and as a description of the priorities of a group of researchers and teachers was short-lived, partly on account of its own theoretical limitations, some of which I discuss later, and partly on account of changes in the wider political and economic circumstances which meant that a focus on teachers as agents of change became increasingly unrealistic. The oversimplification of some of its earliest formulations and popularizations and particularly its naive rejection of the concept 'social structure' received their most systematic critique from Whitty (1974). His work led to our joint efforts at reconceptualization in the two collections that we co-edited (Whitty and Young, 1976; Young and Whitty, 1977) and later his own book (Whitty, 1986). The two collections represented an end of the new sociology of education as a distinctive approach in the UK, although some of its ideas were picked up later by those developing the sociology of the curriculum (e.g. Goodson, 1987), and in different ways in other countries (Ladwig, 1996; Muller, 1996). It was marginalized in a leading Anglo-American Reader in the sociology of education (Karabel and Halsey, 1977) but was taken up and developed in the field of curriculum theory in the USA, most notably in the work of Apple, Wexler and Giroux. It is interesting that much later there was a sudden burst of commentaries and reviews by Canadian and French researchers (Forquin, 1983; Trottier, 1987).

Why then is the 'new sociology of education' worth bothering about nearly two decades later? Why should we assume that there are significant lessons to be learnt from this brief flowering of intellectual radicalism that perhaps owed more to a political naiveté born of the aspirations of the cultural radicalism of the 1960s than to systematic research and theory? The aim of the remainder of this chapter is to answer these questions.

Early Responses

I should like to discuss briefly a number of quite diverse responses to the 'new sociology of education' in the 1970s before attempting a more systematic analysis. My abiding memory of the responses to *Knowledge and Control* in the early 1970s was the level of anger and antagonism generated among political groupings who would have been unlikely to have agreed on anything else. Let us begin with the responses from the 'Right', then unlike in the 1980s and early 1990s, a weak and marginal group in the UK with little influence — particularly in relation to education. The best example of a Right-wing response was a publication in 1977 of a report with the title *Marxist and Radical Penetration: The Attack on Higher Education.* It told of teachers coming into the schools 'with *Knowledge and Control* in their blood stream' ready to 'soften up British youth for the Trotskyist take-over'! Less polemical but showing no less anxiety, were the responses of a number of liberal and conservative philosophers — and even some sociologists — who wrote newspaper and journal articles with titles like 'The abyss of relativism' and 'Knowledge out of control' (Pring, 1972). They warned of the dangers of bringing the heady ideas of the sociology of knowledge from its safe and rarefied place in debates about epistemology into the practical arena of curriculum decision making.

There are, of course, many historical parallels to these attempts to restrict potentially subversive ideas to an elite, by Churches and politicians as well as by educationists. For example, in nineteenth century England religious leaders were largely successful in keeping geology out of the school curriculum on the grounds that it might undermine young people's faith in God. However, in the 1970s it was not faith in God but in Western Civilization that was the issue. In suggesting that the academic curriculum might not be a benign selection of the 'best in the culture' but a particular elite's selection of knowledge largely in the interests of preserving its own position — the 'new sociology of education' was seen as challenging something almost sacred. Perhaps the strange thing in retrospect is the surprise and hurt that such reactions invoked. I doubt if those who identified with 'new sociology of education' are the only radical intellectual group in history who not only wanted to subvert the established institutions of education but also expected to do it unchallenged! This surprise, of course, raises much wider issues about the contradictory position of middle class radicals in prestigious institutions like universities (Jaccoby, 1997).

The response from a section of the left in education, particularly those linked to the Communist Party, was very similar to that of the Right. For them the academic curriculum was something that the labour movement had fought to get access to for their sons and daughters. At a time of at least some increase in educational opportunity, such questioning as that proposed by the new sociology of education was seen as a threat to the whole basis of a left educational politics committed to working with the educational establishment to extend access. A number of articles appeared in journals with a wide circulation amongst teachers (e.g. Simon, 1975) which attacked the 'new sociology of education' for suggesting that the academic curriculum was biased in social class terms and could not be the basis for a truly comprehensive education. They claimed that such arguments appeared to give legitimacy to the academic exclusion of working class children. The 'new sociology of education', it was asserted, was 'encouraging educational apartheid' and in a phrase I remember well, 'preparing working class pupils to be little more than helots'. Other less formal and less public responses came from individual teachers and teacher educators. For example, one wrote, 'it (*Knowledge and Control*) gave me the confidence to think what I had always intuitively felt but not had the confidence to express'. Something of the latter feeling was expressed in a recent contribution to 'The Guardian's' *Don's Delight* column in which John Evans, Professor of Physical Education at the University of Loughborough, referred to *Knowledge and Control* as the 'book that changed my life'.

Practical Outcomes

I would like to link these observations to one final point about responses to *Knowledge and Control*. The 'new sociology of education' was associated with both a critique of the academic curriculum as a form of domination and with supporting non-hierarchical forms of pedagogy, student-centred as opposed to subject-centred learning and breaking down the barriers between school and non-school knowledge. In the very different political climate of the 1980s, both the critique and the alternatives were represented within English educational policy but in quite different contexts from those hoped for or expected by those associated with the 'new sociology of education'. From as early as 1976 there was criticism of the English academic curriculum as a contributing cause to Britain's industrial decline. It was seen as deflecting successful students from their proper future in high technology industries and denying slower learners the possibility of gaining the kind of practical skills they would need if they were to obtain jobs (Barnett, 1987). At the same time, we find a non-hierarchical pedagogy (expressed in the idea of the 'negotiated curriculum' and later a learner-centred curriculum) forming part of programmes for low achievers and the young unemployed. Such courses were rather euphemistically called pre-vocational but all too easily excluded those they recruited from progressing either to specialized vocational or academic studies (Ranson, 1984; Green, 1984; Spours and Young, 1988). This particular issue is discussed further in Chapter 4 of this book.

It was this contradictory combination of outrage from the left and right, anxiety from liberal academics, and a sense of emancipation from some teachers that suggests to me that a more critical examination of some of the assumptions of the sociological critique of the academic curriculum is necessary. The fact that some of the alternatives implicit in the critique were and still are being incorporated into what are highly divisive vocational programmes gives the issue an added urgency. I shall argue that the critics of the 'new sociology of education' were, in important ways, right. This in no way denies that there was undoubtedly something emancipatory in the connections that the 'new sociology of education' made between concepts of knowledge in curricula and the distribution of power in society nor that a social theory of knowledge, freed from its weaknesses, is vital if research on curricular alternatives is to have a future. In the next section, therefore, I review two of the explicit claims of the 'new sociology of education'.

What Was New in the New Sociology of Education?

In relation to its claim to be offering 'new directions', I shall consider three issues that were central to the 'new sociology of education':

- the question of educational inequalities
- prioritizing the curriculum as topic for sociology of education
- emphasizing teachers and teacher educators as agents of progressive change.

What was not recognized at the time but is striking in retrospect was the extent of the similarity of political concerns between those identified with the 'new sociology of education' and those whose work it criticized — AH Halsey, Jean Floud, JWB Douglas and David Glass are the most obvious examples. For both groups the primary political issue about education in England and Wales was the persistence of social class inequalities. Furthermore, in so far as work in the 'new sociology of education' was explicit about what it meant by social class, it took over the broad distinction between manual and non-manual occupations that was used by the earlier sociologists to differentiate members of the middle and working classes. At the same time the 'new sociology of education' drew on writers such as Raymond Williams to give a more explicit cultural meaning to class inequalities and gave considerable emphasis to the theoretical and methodological issues that set it apart from the earlier tradition. The 'new sociology of education' was therefore making some quite definite, though at the time not explicit, assumptions about the nature and role of academic work in education that at least need examining.

It would be my view, at least in retrospect, that there were elements of inter-professional and perhaps even inter-generational rivalry in the 'new sociology of education' position that led it to stress theoretical differences within the discipline rather than political similarities. As governments, certainly in Western Europe, develop a growing range of strategies from persuasion to bribery to bring academics into line, the perspective adopted by the 'new sociology of education', which treated academic work as an almost autonomous source of educational influence and expertise, seems increasingly untenable. If the 'new sociology of education' had emphasized the political importance of overcoming educational inequalities rather than its theoretical distinctiveness, it would have sought alliances with politically sympathetic survey researchers of the earlier tradition in sociology of education rather than seeing them as a kind of 'old guard' or professional opposition. There is also a deeper point to which I cannot do justice here. It could be argued that the 'new sociology of education' tried to replace a reformist politics around social class inequalities with a radical though underdeveloped 'cultural' politics. However as they both neglected questions of gender and race (Acker, 1981), it is not surprising that neither the 'old' nor the 'new' sociology of education was able to deal adequately with the issue of educational inequalities.

The most distinctive and still to me most important contribution of the 'new sociology of education' was to make the processes of selection and exclusion of knowledge, both in the classroom and in the wider society, the central topic for the sociology of education. The argument that the processes of classroom interaction could be shown to embody power relations between teacher and students *and* in the wider society was both important and at the time new. However, there was also a tendency to treat these processes as if they were the only legitimate concerns of the sociology of education and therefore to neglect the concerns of earlier researchers with the wider processes governing pupil access to selective education. The sociological analysis of the curriculum would undoubtedly have been strengthened by developing research to link the process by which pupils were selected for different types of school (and streams within schools) with the processes by which knowledge was selected or excluded in the curriculum.

The final distinction between the so-called old and 'new' sociologies of education was in their views of their audience. The earlier work saw itself within the Fabian tradition of policy-oriented research. It assumed that politicians and educational administrators were reasonably rational people who would act on carefully researched findings and that they shared the researchers' concern with eliminating inequalities. This point is well demonstrated in a later example of work within that tradition (Halsey, Heath and Ridge, 1980). The 'new sociology of education', on the other hand, implicitly distrusted such people as 'part of the establishment' and directed its attention towards other academics, particularly teacher educators as well as to teachers themselves. Thus one audience or agency of change was replaced with another. No attempt was made to analyse the role of the state and the relationships between different actors within it, nor to discover whether teachers were in fact responsive to the new sociological ideas and how, if they were, they could become agents of change independently of or even in opposition to administrators.

Despite its radical politics, there were ways in which, at least in some respects, the 'new sociology of education' was quite conservative. By cutting itself off from educational policy makers, the 'new sociology of education' assumed that the old idea of academic freedom would continue to be the basis for its autonomy, and somehow, as suggested earlier, allow it to be an agent of radical change. In the next section, I take a number of examples to illustrate the problems that arise when academic work with progressive purposes gives more emphasis to its autonomous role as a discipline than to an awareness of its position in the wider balance of political forces.

The 'New Sociology of Education' and the Curriculum

The most distinctive feature of the 'new sociology of education' was its focus on the school curriculum and, as indicated earlier, this was also something that gave its critics most anxiety. The focus on the curriculum arose directly out of the search for an alternative explanation of working class school failure to that provided by the earlier sociology of education; this had developed the concept of educability which brought together a range of causal factors in the cultural backgrounds of low achieving working class students. In its more simplistic forms, the concept of educability offered solutions of (a) educational expansion, and (b) compensation for cultural disadvantages, as if the cultural form of educational provision played no part. In direct opposition to this approach, the 'new sociology of education' focused directly on the selective features of the academic curriculum as the major source of the unequal distribution of education. As I argued in Chapter 1, with its separate single subjects, its hierarchies of valued knowledge and its exclusion of non-school knowledge, the academic curriculum was seen by the 'new sociology of education' as an instrument of social class exclusion. The ideological power of the academic curriculum was identified by the success with which it was able to convince people that it was the only way of organizing knowledge that enabled students to develop their intellectual capacities. It therefore gave legitimacy to the view that those who did not succeed in its terms were, in effect, ineducable.

As a framework, the sociological critique of the curriculum gave rise to a number of empirical studies of struggles for curricular legitimacy that lent support to its claims (e.g. Young, 1972; Vulliamy, 1976). Its weakness was the way it slipped from being an analytical perspective on curriculum practice to being what might be described as a kind of 'oppositional description' of how the curriculum really was. This slip from analysis to description had the effect of treating the academic curriculum as if it had only ideological power; in other words the focus was restricted to how the curriculum sustained the existing unequal distribution of power in society. This meant that the cultural power of the curriculum as a source of real understandings, which despite its ideological 'packaging' gave at least some students an understanding and control in the world in which they were going to have to live, was neglected. The sociological analysis of the curriculum as a form of ideological power meant that the only alternative was no curriculum (a kind of deschooling) or some notion of a curriculum based on experience, a notion referred to in the previous chapter and very well criticized by Hall (1983). A number of sociologists attempted to solve the problem of the relationship between ideology and culture in the curriculum by drawing on the idea of a working class curriculum (Cohen, 1984; Whitty, 1986) based on 'really useful knowledge', a Chartist idea from the early nineteenth century (Johnson, 1980). The idea that there could be knowledge that was located in the circumstances of a particular social class made some sense in the very specific and short-lived Chartist experience when skilled craftsmen owned the means though not the relations of production. However, whether the concept of 'really useful knowledge' can be given any meaning over a century later, is far less clear, as Johnson himself pointed out (Johnson, 1980). Decisions about workplaces are less and less in the hands of owners, in the nineteenth century sense; they are increasingly removed from centres of production to centres of research and planning which in many cases are not even in the same country.

I would like to summarize the three weaknesses which I see as contributing to the failure of the 'new sociology of education' to fulfil either the hopes that some of us had for it or the fears of others. First, it lacked a political analysis of the role of academic work in education. This meant that it tended to overemphasize disputes within the discipline and failed to build links with other educational researchers with whom it differed over method and even theory but not over values and purposes. It also tended to over-emphasize the importance of educational research in contributing to educational change; thus with some irony, the 'new sociology of education' ended in a similar position to those who argued for the independence of educational research from policy and practice. Second, in emphasizing how the curriculum perpetuated educational inequalities through the process of academic exclusion and in neglecting the role of organizational structures, it gave a misleading autonomy to teachers as agents of curriculum change and neglected the links between the social class basis of curriculum knowledge and the social class basis of student selection. Third, in failing to distinguish the ideological power of curricula in legitimizing selection and exclusion and its cultural power in providing access to powerful ideas, it had no criteria for developing and assessing curricula alternatives.

Writing in 1997, it is my view that in questioning the objectivity and autonomy of the academic curriculum and in demonstrating its socio-historical character, the 'new sociology of education' was tackling an issue that remains as important today as it was 25 years ago. However, it failed to be specific enough about how the social character of the organization of knowledge in the curriculum should be conceptualized. The 1960s and 1970s were a period of considerable educational expansion in all Western countries and the goal of greater equality in education was widely shared across the political spectrum. It was also one of those rare times when forms of cultural radicalism appeared, at least in some circles, as normal. This was the context in which it was possible for the 'new sociology of education', as well as similar developments in philosophy and psychology, to raise some fundamental questions that went to the heart of what education in a modern industrial society was about and what such a society thought about itself. Similar questions were being asked by the burgeoning groups of the new left and in almost every academic discipline (Pateman, 1971). For the sociology of education the question was whether the greater equality, which was widely supported, could be achieved without some substantial changes in our ideas about knowledge and how it should be organized in curricula. The political responses I referred to at the beginning of the chapter were an indication of the kind of interests threatened in even conceiving of such changes, let alone that they might be a practical possibility. The sociological critique of the curriculum, in that it attempted to invert the balance of power away from experts to the community, was democratic, at least in theory. However, it lacked popular support beyond small groups of teachers and teacher educators and, because it lacked both a strategy and practicable alternatives, it failed to gain support from progressive administrators or other academics. It exemplifies well the limitations of a model of research that might be described as 'critique without alternatives'. The much greater professional support gained by what was in many ways a no less radical analysis of the post compulsory curriculum in the early 1990s (Finegold et al., 1990) and which is discussed in Chapter 5 and later chapters of this book illustrates the point well. *A British Baccalaureate* (Finegold et al., 1990) was not just critique; it did offer an alternative, even if eight years later it is still far from being realized.

Conclusions

This chapter has focused on a relatively small incident in the history of educational studies in the UK. However, the issues raised concerning the fate of the 'new sociology of education' do, I would argue, have wider implications both for educational studies and the curriculum as well as for the broader role of university-based educational researchers. I would like to conclude with a brief consideration of one of the implications of the previous analysis which strikes me to be of particular relevance today. It relates to the anti-positivist view of knowledge that the 'new sociology of education' shared with many others at the time and since. Despite the differences between the 'new sociology of education', which was initially inspired by phenomenology and a pragmatist sociology of knowledge (Young, 1971; 1973), the Marxist sociology of education of the late 1970s and 1980s (Sharp, 1975) and the post modernist variants that followed, they share a basic principle in common of seeing knowledge as 'socially constructed'. It seems likely that the more intensive criticism that was brought to bear on the 'new sociology of education', at least relative to the later variants, reflected its distinctive concept of social constructivism. It tried to link knowledge to the structures of power in society **and** to the processes of social interaction *in the classroom* (Keddie, 1971). It thus appeared to offer the basis for a strategy of radical change. In practice, the two strands of the analysis of the relations between power and knowledge became severed as structuralist and anti-structuralist versions of the sociology of education were set against each other and any practical or policy implications of holding the two sets of ideas together were quickly lost. The question remains as to why links between structuralist and constructivist views of knowledge, which were part of the new sociology of education at the beginning, became severed and whether this separation might account for its demise. There are a number of possibilities. The first is that the two approaches are intrinsically incompatible and that adherents of each will pursue different intellectual journeys as they have in the past with little direct relevance to policy or practice. I reject this possibility in so far as it applies to education which is, by definition, a practical activity. In other words, unlike most other academic disciplines, educational theories depend on practice and therefore cannot avoid in some sense relating back to it. The second possibility is that social constructivist views of knowledge can, except in the most trivial sense, only lead to relativism and the arbitrariness of all judgments. From this point of view the policy and practical implications of such theories are minimal and at best they are relegated to the margins of academic life as was the case of the old sociology of knowledge. I reject this view both practically, as undermining any rationale for educational studies in the university, and theoretically as being little better than the mirror image of the objectivist view of knowledge that it criticizes. The fact that powerful concepts have been socially constructed in particular contexts for particular purposes does not make them less powerful. Even well tested theories in the natural sciences contain contextual elements which shape how they are used. The third possibility is that the original theory in *Knowledge and Control* was inadequate or at best little more than an aspiration that certain links were important. I reject this conclusion as true but inadequate on its own; it can only lead to the misguided search for better theories, as if education was like a natural science. In some ways the post-modernist ideas that replaced earlier forms of social constructivism in the sociology of education are 'better' theories to the extent that they are more comprehensive in making structural and interactionist links between power and knowledge. However, they are, if anything, further from bridging the gap between theory and policy and practice than the ideas they replaced. The final possibility is that the problem with the 'new' sociological approach to knowledge and the curriculum was not just that it had theoretical inadequacies but that it was shaped by the location of researchers in the universities who were insulated from both policy and practice. The issue to which I will return in the final chapter of this book is therefore not only what new theory of knowledge is necessary but what new relations are necessary between universities, as sites of knowledge production, and the sites of policy and practice where educational ideas become and often fail to become practical realities. Only with such a dual focus will it be possible to avoid the break that characterized the demise of the 'new sociology of education' and left radical ideas to become little more than academic debates.

Section 2

Academic/Vocational Divisions in the Curriculum of the Future

Bridging Academic/Vocational Divisions in the 14–19 Curriculum: A New Perspective on Linking Education and Work

The first chapter of this book suggested that the secondary curriculum could be analysed in terms of the *stratification of knowledge* and that there were links between the stratification of knowledge in the curriculum and the patterns of social inequality and distribution of power in the wider society. A key example of this relationship between the curriculum and social stratification is the academic/vocational divisions that separate *education* in the subject-based curriculum from training in work-related skills and the way this division reflects and is reflected in the organization of work and, in particular, in the division between mental and manual labour. The political issue, though hardly debated except in the rarefied world of left-wing journals, was whether these divisions reflected the distribution of intellectual capacities in the population, or whether they were no more than a historically specific form of social organization which educational divisions merely confirmed.

Prior to the 1980s, at least in the UK, academic and vocational programmes were almost completely separated from each other and though the divisions between them were sharp, in terms of the future life chances of students, the problems they gave rise to were not widely debated. The most visible division in the secondary curriculum was the legacy of the old division between grammar and secondary modern schools that was a characteristic of the curriculum of the new comprehensive schools of the 1960s and 1970s. This division was between what might be called the 'strong' or 'grammar school' version of the subject-based curriculum and the weak 'secondary modern' version with less subjects and less content supplemented by classes in woodwork, metalwork and domestic science. The latter was only 'vocational' in the implicit sense that it gave clear messages about the kind of jobs that it was expected that young people on such courses were destined for. There were debates, discussed in earlier chapters, about the viability of an alternative to the subject-based curriculum that took more account of the everyday life experiences of the majority of pupils and about a modern version of a 'practical' curriculum. Vocational courses, on the other hand, involved only a minority of 16 year olds; they were not available in schools, were mostly part time and largely associated with work-based apprenticeships.

By 1988 when the article (Spours and Young, 1988) on which this chapter is based was written, there were few jobs for pupils leaving school without qualifications and such pupils either stayed at school or college or entered work based training schemes. The government response to these new 'stayers on' was to put a new emphasis on how schools should prepare young people for employment; this led to a series of attempts to 'vocationalize' the secondary curriculum which culminated in the Technical and Vocational Education Initiative (TVEI) which was launched in 1983. It was the growth of what became known as pre-vocational programmes in schools and colleges that began to make visible the academic/vocational divide in secondary education and the problems of progression that it generated. Though often welcomed by students, especially if they included work experience, these programmes served to exacerbate the problems they were designed to solve. Being based in schools and colleges, they were not able to provide real workplace skills, even when jobs were available. On the other hand, the new programmes, designed as alternatives to the subject-based curriculum, did not provide students with the knowledge they needed to progress to further or higher education. Responses by teachers to the new programmes varied. Some accepted an inevitable differentiation of the upper secondary curriculum as the numbers staying on in school after the age of 16 expanded; some saw such programmes as anti-educational in that they denied students, largely those from working class homes, any access to the 'real' knowledge of the academic curriculum; others identified with the more simplistic versions of the sociological critiques of a subject-based curriculum discussed in Chapter 1 and saw the new programmes as a potential basis for a more comprehensive curriculum for all students from the ages of 14 to 19.

None of these responses addressed the extent to which the secondary curriculum, whether subject-based and divided into weak and strong forms, or in the newly emerging divisions between subject-based and vocational programmes, was appropriate to making available the skills and knowledge that young people were likely to need in the twenty-first century. This chapter begins to address this issue, initially from the point of view of history teachers, who in the 1980s were feeling increasingly marginalized, both by the drop in numbers of pupils opting for their subject at the age of 14 and by the general vocational drift of the government's curriculum policy. It argues that the changes in the organization of work and, in particular, the breakdown of divisions between mental and manual labour in the occupational structure, raise fundamental questions about the adequacy of a 14–19 curriculum based on academic/vocational divisions which separate programmes based on subjects from those aiming to prepare young people for employment. Instead of arguing that the subject-based curriculum should be dropped, at least for some pupils, as has been a feature of the new vocational courses, it proposes a new and more *connective* role for subjects for all students, integrated with the experience and understanding of the world of work.

School subjects are ways of providing access to concepts and bodies of knowledge that have evolved historically; however, alone or taught as 'ends in themselves', they cannot be the basis for a 14–19 curriculum for the future. The argument that is developed, which remains no less relevant 10 years after the first version of this chapter was written, is that the 14–19 curriculum needs to combine access to subject knowledge with an understanding of the changing nature of work for all students. In making the case for reassessing the relationship between the curriculum and work, the chapter begins by outlining the policy context of the late 1980s when the National Curriculum was about to be launched and TVEI had been extended to all secondary schools. The following section steps back from the policy context and looks at alternative ways of conceptualizing the meaning of vocationalism by drawing briefly on the interpretations of Dewey and Gramsci. This leads to an approach for bridging the divide between academic subjects and the world of work by developing their 'vocational' aspects. A series of issues that follow from this approach are then discussed; making school subjects more 'connective', integrating work experience in the 14–19 curriculum and some of the dilemmas facing teachers are examined. The chapter concludes with two observations on how the argument of this chapter from the analysis in the 1988 paper. The first relates to the role of subjects and the second to a point implicit in the 1988 paper and concerns the critical role of qualifications in shaping curriculum options.

Late 1980s Strategies for Reforming the Secondary Curriculum

Two major criticisms of the secondary curriculum were made by the Conservative governments in the late 1980s. The first which dated back to Mr Callaghan's 1976 Ruskin speech was that the curriculum was not sufficiently responsive to the needs of industry and commerce; the second was that the freedom of schools to choose their own curriculum was a major cause of the low levels of attainment of the majority of pupils, especially in mathematics and science. Both criticisms can be seen as a reflection of the continued and deepening crisis in the subject-based curriculum that had changed little in structure since the beginning of the century.

Two separate and seemingly contradictory responses emerged from these criticisms and the various unfavourable comparisons which they implied with the educational performance of economically more successful countries such as Germany and Japan. The first, from 1981 onwards, was the attempt to *vocationalize* the secondary curriculum and give more emphasis to making students more employable when they left school. This policy of 'vocationalization' was exemplified by TVEI and the Certificate for Pre-vocational Education and culminated in the 1990s with General National Vocational Qualifications (GNVQs) being made available in schools.

The second response was the proposal, in the Conservative manifesto for the 1987 General Election, for a National Curriculum, based on traditional subjects, and tested at the ages of 7, 11, 14 and 16. Although not overtly vocational in intent, the National Curriculum was designed to limit the freedom of teachers and give greater emphasis to the 'basic skills' of literacy and numeracy that employers were demanding.

Although both reform strands were seen as consistent by the government, the National Curriculum proposals appeared to teachers to be thoroughly inconsistent with pedagogic innovations such as work experience, activity-based methods and modular assessment that were promoted by TVEI. This inconsistency became apparent later when TVEI aims had to be substantially narrowed so that they became at least relatively compatible with the National Curriculum.

These responses to the problems of the traditional subject-based curriculum can be seen as attempts to overcome its weaknesses for lower achieving pupils without changing it significantly for high achievers. The first National Curriculum orders continued to underwrite a passive view of the learner in relation to knowledge and the traditional view of subjects as 'ends in themselves' separated from any contexts in which the knowledge they gave access to might be applied. The new pre-vocational programmes, on the other hand, with their emphasis upon active learning and 'real life situations', were designed specifically to encourage learning on the part of those pupils who had become disaffected from the subject-based curriculum. However, in rejecting any relationship to subject knowledge they inevitably became the basis for new divisions; a point to which I shall return to later. The remainder of this chapter suggests how the two strands of vocationalism, one represented by the work-related focus of TVEI and the other by the strong emphasis on school subjects in the National Curriculum, might be brought together. It begins by looking briefly, but critically at how two very different educationalists, Dewey, the American liberal philosopher, and Gramsci, the Italian Marxist intellectual, tackled the problem of links between education and work.

Reconceptualizing the Relationships between Work and Education

Any attempt to integrate academic and vocational education has to confront the way both terms have been used in educational debates and policy (Young et al., 1997). This means recognizing the ways in which demands for the 'vocationalization' of education have reasserted themselves again and again since the beginning of state education whenever there has been a new period of crisis in the economy (Reeder, 1979). This tendency is not specific to this country. However, the way in which, in England from the middle of the nineteenth century, the concept of vocation, seen as something unique to the

'liberal professions', was separated from its association with 'vocational education' as a way of preparing people for specific and, usually, low level occupations, was distinctive. 'Vocational' in this sense is invariably linked to 'technical'
as in the Technical and Vocational Education Initiative and vocational courses
are always seen as inferior to and measured against 'academic' courses. Furthermore, they are invariably associated with low ability pupils and seen as cater-
ing for a student population that is as unrepresentative in social class terms as
the intake to Oxford or Cambridge universities.

It is arguable that the ways in which the concept of 'vocationalism' has
been used since the early 1980s is more accurately referred to as 'occupationalism'[5]. The term 'occupationalism' can have two meanings. It refers to
the emphasis on preparing young people for particular jobs rather than for a
'vocation' or adult life in general. However, it can also be used, as in the concept of 'behavioural occupationalism', not as an 'educational ideology servic-
ing production'[6] but as 'ideology of production' designed to regulate education. It is behavioural occupationalism, for example, that underlies concepts
such as transferable skills and skill ownership and the performance definitions
of competence associated with NVQs.

The social origins of educational divisions are very clear in the separation,
in England of the middle class concept of 'vocation as a calling' from vocational education as the preparation of young people for skilled and semi-
skilled jobs. However, the changes in the economy referred to at the beginning
of this chapter are beginning to break down the old occupational divisions
between manual and non-manual work and suggest the need to rethink the
traditional division between 'having a vocation' and vocational education and
its links with the academic/vocational divide which is so embedded in English
culture and history. Two alternative approaches to reconceptualizing vocationalism from very different cultural traditions are now considered.

The first approach is that of Silver and Brennan who describe it as 'liberal
vocationalism' (Silver and Brennan, 1988). They draw on Dewey's concept of
an occupation as both a way of defining the meaning and purpose of work
and as *the* organizing principle for the curriculum. It was based on Dewey's
belief that the best liberal education is vocational and the best vocational
education is 'liberal' in the sense that both are complementary perspectives on
how to prepare young people for adult life. Another possibility is the more
overtly political approach of the Italian Marxist, Antonio Gramsci. Gramsci's
starting point was the link he saw between the possibility of work being an
educational principle and industrial workers being the 'ruling class of the
future' and therefore needing to understand the context of their work and
the economic, social and cultural implications of their skills. He broadened
the concept of vocation from its individualistic association with the notion of
a 'calling' to the idea of all people, at least in principle, expressing a commitment to and an understanding of the worthwhileness of work and what it
could represent if changes in its organization were to take place. Thus, for
Gramsci, to have a vocation, and for education to be vocational, involved

more than (the) mastery of the technical skill and knowledge required to complete an industrial or professional task competently. It (would) also entail an awareness of moral obligation, an appreciation of the political and economic implications of a job of work and often of the aesthetics of 'production'. (Entwhistle, 1979)

Despite their political differences and different locations as a Professor at a prestigious American university and as a Communist Party organizer in Turin, Dewey and Gramsci's views on vocational education had similarities that reflected the period in which they wrote and their shared optimism about the outcomes of the industrial and economic changes that they saw taking place. The problem with Dewey's approach was that although he was aware of the gross social inequalities of his time, he also saw industrial capitalism evolving as a basically democratic force for change into a society in which all could have worthwhile occupations. He was therefore unable to recognize the reality that only a small range of occupations could be the basis for the kind of 'liberal vocationalism' that he argued for. Gramsci, on the other hand, though far more aware than Dewey of the contradictions of industrial capitalism, held on to the Marxist view that industrial working class and therefore industrial work itself, could be an emancipatory force in history and therefore an educational principle. Over half a century after Gramsci's death, the future of industrial capitalism has become much less certain and shows few signs of developing in the direction that he (or Dewey) hoped for.

It follows that neither the idea of an occupation as suggested by Dewey, nor those of work and vocation as defined by Gramsci can, on their own, provide the basis for the integration of academic and vocational learning that they, from their different political positions, espoused. However, in providing alternatives to the increasingly out of date vocabulary of liberal education and its disassociation from the world of work, they do point a way forward. Instead of replacing the knowledge basis of liberal education by the concepts of occupation or work, it is suggested that the two concepts can, in a *connective* relationship that might be described as critical vocationalism, be the dual principles of a 14–19 curriculum. The principles of critical vocationalism would give priority to the ways that young people can relate to work and knowledge and how they can draw on both subject knowledge and their experience and understanding of work in developing their ideas about the future. It would draw on academic subjects to shed light on the social divisions and changes in the current organization of work and draw on the work experience of students to help give meaning and context to subject-based knowledge. It would build on the experience of the schools–industry movement and in particular the work of Jamieson, Miller and Watts who have recognized the importance of students understanding the causes of economic change and how such understanding needs to involve the more active forms of pedagogy associated with work experience (Jamieson, Miller and Watts, 1988).

School Subjects, Work and Bridging the
Academic/Vocational Divide

Although the traditional rationale of the subject-based curriculum has been the teaching of subjects 'as ends in themselves', this did not mean that they had no specific links to a student's future working life. Not only have high achievements in academic subjects always been used as important indicators of general knowledge and skills, but mathematics, the sciences and foreign languages have continued to be crucial requirements for entry into many occupations. The approach developed in this chapter extends and makes explicit these 'vocational' aspects of school subjects by suggesting that their role in providing students with access to concepts and ideas can be integrated with the need that students have to understand the changing world of work that they will face as adults. The approach is based on five principles:

- the 14–19 curriculum for all students should in part be based on explicit links between school subjects and the changing nature of work.
- economic and technological understanding should be part of the core of the 14–19 curriculum for all school students.
- school subjects should be presented both as *bodies of knowledge* to be studied for their own sake and for the concepts they give access to, and as frameworks of understanding which have a history and which can enable students to reflect upon their experience and their future aspirations for learning and work.
- debates about the changing nature of work should be at the centre of the 14–19 curriculum for all students and reflected in appropriate ways in the syllabuses of all subjects.
- work experience should be an integral and *connective* feature of the 14–19 curriculum of all students.

Although this approach was developed in response to the divisive tendencies that emerged in late 1980s curriculum policy, it also reflected a recognition that a curriculum response was needed to the more fundamental changes that were taking place, often referred to as post-Fordism (Brown and Lauder, 1991), in the economies of Western capitalist nations. The main features of these changes are familiar and refer to the declining role of mass production due to new technological developments, the growth of the service sector, the breaking down of old skill barriers and divisions between professional and technical occupations, the creation of new divisions between core and peripheral workers and, not least, the new levels of capitalist integration in what is increasingly referred to as the 'global economy'. It is these changes which led to the reduction in unskilled and semi-skilled jobs and the disappearance of the youth labour market in the 1980s and for the demands for new and more flexible relationships between education and work. It follows that it is these changes that a new relationship between school subjects and the world of work must give students access to.

The economic changes described above make contradictory demands on the education system. They open up new possibilities and present new problems. Large technologically-based corporations are increasingly recognizing the need for a more educated, flexible and highly skilled workforce (BT, 1993). At the same time, however, other multinational corporations, especially in the service sector, such as the McDonalds and Burger King hamburger chains, are offering new low paid service jobs which require little prior training. The processes of technological and economic modernization, although not inherently divisive, inevitably have that potential. A major educational objective of a new 14–19 curriculum must be that it forms the basis for students to gain a greater level of understanding of these changes in the organization of work.

The approach proposed in this chapter breaks with the traditional separation of personal from economic objectives associated with liberal education. Instead of seeing 'education for personal development' as distinct from 'education for employment' (or training) it starts with a recognition that personal experience and economic change have become deeply intertwined both in reality and in popular imagination since the beginning of the 1980s. Compared with previous periods, young people of school age experience a far greater density of messages about economic life and work than in the past. The economic recession of the late 1970s and early 1980s and the restructuring of the economy during the second and third Thatcher governments sharpened the popular perception of 'life chances' as students came to see themselves as market-oriented consumers long before they had any idea of what it might be like to be a producer.

This intertwining of the goals of personal development and employability is reflected in the critical tension between the intellectual demands of academic subjects and the practical demands of changes in the nature of work; both need to be at the centre of the 14–19 curriculum and be the basis for interrogating each other. From the point of view of both teachers and curriculum designers, this tension is expressed in a number of dilemmas that relate, among other things, to the curriculum role of work experience and careers guidance and to the need for new ways of approaching work as a curriculum issue (this issue is explored further in parts of Chapter 7).

Dilemmas for Teachers in Linking Education and Work

The first dilemma facing teachers arises from the widely known fact that many students, and especially those who have failed or lost interest in the subject-based curriculum, respond positively to work experience. On the other hand work experience is invariably seen by them as 'a thing apart' with little connections to school work; in other words a student's positive involvement in work experience can have negative outcomes from the point of view of its educational outcomes. Two issues arise in considering this dilemma. The first is how can the positive involvement in work experience on the part of low achieving pupils be the basis for helping them to see the relevance of school subjects; the second is how can this aim be built into the overall curriculum objectives of schools. The second dilemma facing teachers is how to extend the understanding that students have of changes in the nature of work when such understanding will necessarily involve drawing on the very academic subjects that many students have rejected as irrelevant. The third dilemma arises from the resistance on the part of some subject specialists to making connections to work and the economy and how this reflects both a traditionally insular view of school subjects and a narrowly vocationalist view of the curricular significance of work. For obvious political reasons, emphasizing work in the curriculum has been presented almost exclusively in terms of employability or occupational preparation. These objectives are then supported within the organization of schools through the close association of work experience with careers education. These narrow links are further underpinned for many teachers by the assumption that most work experience will be of low level jobs which make few intellectual demands on students. If an understanding and experience of work is to be one of the educational principles of the 14–19 curriculum, it has to be defined more inclusively and involve work generally including the whole spectrum of professional, scientific and managerial occupations and the opportunities for progression to them (Guile, 1995).

From the point of view of most students, understanding work cannot escape being, in part, about their future employment and preparation for it, not the least because ideas about future employment are part of the experience and expectations of all young people between the ages of 14 and 19. However, for work to be an *educational* principle for all students, the curriculum must address not only the changing role of work in giving meaning to people's lives. It must also enable students to make sense of developments in the economy, technology and labour processes and how they will structure the employment opportunities that will be available. Furthermore, and of equal importance to the relationships between education and work as employment, are those between work and leisure and between work as employment and as domestic work. Making such connections involves a broadening of the concept of work to relate to far more than paid employment; it also indicates a crucial role for the humanities and social sciences in a curriculum that gives priority to the experience of work and its future. A curriculum framework will be necessary which takes work in all forms as one of the bases for the development of both knowledge (historical, sociological, scientific and technological) and skills (intellectual, technical, practical and communicative).

Subjects, Work and the Curriculum

The separation of academic subjects from work-related knowledge is based upon two premises. The first is that the former represent the goals of educating the whole person and the second that they are the form of organized knowledge that has evolved over time to enable students to gain access to key concepts and ideas. They cannot, therefore, simply be replaced by 'real life'; whether defined in competence terms by employers or as the everyday life of ordinary people mediated by TV and the tabloid press. Nor can they be simply imposed on to work-related problems.

However, school subjects, like academic disciplines, are never as fixed and unchanging as they present themselves to be, nor as unrelated to broader economic and social changes. The approach to the curriculum proposed in this chapter seeks to make explicit the ways that subjects have a history and are not 'ends in themselves' but part of a wider context. This view of subject knowledge can be made meaningful to students if it is used to consider problems and dilemmas that are thrown up through their involvement in work experience. Furthermore, such a role for subjects could be the basis for enabling students who had become disaffected from the academic curriculum, to begin to see its relevance. School subjects, like academic disciplines, have *two* major strengths — they are bodies of knowledge and methods of enquiry. It is both these components, in articulation with the real life experience of students and their concerns about their future as adults, employees and citizens, that could be the basis for a common 14–19 curriculum for all.

Making explicit the links between school subjects and the changing nature of work also has implications for the relationships between subject specialists and other teachers. Instead of seeing their role as exclusively involved in providing routes of access to higher education, subject teachers will need to take on a broader role. As specialists they are members of their own subject 'communities' with links with those in other schools and higher education; however, they also need to develop links with other teachers and those outside of schools such as employers and parents. This idea is taken up in more detail in later chapters through the concept of connective specialization and the idea of teachers being *connective specialists*.

Extending the Role of Academic Subjects in the 14–19 Curriculum

Instead of accepting the division between academic and vocational courses, it has been argued that teachers should help students to draw on academic subjects to interrogate the world of work and use this to extend their relevance and meaning for students. The next section begins to examine what such a proposal might mean.

Each subject embodies a changing set of practices and traditions of its own and a concept, however implicit, of its relationship with other subjects. For example, physics has changed with the introduction of new topics, such as electronics, as well as, for students up to 16, increasingly becoming part of integrated science, rather than a separate subject. Despite the significant influence of technological change on subjects such as physics, the existing 14–19 curriculum gives few explicit opportunities for using such changes to bring different subject specialists together and to explore how their syllabuses might complement each other. If subject specialists were required to be explicit as to how their subjects related to goals of the 14–19 curriculum as a whole, there could be a basis for physics teachers developing common programmes with teachers who specialize in economics and history. Such programmes could have the goals of showing students how particular industrial processes influenced research in physics as well as highlighting the role of science in economic and industrial change.

A curriculum in which one of the roles of academic subjects was to enable students to explore changes in the nature of work would involve developments in those subjects as well as in their relations with each other. Despite the priority given to separateness, academic subjects have always had some relationship with each other — although these have been largely restricted to familiar kinds of groupings, e.g. humanities, natural sciences, languages. Linking the understanding of changes in working life to subject-based knowledge would involve new kinds of relationships between subjects and innovations in pedagogy for which there is little precedent within existing school subject traditions and often with little support within school and college timetables. An example of such a development was the short lived Helix Project in Haringey, North London in the late 1980s which was funded by TVEI. This brought together subject and vocational specialists in the natural sciences, food technology, cultural studies and printing with employers in both industries in the development of a range of integrated programmes. The programmes bridged the traditional academic/vocational divisions between cultural studies and printing and between biological science and food technology and led to a range of advanced level academic and vocational qualifications. It was not a weakness in its curriculum principles that led to the demise of the Helix Project but a combination of the end of TVEI funds and the rigidities of the new vocational qualifications (GNVQs) introduced following the 1992 General Election. This is a point to which I return at the end of this chapter.

Work, Education and the Role of Qualifications

The approach to links between education and work developed in this chapter was a response to the new divisions between academic and vocational learning which economic change and the reforms of the 14–19 curriculum in the late 1980s were giving rise to. The proposals were directed to the 14–19 curriculum and the context was the opportunities that appeared possible through the creative use of the TVEI framework. The approach to the curriculum outlined in this chapter has argued for making explicit the vocational aspects of academic subjects both as qualifications for employment and in providing concepts for making sense of changes in the organization of work. However, it had a weakness that reflects its origins in developments inspired by TVEI. Like TVEI, it failed to take account of the extent to which the outcome of any curriculum innovation designed to develop new relationships between the subject-based curriculum and the world of work will be shaped by the qualifications system, and in particular, by the divisions between academic and vocational qualifications.

The powerful influence of government policy on qualifications is reflected, in the last decade, in how developments have moved in a very different direction from those proposed in this chapter. Integrative approaches to bringing together subject knowledge and an understanding of work such as the Helix Project referred to earlier did not survive the end of TVEI funding. More divisive approaches to *vocationalizing* the curriculum have developed through the introduction of new qualifications such as GNVQs. While the uptake of these new courses suggests they do respond to the needs of under achieving students, the progression opportunities that they give rise to are far less clear (Spours, 1995).

These developments point to the need for a reassessment of the approach albeit not the principles on which the 1988 article was based. All the recent evidence (Hodgson and Spours, 1997) suggests that in England at least we are faced with a qualifications-driven system of 14–19 education and that any strategy for curriculum change that fails to take this into account is doomed to failure. What might be involved in qualification reforms that could be the basis for a curriculum based on the twin principles of work and subject knowledge is explored in Chapter 8. The second change reflects a greater emphasis in this chapter on the positive educational role of school subjects than was expressed in the 1988 paper. This change has both a theoretical and a practical basis. Theoretically, the chapter gives more recognition to the fact that although school subjects have an ideological role as was argued in Chapter 1, both in the process of social selection and in presenting a 'view of the world', they also have an educational role in providing coherent frameworks for introducing new concepts and ideas. Practically, we now have the evidence of the early years of GNVQs (Spours, 1987) and the problems of progression faced by students who follow vocational qualifications which neglect subjects and are based on the assessment of processes not content.

Conclusions

Divisions between academic and vocational learning reflect the continued social function of the division between mental and manual labour and its role in the reproduction of wider social divisions. Although curriculum reform cannot in itself bring about wider social changes in the absence of broader economic cultural and political initiatives, it is a necessary part of such wider changes and can at least lead to more open-ended learning opportunities in which mental and manual divisions are not simply reproduced.

Throughout this chapter the contradictory nature of the curriculum developments of the late 1980s and the potential space for new approaches which they created was stressed. However, there is evidence from international studies (Lasonen and Young, 1998) that proposals for overcoming divisions between mental and manual labour, whether in education or in the workplace, invariably face serious barriers which do not just reflect the conservatism of governments. Despite dramatic changes in the organization of work which point to the need to overcome divisions between academic and vocational learning, they still have important functions in maintaining the existing social order. The decade since the original version of this chapter was written has been one of almost continuous reform of one kind or another. Despite this, there is very little sign that much progress has been made in bridging academic/vocational divisions and, indeed, many of the reforms can be seen as introducing new rigidities rather than new forms of flexibility. Furthermore, the traditional conservatism of specialist subject teachers and the reluctance of governments of both political parties to change existing academic qualifications have been bolstered by the process of academic drift in which more and more students have opted to take A-levels, thus confirming their 'popularity' despite the continuing high failure rate. Some of these barriers to achieving the kind of change discussed in this chapter and the possibilities for overcoming them are discussed later in this book, especially the critical role of qualifications which was less apparent in the 1980s. It may be, however, that, given its linchpin role in providing access to university, the academic track within the 14–19 curriculum will always be uniquely resistant to internal change; it is not by chance that in other European countries it is known as 'le route royale'. At some point, however, it could be forced to change through external pressures. The growing importance of lifelong learning for any country that wants to be competitive economically and the incompatibility of lifelong learning with both insular forms of subject specialization and traditional approaches to work and vocational education may be one such pressure.

Chapter 5

The Economic Basis for the Curriculum for the 21st Century

Introduction

The aim of this chapter is to develop the principles for a post-compulsory curriculum 'adequate to the demands of the next century' (Finegold et al., 1990). There are two issues here — one is quantitative and concerned with levels of participation in post-compulsory education and the other is qualitative and is concerned with the content and quality of learning. The quantitative issue is whether a curriculum, which was established when at most 20 per cent of each cohort continued in education after 15, is appropriate, when at least 80 per cent is expected to continue until 18 and reach the levels of achievement currently reached by only 40 per cent. The qualitative issue is whether expanding participation on the basis of existing curricula, even were it to prove possible, would provide young people with the kind of skills and knowledge that they are going to need in the likely circumstances of the twenty-first century. This chapter explores those circumstances and their curriculum implications.

Starting with the English and Welsh system of post-compulsory education and training has an advantage from the point of view of this analysis as it can be seen as a 'worst case'. It is an example of a highly industrialized country which combines low participation, deep social class divisions and a curriculum which has changed little in half a century or more. Paradoxically, it is the backwardness of the system in England and Wales that may provide us with insights that do not arise so directly in the more advanced systems found in many of the countries elsewhere in Europe (Lasonen and Young, 1998).

Let us consider, for the purposes of comparison, two hypothetical cases of countries in which social class divisions are significantly less than in the UK. One is of a country (and I suggest that the Netherlands may be a good example) which has a divided educational system but one that is not embedded in a deeply divided social class structure. In such a situation it is unlikely that the educational divisions will have the consequences for levels of participation that they do in England and Wales. In other words considerable expansion of levels of participation and achievement are possible in a country like the Netherlands even though the educational system remains based on academic/vocational divisions.

The other case is of a country (and here I suggest Japan as the example) in which the academic curriculum is no less dominant than in England and Wales; however, the process of selection is deferred until the end of secondary schooling. In Japan virtually all students continue their full time studies until the age of 18 or 19 despite the absence of any substantial changes in the traditional academic curriculum.

Neither of the two possibilities outlined above is open for the system in England and Wales which is characterized by a continuing cleavage between social classes, a deeply divided system of qualifications and a narrow and elitist academic curriculum. It may be that it is the very impossibility of reforming the existing system that has led to a more radical analysis emerging and finding support (Finegold et al., 1990; Young and Watson, 1992). Furthermore, in taking academic/vocational divisions and therefore by implication, the interrelationships between the curriculum and a changing occupational structure as its focus, it may be that such an analysis will give us some insights into the curriculum that will be necessary in the twenty-first century. It is to this analysis that I now turn.

Divided Qualifications; Divided Curriculum

The Institute for Public Policy Research Report, *A British Baccalaureate* (Finegold et al., 1990), remains, eight years after publication, the most comprehensive critique of post-compulsory education in England and Wales that has yet appeared. Its analysis was distinguished in two ways from the plethora of other reports that appeared in the 1980s. It began by restating the widely held criticisms of the narrowness and exclusiveness of the academic route — only 30 per cent of the cohort take it and the vast majority take only two or three (2.3 on average) A-Level subjects — and of the poor quality and relative scarcity of 'vocational' alternatives (over twice as many students obtain A-Levels as the equivalent vocational qualifications (GNVQs). However, the report went on to argue that the cause of these weaknesses could not be found solely in the inadequacies of the separate routes but in *the divided system itself*. In other words, they are the direct outcome of having separate academic and vocational tracks leading to separate *qualifications* in the first place. The report's prescription for a *unified system of qualifications* that 'will end the division between education and training' followed from this argument. Second, the report did not just focus on the structural issue by drawing a distinction between a divided and a unified qualifications system. It also considered the implications of a unified system of qualifications for curriculum policy and practice.

The report began by reviewing the failure of a variety of attempts during the 1980s to reform the two (academic and vocational) tracks. Two such reform strategies are worth referring to as they reflect examples of 'borrowing' from other countries. First, there were attempts to diversify the academic track

(A-Levels) in order to give it a broader appeal and make it less exclusive — what might be called *the French solution.* Second, there were the efforts to enhance the status and content of vocational programmes along German lines. The report concluded that in the UK, these reforms strategies inevitably came up against the barriers of a divided system and, in particular, its assumption that sometime between the ages of 14 and 16 young people can be divided into two groups — the academically gifted (at least relatively) and the rest.

Attempts to diversify A-Levels have been restricted by two fundamental features of the English academic track. First, it is explicitly designed for selecting the 'top 30 per cent' and its normative referenced model of assessment is geared to this, despite some recent modifications to introduce elements of criterion referencing. The year by year increases in the proportion of candidates achieving higher grades at A-Level have been used by some as evidence of falling standards of marking not of the improved level of performance of the system. The second feature of A-Levels is that they are not a *curriculum framework* capable of reform and modification like the French Baccalauréat. They consist of individual subjects clearly separated from each other with their own rules and traditions.

The barriers confronting attempts to enhance the status and content of the vocational alternatives to A-Levels are different but no easier to overcome. Quite apart from the Competing Examining Boards and the lack of clarity of progression routes to higher levels, vocational qualifications face the fact that regardless of their content, they continue to be judged by employers, university admission tutors and students as inferior. By 1998, and despite some rationalization of Examining Boards and the emergence of GNVQs as the dominant full time vocational route, this situation has changed little.

The IPPR Report goes on to identify six main weaknesses of the divided system in England and Wales as follows:

- it is based on nineteenth century assumptions (now increasingly challenged) that industrial economies require the separation of mental and manual labour which provide the justification for academic/vocational divisions,
- it is a system dominated by *selection* when the problem now and in the future is how to increase both the quantity and quality of *participation* of students at 16+,
- it is inflexible in that it separates students into academic and vocational tracks and makes movement and transfer between them extremely difficult,
- it inhibits innovative study combinations that can link theoretical and applied learning across the academic/vocational divide,
- it exaggerates differences between high and low prestige institutions and programmes, reinforces the process of educational stratification and leads to the particular devaluation of vocational education and training that characterizes the system in England and Wales,

- in combination with the unique structure of the labour market which provides incentives for early school leaving, it locks the country into a 'low skills equilibrium'. (Finegold and Soskice, 1988)

Finally, the main focus of the report's analysis is on the strategic role of qualifications in determining educational opportunities and how a divided system of qualifications is inevitably dominated by its function of selecting young people for higher education or employment. A qualification system that is dominated by selection limits both levels of participation and achievement and the possibility of innovative curriculum reforms. Meanwhile, the Conservative government, in its proposals for what was referred to as a *modern* system of qualifications in the 1991 White Paper *Education and Training for the 21st Century* decided to stick firmly to a divided system, albeit in a somewhat reorganized and rationalized form. It is therefore not surprising that it was the IPPR Report's proposal for a *unified qualification system* that stimulated greatest interest. The specific recommendations of the report were for:

(i)   A single national Qualifications Authority to replace the separate regulating bodies (the Schools Curriculum and Assessment Authority and the National Council for Vocational Qualifications).

(ii) A single integrated diploma, normally to be achieved at 18, to replace the current alternatives of either a cluster of A-Level subjects (and in some cases AS-(half A) levels) or one of the range of vocational qualifications that are (at least in theory) available for students after 16.

It is interesting that, eight years later, the first proposal, for a single regulatory authority, the Qualifications and Curriculum Authority, is in place. However, the tentative suggestions for an Advanced Diploma or Overarching Certificate put forward by Dearing (SCAA, 1996) (see Chapter 8) and echoed in the new government's consultation document, *Qualifying for Success* (DfEE, 1997) indicate how far we are from the second.

This focus on the interdependence of the qualifications system and the curriculum is a recognition of the neglect of qualifications in previous analyses of the 14–19 curriculum, such as that discussed in Chapter 4 in which very little attention was given to the role of qualifications. Differences in qualification systems, it was argued, are the

> key factors that distinguish between systems of post compulsory education
> with high and low levels of participation. (Finegold et al., 1990, p. 14)

They differ, the report suggested, according to the priority they give to *selection*, the *setting* of standards and the *empowerment* of students to learn. The report, in showing how the qualification system in England and Wales is characterized by the dominance of its selective function, and its use of exclusion as the main means of maintaining standards, went a long way to explain the persistence of low participation and achievement. The importance given to qualifications in the report also reflects the dominating role that assessment, and in particular terminal examinations, has had on post-compulsory education in England and Wales (Wolf, 1992). In the absence of any direct role for the state, Examining Boards, which are mostly either private charities or owned by the universities, exert considerable power. They remain the linchpin of the qualification system and have a stranglehold over the curriculum. The IPPR proposals for a unified system of qualifications and a single diploma at 18+ were not therefore only about reforming the curriculum. They involved major institutional changes and posed a threat to major vested interests — not only the Examining Boards but potentially also the private secondary schools, one of whose main attractions to parents is their examination successes. In countries where the state has a more direct role in the curriculum, the *separate* significance of qualifications is likely to be much less. There are already indications of this in England and Wales in the compulsory phase of education (5–16) since it has been regulated through the National Curriculum as well as by the Examination Boards. It is also likely that the stronger regulatory role of the new Qualifications and Curriculum Authority will reduce the autonomy of the Examination Boards in influencing the curriculum at 16+.

As stated at the beginning of this chapter, the curriculum issue identified in the IPPR report was not only concerned with how to raise the levels of participation in post-compulsory education: it also focused on the content and quality of learning. The report makes clear the inappropriateness, for the learning needs of young people who will be adult citizens seeking employment in the twenty-first century, of both the traditional academic curriculum of A-Levels as well as a curriculum based on occupationally specific skills. It is therefore the social and economic basis of a new *curriculum* that is the main focus of this chapter and to which I now turn.

The IPPR report's proposals for the curriculum follow from the argument for a unified qualifications system. Instead of having separate academic and vocational courses, a future post-compulsory curriculum would consist of a range of theoretical and applied modules *within a single unified system*. Students then would choose from within a number of routes or pathways according to their interests and aspirations and taking account of their previous achievements. However, replacing a curriculum based on separate academic and vocational tracks by one consisting of a unified modular system is not just a new way of organizing the curriculum, like replacing school subjects with interdisciplinary themes. Academic/vocational divisions have their origins in a culture which associates manual work with low status and in an economy which is based on the separation of mental and manual labour. A unified curriculum, on the other hand, would not separate the preparation of young people for employment from the wider role of preparing them to become citizens in a democratic society. It follows that such a curriculum implies that a very different form of economy is emerging to that which has been dominant in industrialized societies for the last century.

In considering the grounds for such a curriculum and in beginning to specify the form that it might take, it is necessary to examine the economic basiś of the current separation of academic and vocational education and what indications there are that it may be changing. I shall draw on the growing body of research in a number of countries that suggests we are at the end of an industrial era dominated by mass production of goods and services, and that there are signs of a new mode or production emerging, variously characterized as *post Fordism* and *flexible specialization* (Piore and Sabel, 1984; Mathews, 1989; Murray, 1988). All these writers recognize that the changes they describe are not inevitable and that they are political as well as economic. However, what is important from the point of view of this chapter is that they all point to the emergence of new relationships between education and the economy. Whereas, under mass production, the economy set severe limits on the development of the education system, an economy based on flexible specialization depends on prior educational and political changes. We are, it is argued, entering an era of education-led, or, more broadly, human resource-led economic growth, when, as Reich (1991) and others argue, it is *national systems of education and training* rather than *national economies* that will determine the fate of nations.

Specialization in the Curriculum: Beyond the Specialist/Generalist Distinction

Early and narrow specialization has for a long time been regarded as a distinctive feature of English and Welsh post-compulsory education, and has increasingly been seen, even in official reports, as a major weakness (DES, 1988). This narrowness is expressed by the fact that the majority of those on the academic track can and do restrict their studies after 16 to the sciences and mathematics or humanities/languages alone. The International Baccalaureate, Scottish Highers, as well as most post-compulsory curricula elsewhere in Europe offer a much broader curriculum with a generalist rather than a subject-specialist focus. A parallel distinction between narrow and broad curricula can be made in describing English and other European vocational qualifications. English and Welsh vocational qualifications, even when they are not occupationally specific tend to limit the horizons of students to particular occupational areas, whereas other European models adopt a Baccalaureate-type approach combining occupational and general education (Watson, 1991).

In the case of England and Wales, the issue of specialization has usually been posed in terms of the absence of any kind of framework such as is provided by the Abitur or Baccalaureate that might compensate for the unique narrowness and exclusiveness of single subject A-Levels. Virtually every other country has some form of baccalaureate or matriculation at 18+. However this is to concentrate only on the peculiarities of this country and neglects a second dimension of specialization which is not specific to England and Wales, the separation of knowledge from its application through the persistence of academic/vocational divisions. Furthermore, a concentration on subject and vocational specialization alone can all too easily lead to the neglect of the academic/vocational divide as itself is a form of specialization and to the assumption that a unified curriculum would necessarily involve less specialization.

The alternative approach that will be adopted in this chapter is to recognize that the pressure to shift away from subject and vocational specialization arises from deeper changes in the *form of specialization* not just as it appears in the curriculum but in the wider division of labour and occupational structure of society. The IPPR proposals for a unified curriculum did not propose a move away from specialization but a move towards more integrative or *connective forms of specialization* which are not based on either insulated subject divisions or academic/vocational divisions. In curricular terms *connective specialization* emphasizes the importance of developing new types of cross-subject skills and understanding as well as the ability to innovate and to apply and use learning in different contexts. Reich (1991) refers to such skills and knowledge as *symbolic analysis* and from a slightly different perspective Zuboff (1988) refers to *intellective skills*. Such educational priorities are frequently identified by leading edge companies (British Telecom, 1993), but without indicating how they might be expressed in the curriculum. Before exploring these possibilities for a *curriculum of the future*, it is necessary to consider why specialization is such a crucial issue in post-compulsory education at this time.

Specialization as an Integral Aspect of Modern Economies

A high level of occupational specialization is an integral aspect of the state and the economies of modern societies and it is a crucial reason why such societies have been so vastly more productive than those that they evolved from. The first substantial increase in specialization occurred with the emergence of the modern state in the last decades of the nineteenth century. It developed further through the expansion of industrial economies in the twentieth century with the growth of mass production. As Piore and Sabel (1984) put it:

> the extensive division of labour in mass production (was characterised by) both the break between conception and execution of tasks and the highly specialised character of almost all production jobs.

The consequences for the newly emerging system of mass education were twofold. Curricular specialization was fuelled by the rapid development of knowledge expressed in the growth of and divisions between new subjects and vocational areas. At the same time school-based 'education' and work based 'training' became increasingly separate with the development of mass production. This made it possible:

(for the system of production) to rely on two separate institutions for training employees: the formal education system and the firm itself. The formal education system . . . providing abstract knowledge of products and production . . . the firm (providing) training for the fraction of the workforce that needs skills . . . (Piore and Sabel, 1984)

Thus the main features of what will be referred to as *divisive specialization* were established — the divisions between academic subjects and the separation of education and training.

Mass Production and the Development of Divisive Specialization

The correspondence between education and the economy in industrial societies has always been somewhat tenuous. Education is shaped by many historical mediating influences other than the economy or its leading productive processes. The parallels that can be drawn between economic organization and the curriculum in the era of mass production may relate less to the direct influence of the economy and more to how the economy and the education system have themselves been shaped by similar cultural and political histories (Green, 1990).

In England and Wales the new social divisions between managers (nearly always owners at this time) and factory workers emerged in the early nineteenth century in an environment still culturally and politically dominated by the feudal aristocracy and, in the new factories, by the craftsmen who controlled the tools and new machines. The education of craftsmen took place almost entirely within the apprenticeship system and developed separately from the growth of mass elementary education. Thus, the terms were set for the early and sharp separation between academic study and vocational education which was to become the basis for the uniquely *divisive* form of curricular specialization that was to emerge in England and Wales. Relations between the expanding industry and services in the later nineteenth and early twentieth century and the education system were mediated by a divided qualifications system consisting of two largely separate tracks; these were an academic track dominated by subject-specialization and terminal examinations and an occupationally specific vocational track consisting of work-based apprenticeships. Such a selective system also ensured that large sections of the population received only elementary education and had no opportunities to gain qualifications of any kind.

It was not until the 1980s that a British government decided to rationalize vocational qualifications and to attempt to extend them to the majority of the working population. The method it adopted, when the National Council for Vocational Qualifications (NCVQ) was established, was through the precise specification of job competencies for different occupations. There is some irony, in NCVQ being launched at a time when systems of production based on the rigid specification of jobs were increasingly being questioned as the continuing basis for maximizing productivity. It is therefore not surprising that by the late 1990s the system of qualifications and curricula for post-compulsory education in the UK are at a point of contradiction. There are (largely political) forces committed to maintaining inherited divisions with their powerful selective and restrictive functions and there are the growing demands (largely industrial and professional) for a broader curriculum as the basis for educational expansion. Increasingly, the latter groups are recognizing that such expansion is not possible within a divided system.

These contradictions do not just express the problems of expansion and the difficulties of gearing a curriculum dominated by selection to promoting increases in participation. They also raise the question, mentioned earlier in this chapter, as to whether a divided curriculum can deliver the kind of skills and knowledge that are going to be needed if the country is to be competitive in the economic context of the twenty-first century. In order to gain some insight into what new combinations of skills and knowledge might be needed, it is necessary to review briefly the arguments about current economic changes and how they are expressed in changes in the form of specialization. It will then be possible to consider in more detail their implications for the curriculum.

New Concepts of Specialization in the Economy and Education

The idea that we are at the beginning of a new economic era is much contested and its possible form and destination are far from clear. Different analyses give different emphasis to cultural and economic changes. This chapter is primarily concerned with the latter — in particular with changes in the organization of work and the structure of occupations. The emergence, in the economies of advanced capitalist countries, of what has been termed 'post Fordism' has been widely commented on. It is a rather loose, albeit evocative term which refers to the appearance of a collection of industrial innovations such as flexible specialized production, new uses of information-based technologies, flatter management structures, and a greater emphasis on teamwork. Mathews, Hall and Smith (1988) describe the changes in this way:

> The industrial system that has dominated the twentieth century — a system based upon mass production, mass consumption, Taylorised fragmentation of work and deskilling — is visibly dying, and creating economic chaos as it is forced from the historical stage. A new industrial system is being born — based upon technologies of microelectronics and new materials, intelligent production, human-centred organisation, worker responsibility and multiskilling . . .

The forms of specialisation within the economy are in fact changing. They are reversing the concept of mass production and introducing the process of 'flexible specialisation'.

Flexible specialisation involves the combination of general purpose capital equipment and skilled, adaptable workers to produce a wide and changing range of semi-customised goods. Manufacturing flexibility and market responsiveness go hand in hand, allowing companies to tailor their output to sales trends and carve out new market niches by adapting products to customer needs.

The actual extent of such developments and their likely extension in particular countries is open to question as are their social consequences. What is not in doubt is that changes from a system of mass production to one based on flexible specialization make quite new intellectual demands on employees at all levels. The social, intellectual and essentially *educational* basis of the new forces of production are well recognized by Castells (1989) when he states that it is the

structurally determined capacity of labour to process information and generate knowledge that is the material basis of productivity and the (modern) source of economic growth. Yet this symbolic capacity of labour is not an individual attribute. Labour has to be formed, educated . . . etc.

. . . In addition . . . social institutions . . . and the overall structure of society . . . will be key elements in fostering or stalling the new . . . productive forces. The more a society facilitates the exchange of information flows, the decentralised generation and distribution of information, the greater will be its collective symbolic capacity.

But the argument can be taken further. A high-participation education system linked to a high-skill system of production would require a curriculum which was congruent with it. In other words it too must exhibit features of flexible specialization. Hickox and Moore (1991) make the point that it may only be in a 'post Fordist' phase with the vastly increased pressures on industrial capitalism to raise productivity that we can begin to talk with any realism about a correspondence between education and the economy. They point out that managers of the future will have to learn that their only new sources of productivity are the potential intellectual capacities of their employees.

The new forms of work organization associated with flexible specialization set quite new criteria for the curriculum. Instead of the traditional screening role of academic/vocational divisions, the emphasis will have to be on new and innovative kinds of connectiveness between knowledge areas with different forms of specialized study interwoven with a generic core of knowledge and skills for all students. It is debatable whether such criteria, despite their origins in the demands of new occupations, should be described as a modern version of general education or an advanced form of vocational education.

From the point of view of the curriculum there are two key issues; increasing flexibility — the opportunity for individual students to make choices and combine different kinds of learning in new ways — and improving coherence — the sense of clarity that students need in order to know what they need to learn and where a particular course of study or cluster of modules will lead them. The IPPR report concluded that this combination of flexibility and coherence could be achieved through a modular curriculum, provided there were also clear sets of pathways or routes for students to identify with. This model of the curriculum has some parallels with new forms of network organization in which teams of employees are given maximum autonomy within a clear set of overarching purposes (Morgan, 1988). This parallel is developed further in Chapter 6.

It is not surprising that the educational implications of this new era have been interpreted as being 'anti-specialization' — particularly with the recent emphasis upon generic problem-solving and the dissolution of curriculum barriers (Brown and Lauder, 1991). However, as was mentioned earlier, this is incorrect; the change is not away from specialization but towards new forms that can (at least in principle) free specialization from its association with selection and insulation. **The separation of specialization from its association with divisions and the insulation of subject areas is the key basis for distinguishing between a divided curriculum or 'curriculum of the past' and a 'curriculum of the future'.** This is the key argument of this chapter and one to which I will return.

The issue of new forms of specialization is central to whether changes in industrial economies can be the basis for a new curriculum. The productivity of industrial capitalism up to the middle of this century depended on what has been termed here *divisive specialization* or increasing the division between mental and manual labour. Specialist engineers and managers, at least up to the 1970s, designed systems of production which depended less and less on the skills and knowledge of the majority of employees (Noble, 1979). This system was the most productive the world had ever known and, as knowledge grew, specialization took the form of the principles of scientific management being applied to more and more areas of manufacturing and increasingly to the service sectors. It is this system of production and its dominant form of divisive specialization that is under challenge by systems that depend on maximizing the innovative contribution of all employees (Prospect Centre, 1991; NEC, 1992). The origins of this change are twofold — the 'globalization' of economies and the massive increase in the potential for competition that goes with it and the productive potential of information-based technologies.

A form of work organization which seeks to maximize the intellectual potential of all employees cannot rely on a curriculum that limits itself to providing a small proportion of the population with highly specialist knowledge, while, at the same time, neglecting the level of attainment of the majority.

Again Piore and Sabel (1984) make the point clearly when they state that in production systems based on flexible specialization:

> designers must be so broadly qualified that they can envision product and production together (something not learnt by) book learning alone . . .

> Production workers must be so broadly skilled . . . to be able to collaborate with designers to solve the problems that inevitably arise in production.

In other words, the organization of production has to become part of a new paradigm. Such a paradigm will increase the scope for choice, personal flexibility and high performance and enable the highest possible number of people to innovate in a constantly changing world. This form of 'flexible' or 'connective specialization' contrasts sharply with the 'divisive specialization' that underpins academic/vocational divisions. Before exploring further this idea of *connective specialization* as a curricular concept, it is necessary to consider the curricular implications of the dominance of *divisive specialization*.

The Language of Divisive Specialization and Its Curricular Implications

One consequence of inheriting a deeply divided system in which academic and vocational tracks are so embedded in the institutions and the social structure is the absence of any overarching concepts that link knowledge and skill. Without such concepts it becomes difficult to develop the idea of flexible specialization in curriculum terms. The comparison between the vocabulary and concepts available in English with the potential of French terms such as 'formation' and 'qualification' and the German term 'bildung' are very striking. In English, most of the terms and concepts which we have for discussing education and training, though never precisely defined, have limiting and often highly divisive meanings. They were established in the discourse and institutionalized in the last part of the nineteenth century but remain extremely powerful. It is possible to list some examples as follows:

Knowledge —	which usually refers only to academic subjects
Science —	which unlike in German refers only to the *natural* sciences
Technical —	technical education in England is associated invariably with manual work and low status occupations
Academic —	means detached (but with high prestige)
Vocational —	is defined in contrast to academic and relates to preparation for specific occupations
Skills —	are associated with the manual activities of craftsmen
Competencies —	are defined in terms of observable performances

This is the vocabulary of a deeply divided system. It is also the vocabulary of a society deeply rooted in its past, with limited intellectual resources for change or even for coming to terms with the present let alone the future.

A further consequence of the role of academic/vocational divisions as a dominant form of specialization in the UK is the extent to which rigour and standards, almost entirely associated with A-Levels, have been separated from both personal and social education and the preparation of young people for future employment; the latter curriculum goals tend to be associated with the needs of 'academic' failures. This association of rigour with academic subjects and their forms of assessment is well exemplified by the current attempts to give parity of esteem to GNVQ's through introducing externally set and marked tests. A curriculum of the future has to bring together the aims of rigour, relevance and personal development, which appear so irretrievably separate in a divided curriculum, in new and more integrated forms of assessment.

Although it is difficult to find examples of *connective specialization* in the UK, this does not mean that the process of specialization, albeit within the divisive form, is not changing. I will describe these changes in terms of the distinction between *sectional* and *corporate* forms of divisive specialization. The latter refer to horizontal and vertical developments within and between occupational groups. I shall contrast these developments with the possibilities of *connective* specialization.

Forms of Specialization and Their Curriculum Implications

The *sectional* form of divisive specialization refers to how, in response to changing circumstances, members of professions and groups of craftsmen within an occupational area traditionally identify with their fellow professionals or craftsmen and form associations (and trade unions). In curriculum terms it describes the associations of academic or vocational subject specialists, many of which were established at the turn of the century. Exaggerated subject specialization is characteristic of a divided curriculum and subject associations are particularly strong in the system in England and Wales.

The curricular priority which characterizes the *sectional form of divisive specialization* is an exclusive concentration on subject-specific content. However, this is not an inevitable feature of the behaviour of subject specialists or craft teachers. It refers only to their historically insulated forms of organization in a divided curriculum. In the context of the much broader notion of educational purposes associated with a 'curriculum for the future' identification with subjects and occupational areas can become the basis for developing teams of *connective* specialists.

Corporate specialization is illustrated by a number of developments that can be found in both the economy and in education that are expressions of limited vertical integration. In industry it refers to how different groups of specialists (both craft and professional) and also employees and senior managers within a firm can, in the face of external threats (e.g. global or even national competition) identify common purposes beyond their 'sectional' interests. Corporate specialization is much more frequently in evidence in countries other than the UK, as is indicated by the frequent reference to examples of co-determination between unions and employers in Sweden and Germany. The absence of corporate specialization in the UK is partly because in the past UK employer/union relationships were so often adversarial. More recently it reflects the extent to which such relationships have been actively discouraged by the neo-liberal economic policies of government.

The two main curriculum priorities of the *corporate* form of *specialization* are the broad notions of integrating natural and social sciences which bring groupings of subject specialists together and the idea of transferable (or 'core') skills which transcends and complements occupationally specific skills or subject-based knowledge. The former developments have, as discussed earlier, been limited by government determination to maintain the selective function of A-Levels as single, separate subjects[8]. The idea of core skills continues to be widely supported by business and industry and government (CBI, 1989, 1993; SCAA, 1996; DfEE, 1997) and has been seen as a basis for collaboration across the education/industry divide. As with forms of subject integration, the implementation of core skills has been profoundly limited by the divided system of qualifications (Young, 1991; Young and McDonald, 1997; Young, Hayton and Leney, 1997).

The *corporate* form of *divisive specialization* can be seen to represent a transitional and even contradictory phase. It is transitional in the sense that its curricular priorities emphasize breadth and the idea of 'core skills' in ways which go beyond the traditional forms of divisive specialization. It is contradictory to the extent that the broad notion of skills that is being sought after in potential employees by leading edge companies (British Telecom, 1993) is very different from the narrowly defined job specific concept of NVQs or even the numeracy and literacy included in GNVQ's that employers are supposed to want.

In developing their concept of *flexible specialization*, Piore and Sabel write about 'envisioning product and production together'. In relation to the curriculum I prefer the term *connective specialization*, as it refers explicitly to the interdependence of different specialists and contrasts with the insularity of traditional subject specialists. It emphasizes the importance of specialists, whether physicists, designers or guidance staff, for example, sharing an overall sense of the relationship between their specialization and the whole curriculum. In other words, whereas divisive specialists see the curriculum from the point of view of their subjects, connective specialists need to see their subjects from the point of view of the curriculum. The concept of connective specialization gives renewed importance to the curriculum as a way of expressing educational purposes.

In the sense used here, connective specialization is concerned with the links between combinations of knowledge and skills in the curriculum and the wider democratic and social goals of education. At the individual level it refers to the need for an understanding of the social, cultural, political and economic implications of any knowledge or skill in its context, and how through such a curriculum, an individual can learn specific skills and knowledge but also the capacity to take initiatives and responsibility, whatever her or his specific occupation or position.

In the context of such a deeply divided curriculum as in England and Wales, it is not surprising that it is difficult to find evidence of *connective specialization* as a curriculum reality. As a curriculum concept it points to the interdependence of the content, processes and organization of the curriculum. As a definition of educational purposes it seeks to transcend the traditional dichotomy of 'the educated person' and 'the competent employee' which define the purposes of the two tracks of a divided curriculum. One example of an attempt at a more elaborate definition of connective specialization suggests that it should include:

> fundamental elements based upon new needs of an age of science, techno-logy and innovation including maths, science, technological studies so that an education system produces . . .

and aims to encourage

> well-rounded, technologically literate citizens who have some insight into the processes of scientific and technological development, and the capacity and will to keep returning to the system to sharpen and broaden their skills and understanding. (Mathews, Hall and Smith, 1988)

To these themes might be added

- economic, political and sociological understanding as part of the pre-paration for active and democratic citizenship,
- the development of modern languages and understanding as tools for the new internationalism,
- aesthetic and cultural understanding as a means of becoming 'competent cultural practitioners'. (Hurd and Connell, 1988)

How connective specialization will be expressed concretely will vary from country to country and depend on historical circumstances. In England and Wales, where divisive specialization remains dominant, elements of connectiv-ity are only found in some of recent attempts to create local *integrating frameworks* and networks. These may take the form of credit frameworks to assist progression and student transfer, new forms of compact between schools and colleges and employers or colleges and higher education or groups of teachers meeting to write modules or to develop learning resources within shared cur-riculum purposes (Young et al., 1994). Each case represents an attempt to express the curriculum aims of *connective specialization* within and between institutions when such changes are limited by the constraints of a divided qualification system. There are signs however, that industrial interests,· at least as reflected in the CBI (CBI, 1993) are going beyond their traditional positions and arguing for a more integrated system.

Summary and Conclusions — A Curriculum for the Future?

The aim of this chapter has been to examine analyses of changes in work organization and the economy and to suggest that they point to a new basis for overcoming the academic/vocational divisions that dominate the post-compulsory curriculum in England and Wales. Starting from the narrow and exclusive form of curriculum specialization found in England and Wales, the focus of the analysis has been on the theme of specialization and the inter-dependence of changes in the *forms of specialization* in the economy and the curriculum.

It was argued that current economic changes could provide the basis for a very different curriculum for the future. Such a *curriculum*, it is suggested, would need to build on and give specificity to the principles of;

- breadth and flexibility
- connections between both core and specialist studies and general (academic) and applied (vocational) studies
- opportunities for progression and credit transfer
- a clear sense of the purpose of the curriculum as a whole

which were originally outlined in the IPPR Report *A British Baccalaureate* (Finegold et al., 1990).

At the end of their book Piore and Sabel (1984) state that whether societies of the future will be based on mass production or flexible specialization will 'depend in part on the capacity of nations and social classes to envision the future that they want'. This chapter extends their argument by proposing that if the UK is to have an economy based on flexible specialization it has to develop a curriculum that is designed for that future. In the UK, despite the result of the General Election in May 1997, this future still looks very distant. We need to remember that futures have to be made, they do not just happen; as Gramsci wrote

> What 'ought to be' is concrete . . . it alone is history in the making and philo-sophy in the making, it alone is politics.

Chapter 6

Modularization as a Strategy for Unifying the Post-compulsory Curriculum

Introduction

In this chapter I want to examine the links between two related curriculum strategies, the outcomes approach to defining the curriculum and modularization as a way of organizing a flexible curriculum into small blocks of learning which can be combined together in different ways. I shall consider how together these strategies might contribute to the broader goal of unifying the post-compulsory curriculum. The criteria that I bring to the analysis arise from the argument first developed by Finegold and Soskice (1988) that the education and training system in this country is related to the economy through what they described as a *low-skill equilibrium*. Some of the links between education and changes in the economy were considered in Chapter 5. Here, it is the educational implications of moving from a low skill equilibrium that are the focus. The analysis in Chapter 5 started from the assumption that it is only high-skill economies that will stand a chance of being competitive and therefore of being the basis for stable democracies in the next decades. The question I seek to address here is the extent to which modularization, linked to a curriculum defined in terms of learning outcomes, can be the basis of a strategy for moving to a high participation/high achievement system of post-compulsory education. Such a strategy would have two goals. First, it would need to point to ways of overcoming the divisions, the fragmentation, the rigidities and the low expectations of the current system. Second, it would need to provide a framework for developing new combinations of knowledge and skill and the incentives for learners to reach high attainment levels as well as for teachers to develop the new pedagogies that would be needed.

Educational innovations are developed in specific political and economic contexts which shape their implementation (Raffe, 1984; Young, 1993b); modularization and the outcomes approach to the curriculum are no exception. In this country, modularization of the 14–19 curriculum was initially developed as a result of local teacher initiatives in the early 1980s (Wilmott, 1983). In contrast, the outcomes approach was developed at a similar time as part of the Department of Employment's launching of the Youth Training Scheme (Jessup,

1991). I shall examine these very different contexts and how they shaped the *content* of the two developments. To do this, it is useful to separate their *intrinsic logics* as educational reforms — what they were intended to achieve — from the *institutional logics* — the organizational constraints — that shaped their implementation (Raffe, 1992a).

In terms of *institutional logic*, modularization, in that it developed as a local initiative with little national support, can be seen as an expression of the fragmentation and voluntarism that have been characteristic features of education and training in this country throughout the century. The outcomes approach, on the other hand, was initially associated with developing vocational qualifications for trainees on the Youth Training Scheme. Not surprisingly, despite being an initiative of national government, it became a victim of another feature of the UK system, the low status of vocational education and work-based training in particular. Both strategies, therefore, can be seen as part of a *low-skill equilibrium* rather than as ways of moving out of it. However, locating these developments within their *institutional logics* does not negate their *intrinsic logics* (of increasing flexibility, improving access and empowering learners) through which they could (at least in theory) be part of a high-skill/high achievement system. The distinction between *institutional* and *intrinsic* logics is useful in explaining why the ambitious aims of modularization and outcomes approaches have not been realized in practice. However, it does not, on its own suggest how the constraints of *institutional logic* may be overcome. I will return to this question in the last section of the chapter.

The chapter begins by considering how the implementation of modularization and outcomes approaches has been shaped not only by their own limitations as reform strategies, at least when seen in isolation, but also by the wider social and political context within which they were located. I go beyond the conventional use of modularization and outcomes approaches as general curricular strategies and suggest that it may be useful to see them as *generic strategies* that, depending on the context, take different forms which need to be specified. I then identify learner-centredness as a key and contradictory assumption of both modularization and outcomes approaches and examine the problems associated with it in a political era dominated by what might be called an 'anti-professional' political culture. The chapter then takes the issues of access and participation that have been associated with both modularization and the outcomes approach and considers how they have been undermined by the dominance of a highly selective subject-based curriculum. Finally, I link the previous analysis to the argument in Chapter 5 that *connectivity* (or connective specialization) needs to be the key distinguishing feature of a post-compulsory *Curriculum of the Future* (Young, 1994) and suggest how modularization and an outcomes approach would be elements of such a curriculum. I point out that, although implementing a *Curriculum of the Future* would need to be part of a much wider political, industrial and economic strategy, elements of connectivity can be found in the links between a number of recent local and national developments.

Modularization and the Outcomes Approach in the UK Since the Beginning of the 1980s

The different origins and aims of modularization and the outcomes approach to the curriculum, which in many ways are closely related, are themselves reflections of the fragmented nature of education and training in this country. As stated earlier, modularization started as a series of *local* initiatives whereas the outcomes approach had its origins in *national* training policies (Jessup, 1991) launched by the Department of Employment, and later through NCVQ in the mid-1980s. The adoption of an outcomes approach to assessment for YTS certification, and later for NVQs, was an example of the government's determination to move away from a 'provider-led' (or teacher-dominated) curriculum for vocational education to one which was 'learner-led' and in which consumer and, in particular, employer interests were given priority. However, as Keep (1997) and others have argued, employers' major priority has been to keep training costs down and young people wanted jobs not training; a focus on consumers, therefore, meant that a policy overtly designed to raise standards all too easily became part of the 'low-skill equilibrium'. From the point of view of teachers, the close connections of the outcomes approach with NCVQ, together with the narrowness of the competencies of the early NVQs at Level 1 and 2, meant that an outcomes approach was easily seen as anti-educational or, at best, as representing a very limited view of vocational education.

Despite the claims that both strategies would contribute to improving the quality and accessibility of education and training provision, the separate origins of modularization and the outcomes approach are not only an expression of the academic/vocational divide but of tensions between local attempts to increase curricular flexibility and government attempts at rationalization and standardization. On the other hand, two other developments, though limited in their scope by the government's obsession with external assessment and their distrust of teachers, are at least indications of the way that both strategies might be used to bridge academic/vocational divisions and be the basis of a more unified system of provision. I refer to, first, the National Curriculum which, though subject-based and not modular, is defined in terms of learning outcomes and second, GNVQs, which are also defined in terms of broad learning outcomes. Both the National Curriculum and GNVQs, despite the tendency in each case to over-specify outcomes, point to the possibility noted by Jessup (1991) that qualifications defined in terms of learning outcomes could incorporate all types of learning. In the remainder of this section, I shall consider modularization and outcomes approaches separately as generic curricular strategies which, in the UK context, have taken particular forms.

Modularization

As a generic strategy, I shall define *modularization* as the breaking up of the curriculum into discrete and relatively short learning experiences. These may or may not have separate learning objectives and assessment requirements. I shall trace the development of modularization in this country and then discuss the possible role of modularization in raising achievement. In order to do this, I will distinguish three forms that modularization can take — *internal, external,* and *connective* — each of which can be illustrated in recent developments.

Initially modularization of the secondary curriculum had two aims. First, it was designed to be the basis for curricula and accreditation for the new kinds of learning that were being encouraged by TVEI but were not deliverable within the divisions of the traditional subject-based curriculum. Second, assessment at the end of each module meant that it could be more directly related to the learning experiences of students and so be more conclusive to raising attainment than conventional forms of terminal assessment. Spours (1989) suggests that these initiatives are best described as *modular developments* rather than seen as examples of *modularization* as they were only modular *within* particular qualifications. For the purposes of this chapter, I shall refer to modular developments within qualifications as the process of *internal modularization.*[9]

The modular GCSEs of the 1980s took on certain of the features of teacher-assessed Mode 3 O-Levels of the 1970s. By being associated with providing access to those students who had been excluded by more conventional routes, modularization came to be seen as appropriate for less able students, and therefore to be linked to a relaxation of standards. It was this influence of *context* (low level courses designed for lower ability students) on *content* (the process of modularization) (Raffe, 1984), in a political climate in which maintaining standards was seen as linked to externally marked terminal examinations, that led, in the 1990s, to the demise of pre-16 modularization.

As TVEI began, in the late 1980s, to have an impact on the curriculum after 16, schools and colleges became increasingly aware of the problems of progression and of the confused 'jungle' of often non-comparable qualifications. *Internal modularization* provided no solution to this problem and schools and colleges began to develop what Raffe (1992a) describes as an *aggregative* modularization strategy and what I shall, in this paper, refer to as *external modularization* across different qualifications. The best examples of *external modularization* were the so-called Y-models in which programmes for 16 year olds were developed with a common first year leading to either an A-Level or BTEC vocational qualification after two years of study. Credit transfer was possible as the modules completed by a student in his/her first year could be credited towards either qualification. There is little research on the success of these developments, though evidence from a local initiative at Gloucester College of Arts and Technology indicated that, in practice, there was very little transfer between qualifications. This would again point to the power of the divided qualifications system in shaping a reform designed to minimize the effect of divisions.

There were important differences between the leading modular schemes The University of Cambridge (UCLES) modular A-Level scheme was devised by an Examination Board and offered to all schools and colleges. It enabled students to combine different groups of modules from a common modular bank in achieving different qualifications. It was a clear example of what I have referred to as *external modularization*. The AEB/Wessex scheme, on the other hand, was a three-way collaboration between schools, colleges, a group of LEAs in the west of England and the Examination Board. The scheme was not just involved in modularizing the curriculum; it was a whole approach to the provision of post-compulsory education which influenced the role of guidance, the preparation of materials and the availability of the learner support that students would need if they were to benefit from the opportunities of choice within the modular system. In linking module design *both* to guidance, supported self study *and* an overall view of the purpose of the curriculum (expressed in the appointment of a cross subject coordinator) the Wessex Scheme demonstrated a number of the features of what I will later refer to as *connective modularization*.

Despite the considerable professional interest in modular schemes that could bridge academic and vocational qualifications (Richardson et al., 1995), attempts by schools and colleges to work with examination boards across the academic/vocational divide came up against the difficulty of their very different approaches to assessment and remained the exception rather than the rule. This situation, however, could well change as a result of the recent amalgamation of academic and vocational boards into unitary bodies. A further limitation on the development and potential of modularization imposed by the previous government that appears to have changed as a result of the General Election is the emergence of a somewhat more flexible attitude to teacher-based modular assessment (DfEE, 1997). The pedagogic advantages of modularization in providing regular feedback to learners is lost if most assessment is at the end of the course rather than at the end of each module.

The Outcomes Approach

Defining the curriculum in terms of outcomes can also be seen as a generic strategy which, like modularization, can take a number of forms. I shall define an *outcomes approach* as one which asserts that the curriculum can (and should) be expressed in terms of measurable learning outcomes. It contrasts sharply with traditional curricula which are frequently expressed in terms of inputs (for example class contact hours and syllabi). An outcomes approach can, in principle, refer to any kind of educational outcome, not just the units of competence with which it has been associated through NVQs.

In parallel with the distinction between three types of modularization, I will distinguish three kinds of outcome approaches which I refer to as *unitized*, *integrated* and *connective*.

Unitized approaches to outcomes are those such as that used in NVQs in which a unit can be assessed on its own and there is no overall curriculum goal associated with encouraging coherence or progression on the part of learners. An *integrated* outcomes approach is exemplified in GNVQs and in the National Curriculum when outcomes are grouped together to form a qualification. An integrated outcomes approach could also be the basis for modular A-Levels. A *connective* approach to outcomes involves groups of outcomes being related both to specific qualifications and to how learners express their purposes in the curriculum as a whole.

As in the case of modularization, the form that an outcomes approach takes, and therefore its consequences, will depend on the context. For example, *integrated* or *connective* outcomes approaches to work based training are much more likely when employers have a strategic approach to training and investment and when trade unions view training as a key element in their negotiations. In the case of the National Curriculum, its official aims are to achieve higher standards in the core and foundation subjects. However, a policy of over-specification of outcomes and little consultation with teachers or parents has resulted in a curriculum which monitors school achievements but provides few incentives for teachers to take more responsibility for raising achievement in their schools. In the case of NVQs, the separation of outcomes from learning processes encourages colleges and employers to concentrate on assessment rather than investing time in devising new pedagogic strategies.

Any form of outcomes approach to the curriculum is radical when contrasted with traditional approaches in its challenge to the link between teaching and learning. This challenge can be seen from the point of view of the student, the teacher and the institution. From the point of view of the student, outcomes provide criteria which allow them to demonstrate that they are qualified without necessarily attending a course of study. Furthermore, if students are thinking of taking a course, outcomes provide them with explicit criteria both for making choices and for judging the effectiveness of the teaching. From the point of view of teachers, an outcomes approach can create the conditions for improving their professionalism by the requirement it makes on them to examine their practices in relation to what they expect their students to achieve. From the institution's point of view, an outcomes approach does not prescribe either time or method of study. Whether this becomes an incentive for an institution to take greater responsibility for achieving outcomes depends both on its overall curriculum strategy and on the incentives for developing such a strategy that the system of funding provides.

In its separation of outcomes from processes and the opportunity it provides for the recognition of prior learning, an outcomes approach is likely to appear more relevant to adults than young people. Nevertheless, the two broad principles that follow from an outcomes approach remain important for learners of any age. They are, first, that the curriculum should be expressed in terms of what a school or college expects a student to achieve and, second, that a school or college is obliged to define its responsibilities to learners. The limitations of all outcomes approaches is that they only refer to outcomes. They can therefore never be the basis of a complete curriculum strategy. Institutions also have to make decisions about input priorities — for example the balance between class contact and open learning time and between formal teaching and learning support time.

In this section, I have argued that the form that modularization has taken and the kind of approaches to outcomes that have been developed reflect the context of their implementation as much as their *content* as innovations. There appears to be nothing *intrinsic* to either modularization or outcomes approaches that links them to low level programmes or a low-skill equilibrium. However there are two features of the way they have been developed that reflect a political context in which consumers have been given priority over providers (of qualifications) and make it likely that both strategies will be associated with low standards in practice. These are, first, a neglect of learning processes and, second, a tendency to devalue the professional expertise of teachers. In the next sections, therefore, I deal with a key aspect of the content of both innovations that relate to these issues — their focus on learner-centredness.

Some Problems with the Idea of Learner-centredness

Both modularization and outcomes approaches can claim to be learner-centred approaches to the curriculum, though from rather different points of view. Whereas an outcomes approach starts by describing what a learner can expect to achieve or by defining criteria for recognizing learning that has already been achieved, modularization focuses on students as *managers of their own learning* who need feedback to provide a basis for improving their own learning strategies, and as *decision makers* and *choosers* of learning programmes.

The idea of the active learner who takes responsibility for her/his own learning is an attractive one and is a recognition of something which traditional content-dominated models of education have all too easily forgotten. However, in practice, there are some fundamental problems with the concept of learner-centredness which are magnified in a political context in which the government distrusts the expertise of teachers as a professional group.

A more learner-centred curriculum implies that students should be given more opportunities to make their own learning decisions. However, the capacity to make learning decisions cannot be separated from the level of learning reached. The ability to make learning decisions is itself something which has to be learned, something recognized in the fashionable idea of 'learning to learn'. Raising levels of overall achievement involves increasing the capacities of those groups of students and trainees who have in the past shown that they lack either the motivation or the capacity to learn. It follows that if a learner-centred approach is to address the problems of low achievers it cannot just be concerned with access and choice; it must be about new pedagogies, new relationships between teachers and learners and the development of new learning strategies. In other words, a learner-centred approach, even if it begins by separating outcomes from processes, has to be complemented by a focus on how learners are supported by teachers. This may of course involve a number of activities such as guidance and diagnostic assessment which have not in the past been seen as central to the work of teachers (Shackleton, 1988).

Giving up some of their traditional practices will mean placing more, not less responsibility on teachers. Counterposing teacher-centredness with learner-centredness, particularly within the context of an outcomes approach which gives so much attention to assessment, can all too easily distract attention from the development of a learner-centred pedagogy.

My critique of a learner-centred curriculum has focused on the limitations of approaches that over-emphasize the active role of learners; it has argued that they neglect the need for new roles for teachers and trainers. In suggesting that students or trainees will learn by themselves if certain barriers, such as college attendance at particular times, are removed, the proponents of learner-centredness may be searching for a modern version of the old apprenticeship idea of 'learning by doing'. Whereas, at least in the apprenticeship model, there was some institutional support for the apprentice to learn from experience, in the new model learning is entirely up to the individual; all that outcomes-based qualifications can provide are evidence criteria for assessing competence or attainment.

A learner-centred curriculum may appear attractive, if the main objective is to reduce the role (and the cost) of teachers. However, the question remains as to what value would be attached to qualifications that depend less and less on teaching. It is difficult to see how learner-centred approaches can, on their own, get beyond encouraging students to learn by trial and error. This would not seem to be a basis for raising levels of attainment or preparing young people for a world of work in which more and more jobs are likely to require conceptual knowledge and skills that cannot be learned on the job alone.

This section has focused on one of the main features of both modularization and outcomes approaches — their shift from a teacher-centred to a learner-centred curriculum. The limitation of learner-centred approaches is that, in the context of wider efforts to reduce the influence of teachers and professional educators, they lead to the neglect of the need for new pedagogies and more broadly the need for a new kind of professionalism among teachers. The next section turns to another aspect of the curriculum which learner-centred innovations neglect — its content.

Modules, Outcomes and Content: A New Approach to the Organization of the Curriculum

I argued in the previous section that modularization and outcomes approaches tend to polarize learner-centredness and teacher-centredness. In this section, I want to turn to another polarization, that between content (for example syllabi, textbooks and bodies of knowledge) and the specification of learning objectives. In polarizing learner- and teacher-centredness the issue of pedagogy remains unresolved. Similarly when outcome-led curricula are presented as alternatives to those that are content-led, we are left with the question as to what organization of knowledge could replace the traditional view of curriculum content defined in terms of school subjects or occupational fields.

School subjects developed with mass schooling and cannot be seen as in isolation from its other features in the UK such as low participation, narrow forms of specialization for older pupils, a neglect of generic knowledge and skills and the absence of any model of general education. However, despite these weaknesses subjects persist as the dominant organizing form of the 14–19 curriculum. In the remainder of this section, I want, therefore, to consider a number of ways in which a modular curriculum based on learning outcomes might provide an alternative way of addressing the organization of knowledge in curricula that would be the basis for overcoming these weaknesses.

Incentives for Learning

The IPPR report (Finegold et al., 1990) argued that selective A-Levels and low status vocational alternatives serve to keep down participation and achievement. The issue here is the extent to which incentives might be different within a modular system based on learning outcomes. The evidence provided by Raffe (1992a) from a survey of students on the Scottish National Certificate (a modular and outcomes-based vocational qualification) is that, while its greater flexibility was welcomed by students, this did not lead to increases in participation or achievement. The reason, Raffe suggests, is that, although modularization does increase choice and flexibility, it does not (and on its own cannot) create incentives for higher performance. Such incentives, he argues, are located in the institutional and wider social context. In the case of the Scottish National Certificate, this context was one in which vocational qualifications were still seen as signs of failure rather than achievement. It follows that if modularization is to promote incentives for learning, it needs to be part of a move towards a less divided system and specific strategies are needed to promote the recognition of vocational qualifications by HE and employers.

Broadening of Studies After 16

The over-specialized nature of the post-compulsory curriculum in England and Wales has been widely recognized, at least since the Dainton Report (DES, 1968). The main structural cause of the problem is the size of existing qualifications, especially A-Levels and GNVQs, in relation to the hours available in a college or Sixth Form timetable. By breaking up qualifications into units of 30 or 40 hours (Rainbow, 1993), a modular curriculum provides the flexibility needed for the development of broader based programmes of study. However, this cannot be achieved by modularization alone; whereas breadth is an aggregative feature of a curriculum, modularization is a disaggregative strategy. Breadth needs to be specified in terms of rules of combination of modules and criteria for balancing specialist and broadening studies (Young and Barnett, 1992). Without such specification, student choices, as well as the modules offered by institutions, will be shaped by the demands of university admission tutors and employers and by their own individual and, on their own, inevitably ill-informed judgments.

Generic Knowledge and Skills

The insulated form of subject specialization that characterizes the post-16 academic curriculum in the UK limits the access of students to any forms of knowledge and skills that are not subject-specific. These new kinds of generic knowledge skills have been described as either overarching capabilities (Prospect Centre, 1991) or the capacity for symbolic analysis (Reich, 1991). Both are ways of expressing the idea that the ability to apply knowledge is as important as the knowledge itself and that knowledge at the interface between subjects may sometimes be more important than the subject knowledge itself. A modular curriculum can offer such possibilities, by allowing different combinations of subject knowledge and applications which can be defined in outcome terms. However, the development of generic knowledge and skills requires the specification of contents, contexts and processes (e.g. industrial experience and working in teams) and therefore would require a curriculum that went beyond a national modular bank and beyond learning outcomes that were linked only to individual modules.

Coherence

Coherence in the present post-16 curriculum is limited in two senses. First, it only applies to some learners — those taking a group of A-Level subjects or a vocational programme that relates clearly to their future plans. Second, in a subject-based and divided curriculum, the possibilities for links between subjects and between subjects and vocational fields are very limited. Again, modular curricula create a whole new set of possibilities, at least in principle. However, without rules of module combination, a common system of credit, identifiable routes and integrated systems of guidance, modularization can easily lead to fragmentation, rather than be a basis for more extensive and inclusive forms of coherence.

Each of these examples illustrates the main theme of this chapter. Modularization and learning outcome approaches to defining curriculum content are not an adequate basis, on their own, for an alternative to the existing organization of educational knowledge. Crucial decisions about content and process remain. In so far as such decisions are not made explicit in a new curriculum strategy, the old tendencies to selection and division of the subject-based curriculum will remain dominant. The final section, therefore, considers the elements of a broader curriculum strategy within which modularization and an outcomes approach could be a part.

Towards Curriculum Connectivity

Modular curricula and outcomes approaches present a radical critique of the existing curriculum. However, they do not, of themselves, provide an alternative framework. Breaking up the curriculum into modules challenges the subject organization of knowledge but is only, at best, half the answer to questions of curriculum reorganization. It fails to address either the criteria for 'breaking up' or the basis on which the parts (modules) should be combined, and who should be involved in the process of recombination. What is needed is a new approach to the organization of the curriculum that links modules and outcomes both to the aspirations and needs of learners and to the goals and purposes of the system as a whole. In order to do this, I link the ideas of *connective modularization* and *connective outcomes* to the idea of a *Curriculum of the Future* (Young, 1994).

Modularizing the curriculum and defining modules in terms of outcomes are the first steps towards the design of a curriculum that could be said truly to involve learners. It is the possibilities that they offer for creating that involvement which make them a crucial part of a *connective* curriculum strategy. However, neither a list of outcomes nor a modular bank constitute a curriculum. On their own, they treat learning as if it was like shopping in a supermarket. Whereas no relationship with sellers is required to shop in a supermarket, except at the cash till, learning *is* a relationship or rather a set of relationships. The concept of *connectivity* starts by recognizing that learning is purposive and a social process that takes place explicitly or implicitly in a 'community of practice' with other learners (Lave and Wengler, 1994). It stresses the need to link the purposes and activities of both learners and teachers with how they relate to developments in the wider society. Teachers might design particular modules in the social sciences or technology that relate to their knowledge and experiences as well as to that of their students. However, decisions on which modules to develop would also need to depend, for example, on the existence of an industrial policy that provided incentives for the development, use and marketing of new construction materials, or of a welfare policy that was part of a new approach to community care.

Connectivity, therefore, does not refer to a particular curriculum model but to how the curriculum purposes of a school or college are expressed in all its activities and how these activities are brought together to articulate and support the purposes of individual learners. In other words, connectivity stresses the interdependence of a school or college's whole curriculum and the elements that make it up — subject and vocational programmes, learner support, guidance etc. and its relationship to broader developments in society.

Concluding Comments

In this chapter I have argued that, despite their potential, modularization and outcomes approaches have severe limitations as curricular strategies. These limitations were made clear by considering the contexts in which they have been developed and the problems of trying to introduce them in isolation. In relation to raising achievement levels or broadening the curriculum, they are at best tools rather than strategies. To suggest what such a strategy might involve, I have used the concept of connectivity which extends Morgan's idea of 'an organization as a brain' (Morgan, 1988) and applies it to the curriculum. It is a way of expressing the idea that the curriculum of the future will need to be a system, albeit a new kind of *open* system. Three features distinguish *connective* from *traditional* models of the curriculum as a system. First, they are open because their concept of purpose is defined in terms of future needs and debates about different futures and therefore cannot be fixed or certain. Second, they emphasize feedback between curriculum purposes and learners' needs. A connective curriculum not only shapes learner purposes, it has to be shaped by them. Third, the concept of curriculum purpose is an element of all the parts of the curriculum such as subjects or occupational knowledge and the relations between them, as well as going beyond the parts; it is not external to the parts.

Within the framework of a curriculum based on connective specialization, modularization offers the possibility of student choice and new combinations of study that can relate student purposes to the options a society has for the future. Likewise, outcomes become not just a method of defining module content and providing evidence on which students can make decisions about what to study; they are ways of expressing links between the knowledge available in schools and colleges and future opportunities for employment and further learning.

Connectivity is a vision of a curriculum of the future but not only a vision. It can point to specific strategies for teachers, whether they are designing modules, recording the achievement of their students or assessing their work. It also recognizes the need to make explicit how such everyday practices are linked to the ways that schools and colleges are themselves part of a wider system and to debates about the kind of future a society envisages for itself.

Chapter 7

Integrating Personal and Social Education into the 14–19 Curriculum

Introduction

This chapter has both a practical and a theoretical aim. Practically, it is a contribution to the debate about personal and social education with a primary focus on the 14–19 curriculum (Inman and Buck, 1995). Theoretically, it presents an argument that, if personal and social education is to be at the centre of the 14–19 curriculum, relations between subjects and the curriculum as a whole need to be reconceptualized. As one approach to this reconceptualization, the chapter draws on the ideas of connectivity and connective specialization introduced in Chapters 5 and 6 and starts from two premises. The first is that secondary education is not just about access to the basic areas of specialist knowledge and understanding (nor, in its later phase, to learning the skills and knowledge appropriate to specific jobs); it is also *and as fundamentally* concerned with the personal and social education of students as future adults and citizens. The second premise is that if the importance of personal and social education is to be more than well intentioned rhetoric, a new approach to the curriculum is required that changes the relationship between personal development goals, the educational aims of school subjects and the whole curriculum goals of schools. Such a new approach to the curriculum does not depend solely on changes in the National Curriculum itself, though the narrowness, bias and rigidity of the compulsory component of Key Stage 4 remain problems and the analysis developed here, which focuses primarily on the individual school, is also applicable to reforming the National Curriculum. The crucial issue is how individual schools define their curriculum purposes and how their specialist subject teaching is developed in relation to the purposes of the school curriculum *as a whole*. Such an approach involves a radical inversion of current practice when the aims of subject teaching dominate other school goals. At least in the short term, the proposals suggested in this chapter are likely to be seen as going against the grain of government pressures on schools to raise GCSE and A-Level results and introduce institutional targets. They will require schools to know far more about how all the activities that make up the school contribute to its overall curriculum goals. Schools will need to develop their *collective intelligence* (Brown and Lauder, 1995) about those internal activities which involve the whole school — such as guidance and learner support as well as about activities such as marking and homework which in many schools are left to departments, and about their external links with primary schools, universities, employers and other secondary schools in their area.

Bureaucratic and Connective Models of Curriculum Integration

In order to make more concrete what might be involved in the changes to which I have referred, I want to distinguish between two ways in which schools might organize their curriculum. I shall describe these as **bureaucratic** and **connective** forms of integration and argue that, while bureaucratic integration will inevitably leave personal and social development at the margin of a school's curriculum priorities, connective integration requires the personal and social development of pupils to be one of its core principles. I shall suggest, that despite the external and internal pressures to maintain the bureaucratic model, there are not only powerful reasons for change but signs that, even within the bureaucratic model, transitional strategies are emerging which exhibit some of the features of connective integration.

Bureaucratic Integration

It is first necessary to outline what I mean by the **bureaucratic** integration of the curriculum. It describes the main features of the traditional secondary school curriculum, expressed clearly in the early National Curriculum orders, though less so, in the revisions introduced by Sir Ron Dearing. It is a curriculum based on relatively autonomous subjects, taught in departments and managed by a Headteacher and Deputies who frequently divided their responsibilities by separating control of the timetable from responsibility for discipline and pastoral care. Once the timetable is decided in such a curriculum, there is very little that different subject teachers need to discuss in common; everything is decided in departments. In other words, it is a centrally co-ordinated curriculum with responsibility for the delivery of teaching delegated to subject departments. In form it is not unlike the organization of production in many factories in the years before and after the Second World War.

The advent of TVEI and the variety of other curriculum developments of the 1980s put this model under strain as a whole variety of new posts with cross-departmental responsibility for assessment, careers, Records of Achievement and vocational education were created. In most cases, these new activities were added to the subject-led curriculum and the whole was literally 'the sum of the parts' and no more. It was not surprising that many subject teachers saw tutorial guidance and other non subject specific activities as encroachments on 'real learning time'. No less surprising was that the whole range of learner support activities, together with much of the pastoral and personal development, should become associated with a curriculum for low achievers. New divisions appeared in secondary schools as Personal and Social Education became incorporated into what was known as the pre-vocational curriculum for older and lower achieving pupils. Some subject teachers assumed that the majority of students lacked both the ability and inclination to cope with specialist study. On the other hand, those who promoted the idea of a personal development curriculum often dismissed school subjects as 'alienating' lower ability pupils. Bureaucratic integration was therefore the organizational basis for one of the major divisions within secondary education between the pastoral and the subject curriculum (Power, 1991) and could be seen as a kind of precursor of academic/vocational divisions after 16. A major problem of the Dearing Key Stage 4 proposals is that linking greater freedom for schools at 14 to a smaller compulsory core and the option of a GNVQ Part I could lead to an even more rigid and earlier version of that divide.

The bureaucratic model of curriculum integration has several implications for Personal and Social Education. First, it is likely to be neglected as a specific curriculum goal since the curriculum continues to be dominated by subject teaching. Other possibilities are that it is either a marginal addition which depends on the chance commitment of particular teachers or it reappears, in the form of social and life skills for low achievers, as a replacement for the mainstream curriculum from which they have been excluded.

Schools are not immune to modernizing tendencies and there are signs that the bureaucratic model is being pushed to its limits. Since the establishment of National Targets and League Tables, schools have been under increasing pressure to be more 'effective' in terms of the numbers and levels of qualifications that pupils achieve. The focus on institutional effectiveness has undermined some of the autonomy of subject departments by encouraging tutoring by subject specialists and the cross-subject monitoring of individual pupil attainments (Spours and Young, 1994). Such developments represent a shift in some features of the bureaucratic model in that they stress the integrative role of the *ethos* of a school and the sharing of goals; they imply less reliance on the old hierarchical, delegated structure of responsibility.

One of the limitations of most approaches to school effectiveness is that, despite claims made to the contrary, they take the purposes of a school as given; in doing so, they draw on an *organizational* rather than a *curriculum* view of ethos[10], leaving untouched the content, pedagogy and relations between subjects that are associated with the old model. Furthermore, a top-down approach to improving effectiveness can be resented (and therefore resisted) by teachers and is likely to impinge only indirectly on students as learners. Such approaches are concerned with making existing organizational structures operate more effectively and therefore do not address the possibility that it may be these structures themselves that are part of the problem. The old model of bureaucratic integration was associated with traditional hierarchies and divisions and with maintaining the internal social order of the school; it emerged at a time when the external environment of schools was relatively static and predictable and few demands were made on schools either to be innovative or to raise levels of attainment. The new competitive context that schools find themselves in is very different; it requires them to raise the attainment *of all pupils* by involving them in the management of their own learning and is in direct contradiction to the priorities of bureaucratic integration. It may be that it is in this contradiction between external demands and internal structures that we can identify the sources of change and the possibilities of a curriculum model that takes personal and social education seriously.

There is, however, another factor at work to which I will return later. Creating incentives for change both for learners and teachers depends on the development of a sense of purpose linked to new possibilities for the future. Present policy assumes that purpose for individuals can be left to individual choice and that for institutions it can be left to the market and fear of competition. However successful businesses, on which such 'market' ideas are based, depend on a vision of what people might need in the future if they are to improve productivity and sales. It seems unlikely that schools will change unless teachers and students feel part of such a vision.

Connective Integration

I suggested at the beginning of this chapter that a model for integrating personal and social development into the curriculum would need to invert much current practice; the connective model of curriculum integration does this in two ways. First, it does not start with subjects but with the broader notion of curriculum purposes and how subjects can realize those purposes. Second, it does not start from the requirements of the National Curriculum but with individual schools defining their curriculum purposes and asking how they can fulfil the requirements of the National Curriculum. Schools need to define their purposes in terms of the kind of young person, adult, worker, citizen, and parent that they, in discussion with parents and others in the local community, want their pupils to become and the kind of knowledge skills and attitudes that they envisage pupils will need when they leave school if they are to fulfil such roles. Instead of treating the National Curriculum as something imposed on them, schools need to interpret it as a way of providing a broad specification of content that ensures that what students learn transcends the curriculum and context of particular schools. The point I want to make here is that, in a connective model of curriculum integration, personal and social education becomes one of the sets of criteria a school uses for interpreting the National Curriculum Orders, choosing Examination Boards for GCSE, A-Level and vocational courses and using the discretion allowed to it at Key Stage 4.

For individual schools, one step is crucial in moving towards a connective model. All staff need to endorse the criteria and agree to articulate how their subjects or areas of responsibility would be involved in both supporting shared approaches to teaching and learning and in delivering the agreed outcomes.

The model is **connective** in the sense that subject specialists would be required to *connect* their subject teaching to (a) the overall school curriculum purposes and (b) the way other subjects are contributing to whole school curriculum criteria. The role of subjects would need to be made explicit in four ways; first, by identifying the specialist skills and knowledge they can offer; second, by showing how any of the specific skills and knowledge of particular subjects can contribute to the broader curriculum goals such as personal and social education through collaboration with other subject specialists; third, by identifying the contribution that different subjects can make to raising overall levels of attainment and achievement; and fourth, by identifying the contribution of subject specialists in enabling schools to develop their external links with employers, the community and other education providers.

The school management model needed for delivering a curriculum based on connective integration would be curriculum-led rather than organization-led and would need to be based on goals defined and agreed by the whole staff. The outcome would be quite different from the combination of hierarchical co-ordination and delegation that characterizes the bureaucratic model. Furthermore, quite different relationships would need to be developed between teaching and non-teaching staff who are traditionally separated through the division between pastoral and subject curricula. Incorporating personal and social development criteria into goals for the whole curriculum as well as ensuring that specialist subject goals relate to them will not be easy, when subjects are at least in practice, seen as ends in themselves. For subjects to be *used for* curriculum purposes rather than used to define those purposes requires a vision of the kind of future for which we are preparing young people and for syllabi to be constructed with such a vision in mind. The National Curriculum and most GCSE and A-Level subject syllabi are both based largely on a vision of the past. The 1998 review of the National Curriculum, if linked to the current DfEE consultation on 16–19 qualifications (DfEE, 1997), is an opportunity for a different approach.

From Bureaucratic to Connective Integration

What then are the external forces that schools might gain support from shifting from a bureaucratic to a connective model in their curriculum organization? Schools are under enormous pressure to be more effective, to make do with fewer resources and to enable their students to achieve ever better examination results. Mostly this is experienced as top-down and as a mistaken attempt to impose what are often out of date business principles on schools. I have already pointed to the tensions between these demands and the existing way that schools are organized, particularly as this impacts on teachers as professionals. Teachers do want more of their pupils to reach higher levels of attainment and to raise standards of achievement generally and they are aware that the more students feel a sense of ownership of their own learning, the more they will achieve in curriculum terms. It is for this reason that teachers have responded so positively to the introduction of Records of Achievement and Individual Action Planning and initiatives such as value-added strategies and the ASDAN Youth Award. These developments, all of which arise from teachers finding new ways of supporting student learning, are an indication that the bureaucratic model is under challenge. Furthermore, there is also evidence of the emergence of a *transitional* approach to curriculum integration in which schools develop cross-departmental systems for supporting pupils in improving their achievements. However this shift away from a *bureaucratic* model remains based on a traditional view of curriculum and pedagogy involving the transmission of fixed bodies of knowledge to largely passive learners and is sustained by both the content and the form of the existing National Curriculum. In the strength of its subject divisions, in the relative weakness of its cross-curricular themes and in the limited discretion, even in its revised form, that it gives to teachers, the National Curriculum has provided a boost to the bureaucratic model and made teachers understandably defensive and reluctant to take risks with anything new and untested (Rowe and Whitty, 1993).

A recent report (Spours and Young, 1995) describes work with a group of teachers in developing value-added strategies in Sixth Forms and is an indication of what such a transitional approach might involve. One of the lessons from the development work carried out by the teachers was that such strategies lead to an increasing involvement of students in managing their own learning. It is this student involvement, rather than the statistical or recording aspects of value added approaches, that have been the catalyst for bringing together subject specialists and those involved in the pastoral curricula and for helping subject specialists to see the value of a whole-school or *connective* approach to the curriculum. One of the positive outcomes of linking value added strategies to school improvement (Hodgson, 1997), is that the focus on *learning gain* leads concretely into the questions of motivation and the content of learning and thus to the potential of seeing the personal and social development of students as integral to broader curriculum goals.

Curriculum Change and the Changing Role of Teachers: From Insular to Connective Specialists

Making personal and social development a *whole-school* curriculum priority places new demands on both the senior management of schools and teachers, especially those who have been trained as subject specialists. For managers (i.e. Headteachers and Deputies) it requires them to go beyond organizational definitions of ethos and to begin to define the learning goals of the school. In other words, it requires Headteachers to take on a curriculum leadership role in their discussions with subject leaders and heads of subject departments. A whole-school approach to personal and social education also requires classroom teachers to develop new skills and knowledge. Perhaps more fundamentally, it challenges the basis of the professional identity of subject teachers which has traditionally been based on a relatively bounded and insular knowledge of their subjects. It follows, therefore, that the shift to a connective model of the curriculum would also involve a shift in the role of teachers — in the terms used in earlier chapters, this would be from insular to connective specialists. Part of the resistance of many subject teachers to any move away from bureaucratic models based on insular subject specialisms lies in their fears that the content and depth of subject teaching would be undermined. Furthermore, teachers can all too easily point to the weak conceptual content of non-subject based programmes both in social education (Whitty et al., 1994) and prevocational courses such as CPVE and GNVQs — a point that was raised in Chapter 4.

There are a number of ways in which these forms of resistance might be overcome: in the way that subject teachers are trained, through the professional development programmes of schools and in how subject teachers are involved in the development of personal and social development criteria within the whole curriculum. In this chapter, I shall only dwell on the last point. However before doing so a point made in earlier chapters needs to be re-stated. The shift in the role of teachers from insular to connective specialists is not a shift away from subjects but a shift in how subjects are perceived. Traditionally, insular subject specialists tend to view the curriculum from the point of view of their subjects as ends in themselves; they perceive personal and social education goals as implicit in learning a subject and thus they see any additional PSE time as taking time away from the subject curriculum which is always perceived as 'overloaded'. It is only if subject specialists have a model of the curriculum as a *whole* that it becomes possible to ask how a particular subject contributes to a specific whole curriculum purpose such as personal and social development. To do this is not to dilute a teacher's specialist knowledge but to redefine the role of specialist teachers and the role of subjects. Instead of being a teacher whose specialist knowledge is defined by that which she/he does not have in common with any other teachers, the connective subject specialist is someone who not only has a subject specialism but understands how his/her subject relates to the broader purposes of the curriculum through links with other subjects. The move from bureaucratic to connective integration can be seen as the democratization of specialization operating at the school level in a way that is consistent with the broader social changes outlined in Chapter 5. Furthermore, it can enhance the broader educational role of subject teachers, broaden student learning and extend the range of students who can get access to specialist knowledge.

Continuity and Discontinuity at 16+:
Towards a 14–19 Entitlement

Little research and development on personal and social education has focused on the post-compulsory phase of schooling. However, with the proportion of those who continue to study full time after 16 no longer rising, it becomes increasingly necessary to treat the pre- and post-16 phases of 14–19 education as a continuous whole. Until the 1980s, the organization of provision for those staying on after 16 assumed it was provision for a minority. This minority was initially the 'academic' Sixth Former taking A-Levels and the day release student at college; in the late 1970s, it began to include the 'new' or (one year) Sixth Former and the 'new' full-time FE student, some retaking GCSE and others on various types of pre-vocational programme. Personal and social development after 16 has remained *ad hoc* and informal. In colleges (except Sixth Form colleges) it has hardly existed. In school Sixth Forms, it includes sports, prefect systems, school trips or societies and sometimes classroom-based activities such as general and liberal studies and debating. In its elite form in the Public Schools, personal and social education is taken more seriously as a 'curriculum for future leaders' and strengthened by the possibilities of extra-curricular social education for boarding students. The Public Schools are thus able to compensate for the narrowness of the A-Level curriculum, without, however providing the formal curriculum breadth that is typical of upper secondary education elsewhere in Europe.

Full-time post-16 students are now 70 per cent of each cohort, split roughly evenly between those remaining at school and those going to Further Education and Sixth Form Colleges and mostly on one of the three academic, general vocational and work-based vocational tracks. As colleges are funded only for qualification-linked activities, the earlier *ad hoc* provision of a personal development curriculum for those over 16 is disappearing. A-Levels have no requirement for personal and social development and GNVQ compulsory core skills are limited to numeracy, communications and use of information technology; there are thus no cross curricular themes and no common core for all post-16 students. Some institutions attempt to maintain a personal and social development curriculum through their tutorial system and others register with the ASDAN Youth Award scheme or the Open College Network.

This picture is in stark contrast to systems elsewhere in Europe. Whether, as in France or the Nordic countries, provision is based on full-time study or, as in Germany, it is based partly on the gymnasium and other types of school and partly on an employer-based system of vocational education and training — the dual system, there is an explicit curriculum for all students up till 18 or 19 which includes civics and social studies regardless of the specific programme being followed. Whereas elsewhere in Europe, it is assumed that personal and social development of students continues after compulsory schooling, in England and Wales students are assumed to have completed their personal and social development by 16. The assumption is that the social education of potential leaders continues as in the past through A-Levels and the rest will be prepared through vocational courses or training schemes for their future life as employees.

Like so many important issues facing the education system in England and Wales, the need for a coherent and balanced curriculum for the whole cohort up to 18 which includes Personal and Social Education as a core element, has either been consciously avoided or just has not been thought through. There have been programmes like TVEI which have stressed 14–18 curriculum continuity and given rise to ideas like student entitlement and college charters. On the other hand, the recent policy emphasis has been to encourage student-choice, institutional competition and marketing rather than continuity. Without a 14–19 framework that makes the concept of a core curriculum for all explicit and without funding strategies that encourage institutional collaboration to overcome the discontinuities between schools and colleges, it is difficult to see what increasing student choice could mean, let alone how individual schools and colleges could guarantee any continuity in a student's personal and social education.

In 1995, the Schools Curriculum and Assessment Authority abolished its 14–19 Committee and since then we have had Dearing's 16–19 Review (see Chapter 8), the present government's consultation on 16–19 qualifications (DfEE, 1997) and the projected review of the National Curriculum in 1998. As yet there is little sign that the need for a new 14–19 curriculum vision is recognized and the debate about what it might include has hardly begun. However, under pressure from the increasing fragmentation of programmes and an awareness that staying on in school could be little more than the 'warehousing' of young people before they are returned to the labour market, the concept of a post-16 curriculum of the future is emerging (Richardson et al., 1997). It may be that the dramatic disappearance of the youth labour market (63 per cent of 16 year olds got jobs in 1980, and this had fallen to 9 per cent by 1993) and the rather less dramatic increase in the proportion staying on after 16 will force policy makers involved in the post-compulsory sector to realize that we are in a new educational era in which all young people need a reliable foundation of general education as the basis for their later specialization. Personal and Social Development could then be linked both to the importance of students making choices, to the opportunities from which they have to choose and the consequences of their choice. The next section of the chapter examines some of the wider social and economic changes that are likely to shape debates about personal and social development in the 14–19 curriculum in the next decade.

Personal and Social Development and National Economic Futures

Since Callaghan's Ruskin speech in 1976, the economic role of education has undoubtedly taken precedence, at least in the minds of policy makers and politicians, over its role in the personal and intellectual development of young people. One of the aims of this chapter has been to explore the curriculum implications of countering that tendency. This matters not only because of the intrinsic importance of the educational aims that have been neglected but because it reminds us that the economic role of education is far from clear and that there are no unambiguous learning gains to be achieved by trying to link education more closely to economic needs. In fact, those who argue for a more economy-oriented curriculum turn out in practice to be more concerned with political and ideological outcomes (McCulloch, 1995). Furthermore, it is always easier to claim that a productivity crisis or high unemployment is to do with lack of skills in the workforce than to address the complex issues of investment, planning and management of the economy. From a 14–19 perspective, however, we cannot avoid the world of work and, as economists such as Bowles and Gintis (1976) have long argued, if we do not recognize it explicitly in the overt curriculum, the economy will continue to haunt us through the hidden curriculum. I want, however, in this final section of the chapter to raise a slightly different issue that concerns links between changes in the global economy and the basis that young people have for thinking about their futures.

At some point between the ages of 14 and 19 most young people in industrial societies begin to think about their future in the world of work; they may draw on reading, their experience of careers guidance, of a part-time job or work experience or parental, peer or other role models. In some areas of this country learning from parents can mean learning that most adults are out of work and unlikely to ever be employed; in others, it may involve experiencing the consequences of a sudden lay-off or closure or the equally sudden building of (or, more recently, the decision not to build) a new factory in the locality. Perhaps an even bigger change in the last decade has been the way in which these economic uncertainties have spread from being a problem largely of those in declining industries, such as coal and steel, to being a much broader phenomenon that can as easily affect those who work in banks, colleges or hospitals. It seems likely, therefore, that economic change, often on a global scale, will more and more shape how young people grow up and become adults, parents and citizens and the meaning they give to their gender and cultural identities. It follows that if personal and social education is to have meaning for young people it cannot be separated from how they understand economic changes and how they will shape their lives.

In considering the implications of this argument for the 14–18 curriculum, I want to start from the view that personal and social development is about 'developing the understandings and skills to enable (young people) to shape the world in which they live both now and in the future' (Buck and Inman, 1995), and go on to discuss three ways in which economic change itself bears directly on this aim. First, I refer to the possible changing moral basis of forms of production and business; second, I consider the cultural as well as the economic implications of globalization and, third, I discuss the emergence of flexibility as a focus for possible economic futures.

There are many different ways of viewing the morality of modern production. One is the view of the Adam Smith Institute (though not necessarily Adam Smith himself!) that business is moral and a source of criteria for what is good. Hence maximizing profits is always good and business principles should be applied to any situation where priorities are involved. The educational implication of this view is that business is like justice, truth and concern for others and should be part of any framework of personal development. A more traditional educational view is that business is a necessary evil quite separate from values like the respect for truth that are associated with education. From this point of view, business may be necessary but is not a good in itself. It was this view, sometimes taken to extremes, that the Callaghan Ruskin speech of 1976 and much recent government policy has been against. Charles Handy (1994) has another view that all the best businesses treat profits as a necessary background to doing something that is worthwhile and which satisfies people's needs. The search for evidence and arguments for and against these different versions of the morality of work in a capitalist society is one indication of the complex and ambiguous world we are preparing young people for in the late 1990s. The overriding lesson from analyses of global economic change is that it is going to be harder to continue to separate economic and moral questions. This can be illustrated in relation to two other issues that are frequently debated when considering personal and social education in the curriculum but are not often linked to economic change; I am referring to the issue of tolerance and accepting cultural diversity and the importance of learning to trust other people. These are no longer marginal issues that schools try to equip their pupils with against the pressures of the 'real world'; they are beginning to be addressed by modern business. In the 1950s and 1960s, American and European companies would dump their cheap goods on other parts of the world without caring how they were received as long as some were bought. This is becoming less possible, as companies face more competition both at home and in other countries. A UK company which wants to be successful in another part of the world increasingly needs to come to terms with the local culture in a similar way that members of a multicultural community need to learn about each other. In other words, not only is learning to understand other cultures and value them a vital part of a student's personal development as a future citizen, it can also be a potential basis for enhancing her/his employability.

Another example reflects the new forms of advanced production such as stepper factories where the new 'machines for making electronic machines' are made and where each product is unique and there are no written procedures or defined skills (Kress, 1995). Production workers have to learn to trust each other, take risks and support each other when a decision in wrong. In other words, personal development can no longer be detached from employability; to be a worker in one of the new factories one has to learn to behave morally, be tolerant and respect others.

The point of these examples is not to argue that capitalism has suddenly become benign but that the developments that are shaping our economic future require similar skills, knowledge and attitudes that a young person wanting to shape her or his own life needs to develop. If successful twenty-first century companies are going to be those that listen to their employees and to their customers, then it is important that young people seeking to shape their lives understand why this is so and why it still applies relatively rarely in the UK.

Conclusions

The aim of this chapter has been to reassert the importance of personal and social development and to explore its implications for the 14–19 curriculum. I have considered *first*, the implications of schools developing their own curriculum purposes and what this might mean for specialist subject teachers. My analysis suggests a need to change our traditional concept of curriculum from one in which subjects define purposes based on what I have called bureaucratic integration to one, based on *connective integration*, in which curriculum purposes define the role of subjects and the limits of their role. In considering the possibilities of such a change, I suggested that in current practice we could identify a transitional model which has some elements of connectivity but is still working within the National Curriculum model of bureaucratic integration. I further suggested that in developing whole-school policies for raising attainment, schools come up against the limits of forms of curriculum organization based on the bureaucratic integration of subjects. Second, I drew on a 14–19 perspective and took account of the shaping effects of global transformations in the economy. Here my analysis would suggest that a broad concept of a core curriculum for all post-14 students regardless of the programme that they follow needs to be developed. This could be the basis of a framework to overcome the discontinuity at 16+ and the current absence of any core element for students after they are 16. A number of ways have been suggested as to how such a core might be expressed in curriculum terms. Examples are Crombie White et al. (1995); and Spours and Young (1995). None could be implemented without significant reforms to existing qualifications. I also suggested that no concept of personal and social development for the 14–18 age group would be adequate without incorporating an understanding economic and technological change. ·

The most debilitating aspects of educational policy in the last few years has been an absence of vision and purpose. Perhaps this lack of vision is a failure of imagination on the part of both politicians and educationists; perhaps it is that the educationists of today have had their confidence in visions undermined by post-modernist theories and market economics, unlike those who authored the great education reports of 30, 40, and 50 years ago, which for all their paternalism, did not lack a vision. Whichever of these accounts is nearer the truth, there are two final conclusions from an analysis which focuses on personal and social education as a curriculum issue. The first is, that although the burden on every school, college and university in the country, is to provide a vision for the next generation of learners, it cannot be done at the level of individual institutions alone. When we consider the curriculum as a whole, we need not only the visions of every school in the country but a definition of national educational purposes that goes beyond standards and is expressed in a democratically debated National Curriculum that applies to all students, at least until they are 18 and regardless of whether they are in school or college or of the status of the school. The second conclusion is that, although a student's personal and social education is important and is a much neglected curriculum priority, it cannot, of itself, be the basis for the 14–19 curriculum, for that would be to continue to separate it from the wider social cultural and economic context in which young people grow up. In Chapter 9 when the idea of an advanced level curriculum of the future is developed, I suggest how such a curriculum could be the basis for including Personal and Social Education.

Chapter 8

Qualifications for a Learning Society: Building on the Dearing Review

Introduction

The publication in 1996 of the final report of Sir Ron Dearing's Review represented another stage in the evolution of 16–19 qualifications in England and Wales with its proposals for a National Framework with four qualification levels and a new Baccalaureate-type Diploma at 18+. The recommendations of the Review were in many respects ambiguous, perhaps deliberately so, as it was clearly an attempt to satisfy many different educational and political interests. Responses to the report varied from initial enthusiasm — 'the great fixer has done it again' — to cautious criticism as it became clear that many of the proposals lacked detail and were open to different interpretations.

From the point of view of this book, two related questions about the review need to be asked. The first is whether, as a further attempt to modernize the qualifications system and provide a basis for a curriculum of the future, the Dearing recommendations represent a genuine step forward and, if so, what kind of model of qualification reform does it have. The second question is the nature of the relationship between qualifications and curriculum that the report implies. The Report's strong support for making the three qualification 'tracks' more distinctive would suggest that one of its aims was to reverse such convergence between the tracks as there has been in the last decade. In terms of changing the relationships between the three tracks, therefore, the proposals represented a step back towards greater distinctiveness, not a step towards greater flexibility and a more unified curriculum. On the other hand, the report also made a number of recommendations, such as the merging of the National Council for Vocational Qualifications and the Schools Curriculum and Assessment Authority into a single regulatory body, the proposals for an Advanced Diploma based on four knowledge domains and the breaking up of GNVQs into smaller six — or even three — unit blocks which either establish conditions for, or give pointers to, a more unified and flexible curriculum. The fact that the report makes recommendations with both unifying and divisive implications suggests that any assessment of whether it represents a step towards a more unified system will not be straightforward.

The chapter has three parts. Part I summarizes the Report's main recommendations. Part 2 examines the recommendations and their possible origins from four points of view — the terms of reference of the Review; the context of changes in the system that have taken place since the 1991 White Paper (ED/DfE/WO, 1991); its framework of assumptions; and the possible influence of different professional and employer interests. Part 3 considers the Report's possible consequences in terms of different theories of qualification change, its influence on the prospects for developing a more unified curriculum of the future along the lines suggested in previous chapters, and a possible new relationship between curriculum and qualifications that might relate to a future learning society.

Part 1 — Dearing's Main Recommendations

The report makes 198 proposals. However, its central organizing theme is undoubtedly that a more coherent national framework of qualifications is needed. The main elements that the Report suggests such a framework should include are as follows:

- three distinct pathways — academic, general vocational and work-based vocational;
- National Certificates at each level and a National Diploma at Level 3 to certificate core skills;
- four levels to provide for the equivalence of academic and vocational qualifications, including a new Entry Level;
- a new lateral AS-Level to be taken at the end of one year of study and to be equivalent to half an A-Level;
- re-designing Advanced GNVQs into six- or possibly three-unit groupings
- merging SCAA and NCVQ into a single regulatory body;
- encouraging the merger of the existing academic and vocational examining and validating bodies;
- a new National Traineeship framework, linked to Modern Apprenticeships for 16–19-year-olds on work based schemes.

In summary the Report is concerned to balance proposals for strengthening existing qualifications, especially A-Levels, with those which develop frameworks within which students can combine elements from more than one qualification. Its major continuity with the existing system is its voluntarism — it sees what students do in the 16–19 phase of their education as primarily a matter of individual choice.

Part 2 — Consolidation or Reform? Dearing's Terms of Reference

The key word in the terms of reference for the Review is consolidation. It is clear that this refers to a consolidation of the proposals of the 1991 White

Paper which established the triple-track qualification system based on A-Levels, GNVQs and NVQs. The importance of consolidation as a theme was underlined by the Secretary of State's requirement that the review should have particular regard to:

> maintain(ing) the rigour of . . . A-Levels

> build(ing) on the current development of . . . GNVQs and . . . NVQS

However, the terms of reference also required the review to have regard to:

> increasing participation and achievement and minimising wastage

and deciding whether there might be

> scope for greater coherence and breadth of study post-16 without compromising standards (and) . . . whether core skills . . . should be encouraged as part of the programme of study for more 16–19 year olds. (SCAA, 1996, p. 1)

Even within the terms of reference, therefore, the contradiction between consolidation and reform is apparent. Although explicit in the terms of reference, the origins of this contradiction are wider. Three examples will illustrate this point. One of the stated purposes of the review was to 'support the achievement of the new National Targets' (SCAA, 1996, p. 2) and one of the major new targets for 16–19 year olds is that 60 per cent of each cohort should obtain an advanced level qualification by the year 2000 (a rise of 42 per cent in five years!). This aim has to be set against the requirement in the terms of reference to strengthen A-Levels when they are still, numerically, the main Level 3 qualification for 16–19 year olds and despite the fact that they currently have a 30 per cent drop out or failure rate (Spours, 1995). The second example is the tension between the requirement that the review should look at the scope for more 'breadth' while maintaining the rigour of A-Levels which, at least since Crowther (MoE, 1959), have been associated with the study of a few subjects 'in depth'.

The third example of a contradiction between the demands of reform and consolidation is expressed in the Review's terms of reference to seek:

> scope for measures to achieve greater coherence . . . and (for) strengthening the qualifications framework further. (SCAA, 1996, p. 1)

In the Report, coherence is expressed in at least two ways. First, it is found in the strong emphasis given to a national system of qualifications at four levels. It is also reflected in the Report's support for the merged government department (the Department for Education and Employment), the proposal for merging SCAA and NCVQ, and the encouragement given to academic and vocational examining and validating body mergers. The contradiction appears when these requirements for greater coherence are set against the proposals that A-Levels and GNVQs should be more distinct as a way of maintaining the 'special' character of A-Levels and their association with students of high ability. This tension between consolidation and reform becomes even clearer when moving from the review's terms of reference to some of the Report's specific recommendations. This is a point developed later in this chapter. I first turn to the policy context in which the review was commissioned — in particular, the developments since the 1991 White Paper (ED/DfE, WO, 1991) which was the last major government pronouncement on 16–19 qualifications prior to the Dearing Report itself.

The Policy Context

The 1991 White Paper appeared at a time when a powerful movement towards a unified qualifications system was beginning to emerge. A-Levels were being broadened both in content and assessment (see Chapter 9), there were signs of convergence between the academic and the broad vocational qualifications of the time (BTEC Nationals) and the potential of modularization was being actively explored, at least on a local basis (see Chapter 6). At the same time, a series of reports had been published (e.g. Finegold et al., 1990; Royal Society, 1991) which, for the first time, argued for a unified system and the abolition or phasing out of A-Levels. With its proposals for a triple-track system of qualifications and a reduction in the permitted proportion of coursework assessment in A-Levels to 20 per cent, the White Paper can be seen as a quite explicit attempt both to put a block on these 'unifying' developments and to limit the continued expansion and diversification of A-Levels. Its proposals were designed to direct any further post-16 expansion in participation into GNVQs which had been designed to be clearly distinct from A-Levels (IoE, 1997: Spours, 1997). However, despite the restrictions on coursework assessment, A-Level pass rates continued to increase and a growing number of new applied A-Levels were introduced. The demand for modular A-Level syllabuses has continued to grow and, as the Dearing Report itself notes, some feared that modular syllabi would gradually replace the traditional linear A-Level syllabi. Furthermore, the implementation of GNVQs was turning out to be far from straightforward. They were widely criticized, not only by teachers and academics, but by the government's own Inspectorate; there is evidence that student completion rates and progression possibilities were inferior to those in the qualifications that they had been designed to replace (Spours, 1997). The decision to launch a review of 16–19 qualifications in 1995 and the emphasis on consolidation in its terms of reference can be seen, therefore, as a recognition that all had not worked out as the government had hoped in relation to the agenda mapped out by the 1991 White Paper.

The Dearing Report's Framework of Assumptions

Any report on educational policy engages in issues of public educational debate, both in what it discusses and what it does not discuss, and the Dearing Report is no exception. The most obvious examples of the former are its support for core skills in their current form, its rejection of the need to consider the redesign of GNVQs and its detailed discussion of the advantages and disadvantages of modular and linear A-Levels. The most striking example of a widely debated issue that is hardly discussed in the Report is the role of coursework assessment in A-Levels. However, there are also assumptions at a deeper level which are likely to have had a significant influence on the Report's final recommendations.

The kind of assumptions to which I am referring become explicit when the view of 16–19 education expressed in the Report is contrasted with the provision of compulsory education in other comparable European countries. The report sees 16–19 education as *pluralist* — provision will vary across the country in response to local needs; *divided* — academic and vocational programmes will remain clearly separate and are seen as appropriate for different types of student; and *voluntarist* — no common curriculum requirements are placed on all 16–19 students or on all institutions. These are not only features of educational administration; they represent values associated with diversity, with a view that students can be distinguished in terms of whether they are 'academic' or 'vocational' and with an individualist approach to freedom of choice. It is these values, though they are not explicitly referred to, that are largely endorsed by the Report and that inevitably shape its recommendations.

However, it is again useful to notice a tension between requirements of the Report to be *conservative*, in the sense of protecting these values, and, *reformist* in responding to the pressures on the system as a whole to be more flexible, efficient and attainment-oriented. This tension is exemplified in a number of ways; I will take three examples. The first concerns the Report's discussion of A-Level standards. Despite evidence to the contrary, the Report takes very seriously the view that higher A-Level pass rates could mean lower standards rather than more focused teaching and harder work by students. There are, therefore, a number of proposals for making A-Levels 'stronger' (i.e. more difficult). One consequence of this is likely to be that slower learning students will be forced towards the general vocational track. In other words, the assumption, which goes back a long way in English educational history, is that general (or academic) education is only for the elite. In a similar vein, although recognizing the lack of evidence, the Report supports the view that modular syllabuses, in that they tend to lead to higher pass rates without emphasizing the need to bring together and memorize knowledge at the end of a course, may also lead to a lowering of standards. Its recommendation that all A-Level syllabi should converge towards a part modular/part linear model can be seen as a compromise. It is an attempt to bridge the divide between the *conservative* view that traditional linear A-Levels should be retained as

a demanding test . . . which universities and employers have learnt to respect.
(SCAA, 1996)

and the *reformist* view that modular syllabuses are more efficient instruments
for promoting learning and raising attainment. The psychological assumption
underpinning traditional A-Level syllabi is that the pool of students with high
ability is limited and tests such as three-hour unseen written examinations
need to be devised to identify this 'pool'. In contrast, the modular approach
sees the same 'pool of ability' as expandable and that its size will be significantly shaped by the form of testing, the skills of the teachers and the motivation and study skills of students. It is this reformist assumption that the pool of
ability in the population is not fixed that underpins the idea of progressively
rising National Targets. The report, like government policy, cannot resolve this
contradiction. It reflects conflicting assumptions which go far beyond the issue
of modular syllabi. In South-East Asian and many other European countries
it is an issue that is largely resolved in favour of the reformist view and the
acceptance that there are powerful economic reasons against assuming that
there is some 'natural' limit to the human resources of a country.

In its discussion of the issue of breadth, the Report goes back to the
Crowther Report (MoE, 1959) and its defence of the peculiarly English view
that students learn to 'think' best by having to specialize in two or three
subjects at Advanced Level. Although the Report recognizes that this view may
no longer be appropriate nearly 40 years later, it lies at the heart of the case
for retaining A-Levels in their present form and therefore is not directly challenged. Instead, the option of a new National Diploma in addition to A-Levels
is proposed. The Diploma would offer breadth by requiring study in four
knowledge domains as well as core skills, although single subject A-Levels
would continue for those who wanted them. We have, therefore, the elements
of a Baccalaureate-type award proposed for the first time in England in an
official government report.

This section has considered how Sir Ron Dearing's recommendations
are shaped as much by his assumptions as his overt aims. He is sceptical of
the role of state imposing any curriculum requirements and prefers to leave
students free to choose their 16–19 curriculum. Similarly, he places a high
value on diversity and neglects the possibility that greater diversity can easily
become the basis for new inequalities.

Professional and Other Influences on the Dearing Report

Dearing consulted widely in preparing his Report, both among professional
groups and employers, and received written submissions from many organizations. The policies which appeared to have widespread professional support
(Leney and Spours 1996) can be divided into two kinds according to whether
or not they were included in Dearing's recommendations. There was near
unanimity on the need for a single qualifications framework, the integration of

SCAA and NCVQ and the merging of the academic and vocational examining validating bodies. There were various ways in which respondents went considerably further than Dearing. For example, there was widespread support for the unitization of assessment and the modularization of all qualifications at each level of the National Qualifications Framework to provide the opportunity for broader learning programmes and to facilitate a national system of credit accumulation and transfer as well as a flexible approach to a post-compulsory core that went beyond existing definitions of core skills.

The Review gave considerable importance to the views of employers; they are the first group whose views are referred to. Three features of their views, as summarized in the Report, are worth mentioning. First, employers' concerns tend to be general rather than specific and do not reflect deeply-held views about particular qualifications; second, they make a strong plea for simplicity and clarity as features of any new qualifications framework and third, they see improving core skills as a major priority. The most striking omission in the Report's response to employers' views is the lack of emphasis given to a broader spread of core skills, such as interpersonal skills, management of learning and problem solving in the qualification system. While the employers' views on core skills are warmly endorsed in the Report, their formal assessment is limited to what the Report refers to as the three 'key skills' of application of number, communications and use of information technology. The plea for a wider range of 'core skills' from employers appears to have come up against the requirement, expressed in the review's terms of reference, that existing qualifications should be consolidated or, in other words, not changed.

Part 3 — The Dearing Report and the Process of Qualification Change

Assessing a report such as Dearing's requires not only that it is seen as a product of its terms of reference, its assumptions and the context in which it was launched; it also needs to be seen as proposing a model of qualification change and how qualifications relate both to the curriculum and to wider social and economic changes. This section, therefore, considers three aspects of the Dearing Report, its incremental approach to qualification change, its implicit recognition of the multi-dimensional nature of systems of post-compulsory education, and the question of how both the institutional and wider social and economic contexts shape the consequences of any proposals for reforming qualifications.

Incremental Approaches

A useful distinction can be made, which I also use in analysing the reform of A-Levels in Chapter 9, between incremental approaches to change which leave the system as it is and structural approaches which are designed to change the system itself. Dearing adopted an incremental view of qualification change; it can be contrasted both with structural proposals for a unified system (Finegold et al., 1990), and other incremental approaches such as the proposals in the Joint Statement by the Association for Colleges and others (AfC et al., 1994) and the 'steps and stages' approach developed by the Learning for the Future Project (Richardson et al., 1995).

The *Learning for the Future* 'steps and stages' approach is based on the long term goal of establishing a unified system. It recognized that the process of qualification change is more complex than a once and for all shift from a divided to a unified system that was implied by earlier approaches (Finegold et al., 1990). It also took into account of proposals developed in the 1990s that could not easily be classified as either divided or unified models, but might be seen as representing a step towards a unified model. The Joint Associations Statement that

> (all) qualifications should be brought within a single framework. . . . under one popular title. (AfC et al., 1994, para. 3.2)

was an example of this kind of approach. It was permissive rather than prescriptive and envisaged that existing qualifications would continue to be used. However, there is no doubt that the proposal by the Joint Associations would, if implemented, involve incremental changes from a system of entirely separate qualifications to one in which all qualifications would gradually become part of a common framework. Dearing's proposals for a National Framework were also incremental but in a much weaker sense. He did not propose 'bringing existing qualifications within a single framework . . . under one popular title'.

We have therefore three somewhat different examples of incremental approaches to qualification reform. The proposals by the Professional Associations (AfC et al., 1994) and the *Learning for the Future (LFTF) Project's* (Richardson et al., 1995) 'steps and stages' approach might be described as progressive and evolutionary; they argued for an opening up of more flexible opportunities within the existing system. By defining a clear goal that incremental reforms should lead to a unified system in the longer term, the LFTF approach is the stronger of the two. The Dearing approach, by contrast, might be described as pragmatic and evolutionary; it had no clear vision of the future and the minor changes it proposed were largely in response to pressures on the existing system. The weakness of all such incremental approaches are that they tend to play down the real political interests which are likely to act as barriers to evolutionary change. Dearing, in particular, was so concerned with possible opposition that he offered no overall rationale for why the incremental changes that he proposed might be necessary or where they might lead.

Bearing in mind the requirement on Dearing to consolidate existing qualifications, it is difficult to see what else he could have done. What is becoming apparent, however, is that though they do not have the same prior commitments to consolidating existing qualifications, the new government in its consultation document *Qualifying for Success* (DfEE, 1997) appears to have left itself in a similar position. Incremental changes are suggested but with little vision or sense of direction about where they might lead (IoE, 1997).

The Multi-dimensionality of Qualification Systems

The idea that qualification change is a multi-dimensional process (Raffe et al., 1997) recognizes that qualification systems consist of a number of dimensions and that therefore whole system incremental change, through a series of steps and stages, is only one possibility. Qualification systems can change in some dimensions and not in others. For example, the bodies that regulate qualifications might be merged but certification could still remain divided.

It is useful to view the process of qualification change in terms of a series of inter-related dimensions. Five dimensions can initially be distinguished — government, regulation, validation and certification and assessment — which are hierarchically related to each other although each has some autonomy from the level above.[11] This perspective presents a somewhat different picture of the Dearing Report to that outlined earlier. The Dearing Report's welcome for the establishment of a single government department for education and training (the DfEE) with a single Director of Qualifications, its argument for a single regulatory agency to replace SCAA and NCVQ and its encouragement of mergers between the academic and vocational examining and validating bodies, all point to establishing the conditions for a more unified system and were all by the end of 1997, in place. This does not mean, of course that more administratively unified bodies will necessarily operate more unified validation and certification systems. On the remaining dimensions of certification and assessment, the Dearing recommendations maintain a divided system. However, as more and more students become candidates for qualifications, the economic logic is likely to be for more common systems to emerge and the benefits to schools and colleges of dealing with a single unified Examining Board are likely to accelerate other mergers. It also seems likely that in the more rationalized system that is developing it will be economic and political pressures, on the one hand, and the pressures of implementation on the other that will shape the future direction of qualification change. It is these issues that are considered in a contextual approach to which I now turn.

Contextual Approaches

Notwithstanding the fact that government-sponsored reviews invariably treat qualifications as in some way independent of their wider social context, any attempt to evaluate proposals for qualification reform cannot avoid the social and economic context in which they are embedded. Contextual approaches to qualifications have traditionally seen them as either screening devices and selection mechanisms or as part of the gradual credentializing process that has paralleled industrialization (Dore, 1976; Collins, 1984). However, though such approaches describe the social and economic role that qualifications have played and continue to play, they say very little about the possible role of qualifications in a future society when the vast majority of the population will be qualified. One way of conceptualizing this possibility is through the idea of a 'learning society'. The educational implications of the idea of a learning society are analysed in some detail in Chapter 10. It is both a socio-economic concept and an educational concept. As a socio-economic concept it is the corollary at the societal level of the idea of 'intelligent production' at the level of the firm in which the intellectual capacities of all the employees are developed as a resource for improving the quality of the firm's service or products. As an educational concept, the idea of a learning society represents a profound shift in educational priorities and a transformation of our ideas about what qualifications are for. It involves a shift in emphasis on learning in the preparatory phase, or first 20 years, of someone's life to the importance of learning throughout life and from a stress on learning in schools, colleges and universities to learning in every context where people live and work.

The idea of a learning society, therefore, has profound implications for our view of qualifications that are hardly hinted at in the Dearing Report. Instead of qualifications being primarily, as they are now, a means of selection, either for entry to further or higher education or employment, they become a means of promoting lifelong learning. One way of expressing this change would be from a focus on qualifications as *outcomes* of learning programmes to a focus on qualifying *as a continuous process*. Section 7 of Dearing's Report, which is entitled *Improving Skills for Work and Lifetime Learning*, refers to an Institute of Directors' survey which 'showed almost total support for lifelong learning' (IOD, 1991). However, nowhere in the Report is there a recognition that qualifications might need to be redesigned for this to become a reality.

Conclusions: The Dearing Review; A Step Towards a Qualification System of the Future?

This chapter has considered the Dearing Review recommendations in the light of the policy context in which it was located, its own assumptions and as a response to various pressures and interest groups. It then identified three weaknesses in its approach to qualification change — it makes proposals for incremental changes without a vision of where they might lead; it fails to recognize the interdependence of the different dimensions of qualification systems and it neglects the changing context which will shape the new roles of qualifications in the future. Each weakness can give us some guidelines for how the Dearing proposals might be built on. The chapter concludes by considering three ways of doing this.

A Stronger Framework and Vision

It was argued that Dearing's incremental approach to reform would be unlikely to be successful unless it was linked to a clearer vision of where the proposed changes could lead to. This lack of vision was expressed in the Dearing Report in its very weak concept of a National Qualification Framework which is expressed only in terms of tracks and levels. A possibility that has been suggested (IoE, 1997) is to develop the concept of an overarching certificate at 18+ as a way of pointing to features of a qualification system of the future and the steps that would be needed in getting there. This would involve more common approaches to assessment, establishing the three-unit blocks (or short courses) as the basic components of the certificate and developing the concept of core or key skills to take into account a wider range of personal and intellectual skills that all young people will need in the future.

Extending the Dimensions

It was noted that certain administrative changes, approved or recommended by Dearing are now in place — a single government Department, a single regulatory body and unitary Examining and Validating Bodies. These changes create the possibility of changes on other dimensions; for example, establishing common assessment and grading systems for academic and vocational qualifications and devising ways of bridging the division between full-time students and those on work-based training schemes. The unitary examining bodies will, in the less competitive environment that is emerging, be able to explore new kinds of relationships with schools and colleges now that they are awarding both academic and vocational certificates in the same institutions.

Redefining Qualifications for a Learning Society

By neglecting the changing context which will shape qualifications in new ways in the future, the Dearing Report's recommendations remain basically 'conservative'. It was argued that his essentially credentialist view of qualifications as primarily involved in sorting people out for jobs is increasingly out of date in a society where the priorities must be to motivate people to continue learning throughout life. If qualifications are to act as incentives for learning, then the National Framework cannot end at level 4. The four levels in Dearing's proposals have to be linked to further levels associated with higher education and to ways of encouraging people to progress both horizontally into different fields as well as vertically, as new occupational opportunities emerge. Credit transfer and credit accumulation, on the basis of unitization of the curriculum, will take on much more significance in a qualification framework oriented to lifelong learning. Current qualifications are based on the relative stability of bodies of knowledge (in the case of academic qualifications) and of occupational categories (for vocational qualifications). As relationships between bodies of knowledge (Gibbons et al., 1994) and between occupations become more fluid (Reich, 1991), the balance between individual qualifications and the overall qualifications framework will need to shift from a weak framework with strong qualifications towards a strong framework in which the individual qualifications take on the role of guidelines for learning continuity rather than as gateways to employment. Learners will increasingly rely on updating a Record of Achievement rather than trying to get new qualifications. The role of qualifications as credentials will remain and employers and universities will continue to use base line qualifications for admissions and recruitment. However qualifications also have identity-building functions; increasingly, people decide to get qualified as part of searching for who they are. However, as the qualification system becomes more fluid to reflect the greater importance of qualifying as a continuous process, the identity supporting role of individual qualifications is likely to be reduced and people will need to establish their identity in new ways, through networks and links between institutions (Beck, Giddens and Lash, 1994; Guile and Young, 1997a).

With the pace of economic change forcing more and more people to see becoming qualified as a lifelong and not a once and for all process, Dearing's view of qualifications is disappointingly static and conservative. Nevertheless, he frequently states that his report was an agenda and not a policy. What this chapter has tried to do is to show how that agenda might be broadened as we search for ways of developing qualifications to promote new types of learning. Qualifications are only the 'means', the 'ends' are the learning goals of a society and how they can be extended.

Chapter 9

Beyond A-Levels: Towards an Advanced Level Curriculum of the Future

Introduction

Chapter 1 presented a general sociological analysis of the English academic curriculum in terms of the social stratification of knowledge. However, as was pointed out in Chapter 3, this approach can over-emphasize the role of the academic curriculum in maintaining social inequalities and under emphasize the extent to which the same curriculum also provides access to the bodies of knowledge, the concepts and the intellectual skills that young people need both for further study and employment. The analysis in the early chapters of Part 2 shifted from focusing on the academic curriculum itself to the new economic context of the 1980s and 1990s when not only the academic curriculum was being questioned, but the post-compulsory system of education and training as a whole and how it was shaped by the persistence of divisions between academic and vocational qualifications. Despite this broadening of both debates and analysis, A-Levels as the paradigm example of the academic curriculum, have continued to set the terms for all discussions about the post-compulsory curriculum, both qualitatively in terms of their subject-based model of the organization of knowledge and quantitatively as the curriculum that continues to be followed by most 16–19 year olds. This chapter, therefore, focuses specifically on A-Levels, their resistance to change and possible alternatives to them.

If the definition of an advanced level curriculum is that which prepares 16–19 year olds for study at university, it is A-Levels which still dominate the advanced level curriculum in England and Wales in much the same way as the Baccalaureate does in France. Furthermore, A-Levels remain the linchpin of a system which still allows only one in three students access to any kind of advanced level curriculum; this proportion is just over half of those achieving a similar level in France. At the same time, the economy is changing and the jobs of the future will either be casual and part-time or they will require at least an advanced level qualification. When A-Levels were launched in 1951 they were obtained by only 3 in 100 of each cohort. Of the remainder, nearly all of whom left school before 18, 10–15 per cent went into office or other service jobs, another 10–15 per cent were taken on for either technician or craft apprenticeships at 16, and the remainder got unskilled jobs and left school with no qualifications at all. The peculiarities of A-Levels that make them so different from similar examinations in other countries did not matter so much in the 1950s; a relatively small proportion of each cohort was effected. The fact that A-Levels were closely linked to the selection of candidates for single subject honours degrees at university was also less of a problem, not the least because most degrees at the time were in single subjects. Furthermore, although many of those who began A-Levels failed or dropped out, they could still use their O-Levels to get office jobs or become nurses or teachers.

In considering the contemporary impact of A-Levels, we are no longer discussing the education of one in four or five in each cohort, but the seven out of ten who stay on in full-time education after 16. All their futures are determined by A-Levels in one way or another. Participation falls steadily among those staying on post-16, and includes some of those on A-Level courses; nearly 30 per cent of those who start A-Level courses end up with no additional qualification at the age of 18 (Spours, 1995). However, unlike in the 1950s, there are far fewer office jobs and no nursing or teacher training for those without A-Levels and, of course, far fewer apprenticeships. Among those who achieve good grades A-Levels produce narrow specialists who often have to make arbitrary choices between subjects, many of which they want to continue. Others try for a balanced curriculum but end up with bizarre collections of subjects like Spanish, Economics and Biology. Lower achieving students at 16+ either take A-Levels and risk failure at 18 or have to opt for GNVQs which are as narrow as A-Levels in their way. In contrast, therefore, to the debates about A-Levels in the 1970s and 1980s, the issue is no longer just the future of A-Levels; the issue is the future of 16–19 education as a whole, shaped powerfully by what happens to A-Levels.

It is not only the economy which has changed since A-Levels were launched in 1951 nor just the level of participation in full time post-16 education. The political context is also different. May 1997 saw the first Labour Government elected for almost 20 years. Instead of a government wedded to unchanged A-Levels as the Gold Standard, there was at least some recognition in the new government's consultation paper *Qualifying for Success* (DfEE, 1997), that A-Levels need to be reformed. However, as is made clear in the Institute of Education's response to *Qualifying for Success* (IoE, 1997), the government is far from clear about what it means by reform. In this new context of possible reform but much caution and uncertainty, the traditional criticisms of A-Levels as elitist and too narrow are no longer adequate. A deeper analysis leading to a clearer idea of a new advanced level curriculum is needed. This means beginning by understanding the different functions that are fulfilled by A-Levels and how they are part of a complex system in which schools, colleges, universities and exam boards are locked together.

The Dearing Report (see Chapter 8) argued that A-Levels have reached the limits of the proportion of the cohort which can benefit by them. If this refers to A-Levels *in their present form*, most people would agree. In fact, it is doubtful whether many of those currently achieving only one or two A-Levels benefit much from them. The Dearing report goes on to argue that those who fail or do poorly at A-Levels would be better off on a vocational course. However, this assumes that all slower learning students want to do a vocational course rather than continue with a programme of general education. Limiting student options to A-Levels or a vocational course is only necessary if it is A-Levels that define general education after 16. This chapter will argue that A-Levels are no longer an adequate form of general education if it is to be available to the majority of the young people who stay on in full-time education after 16. It will argue for a new kind of advanced level curriculum and a strategy for achieving it. In doing so it will draw on the concept of *connective specialization* introduced in previous chapters. First, however, we need to be clear exactly about what is meant by the present A-Level curriculum that needs reform, the functions it serves and why it remains so resistant to change.

What Is the A-Level Curriculum and What Purposes Does It Serve?

A-Levels are subject examinations and the Examining Boards examine subjects, not the curriculum. For the Examining Boards there is no such thing as the A-Level curriculum. The term 'A-Level curriculum' refers to the programmes of study that a school or college can offer and a student can choose, based on A-Level subject examinations. The A-Level Curriculum is the responsibility of individual schools and colleges and for each school and college it is different. Despite all the government interventions of the last decade, this situation has not changed. With the removal of most of the powers of local education authorities, individual schools and colleges have a greater responsibility for the 16–19 curriculum than ever before. Schools and colleges have in the past welcomed this autonomy (with the proviso that they see that much of the power to define the advanced level curriculum is in the hands of university admissions tutors). However, with the possible range of 'choices' increasing, schools are beginning to say that they have too many choices and not enough information to assess their implications or a clear enough sense of how the government sees the post-compulsory curriculum developing in the future (Spours and Young, 1996).

The autonomy of schools and colleges in deciding their post-16 curriculum also masks an inequality that has become more marked in the last decade. Although the A-Level grades that students get are treated as the same, regardless of where they have studied, this is far from true for the A-Level curriculum they are offered. HMC Public Schools can offer a vastly superior A-Level curriculum to that offered at any state school or college and it is little wonder that they have so much better results; 80 per cent now get 3 A-Levels (Walden, 1996).

One way of understanding what might be meant by the A-Level curriculum in England and Wales is to contrast it with the similar curriculum offered to 16–19 year olds in other European countries. The characteristics of the two curricula are contrasted in the table below:

The A-Level curriculum in England and Wales	A typical Advanced level curriculum in other European countries
1 (2–4) subjects studied	5/6 + subjects studied
2 Elective, free choice of subjects by students	Student choice constrained by a required core of studies
3 No overall curriculum criteria	Overall criteria define what all candidates should study
4 End of course externally set and marked examinations	Some have no written exams, some use teacher assessment only
5 No relationships between subjects	Some have theory of knowledge course to encourage students to link the different subjects they are studying
6 Individual schools/colleges are responsible for the A-Level curriculum	National requirements define the curriculum for *all* schools and colleges
7 No student has a right to university entry based on passing A-Levels at a particular grade; admission is dependent on individual university selection criteria	Students have a legal right to enter university if national examinations are passed
8 Reliability of results is dependent on the independence of the exam boards and their procedures	Reliability is dependent on state exams or public trust in teachers (Sweden and Germany)
9 Examining is carried out by teachers who teach A-Levels supervised by the Boards and co-ordinated by university teachers	Examining sometimes undertaken by the teachers themselves
10 Linear and modular syllabi	Most syllabi are not modular

NB. These criteria are typical; they do not describe all A-Level examinations or all Advanced level Examinations in other European Countries.

With small variations, A-Levels have, throughout their 46 year history, continued relatively unchanged as the basis of a highly selective and narrow advanced level curriculum. Four interlinked features of social organization of the A-Level system have had a particular role in making them so resistant to change. These are (i) the absence of a national body with overall responsibility for the 16–19 curriculum; (ii) the autonomy of the schools and colleges over what they offer; (iii) the 'free choice' that students have in deciding which subjects to study; and (iv) the freedom of universities to devise their own selection criteria. Even a government committed to changing this system would find it difficult to know where to begin. Another feature of the A-Level system that makes it resistant to change is the interlocking system linking the Examination Boards, university lecturers who usually chair the subject Boards and the teachers who carry out the marking. It is this system which underpins the public confidence in A-Levels and which makes them so resistant to change. Furthermore, it is a system which A-Level teachers know and is, at least for them, relatively predictable. Any change, however educationally sound, is likely to be seen as threatening both by university admissions tutors who are under pressure to recruit the 'best students' and by teachers who are under pressure to increase the numbers of their students getting high grades. It is interesting to note that while the English system maximizes the autonomy of the schools (and university admissions tutors), it places much less trust in individual teachers than other countries. It is almost as if there is a fear that if the mass of teachers in England and Wales were given more responsibility over examining (as is the case in Sweden and Germany), they would forget their professionalism and over-grade their own students, thus lowering standards.

Having briefly identified the main features of the A-Level curriculum, I now want to turn to its wider functions; I will draw on the distinction introduced in Chapter 3 between its ideological and educational functions. Much past and current debate has focused on the political and ideological functions of A-Levels; for example, they have been criticized as being elitist and giving unfair advantages to Public School pupils. It is, of course, true that A-Levels are elitist; but, as the main basis on which students are selected for university, any advanced level curriculum is bound to be elitist to some extent. The key questions are; how elitist are A-Levels, and what functions other than selection, should an advanced level curriculum have? Whereas fewer students passed the Baccalaureate in France than A-Levels until the 1980s, by the end of the decade, twice as many students were achieving one of the new three track French Baccalaureates as achieve 2 or more A-Levels (Watson, 1991). In other words, by remaining so exclusive and as a consequence devaluing other qualifications, A-Levels are part of the reason why levels of post-16 attainment in England are so low. The powerful selective role of A-Levels limits the extent to which they can provide general education to a wide section of each cohort.

However, an advanced level curriculum does not only have a selective role as a gateway to the universities; it also has an educational role. If the educational role of A-Levels is forgotten, not only does this deny the real learning that A-Level students achieve but the only options for the critic who sees them as too elitist is either to argue that they must be abolished or to propose that more students are allowed to pass them. Inevitably, this leads to the charge of lowering standards.

The educational role of A-Levels, as any form of advanced level curriculum, is to provide a way of giving students access to specialized knowledge and the concepts and skills that go with it. However, as can be seen from the table contrasting A-Levels and similar qualifications found in other European countries, they represent very different views of specialist knowledge. The typical European equivalent to A-Levels sets out to offer students a broad based education in the main fields of knowledge, while at the same time allowing them some opportunity to specialize. In the A-Level curriculum there is no attempt to provide a broad-based education; the curriculum consists of a small group of subjects only. Within limits determined by what a student hopes to do on leaving school, the A-Level curriculum does not prescribe which subjects he/she chooses. The A-Level curriculum is not designed to develop any particular capacities; the assumption is that any subject sanctioned by the universities must be a good 'training for the mind'. However, because the educational and ideological roles of A-Levels have been conflated by both supporters and opponents, there has been no research into what kind of 'mind training' is achieved by studying A-Levels or into the different ways in which breadth and specialization might be linked that could enhance and not lower standards. The result is that debates about A-Levels have been limited to critiques of their narrow and elitist character and a general endorsement that they should be broader on the one hand, and the argument that they represent the old standard on the other.

During the long period since 1979 in which the 'Gold Standard' view of A-Levels became part of government policy, this lack of knowledge of the different ways in which A-Levels might be broadened has been of little practical concern; alternatives to A-Levels have not been a political option. As pointed out earlier, there is now a government with at least some commitment to the reform of A-Levels but with no clear idea of what to put in their place. The situation has two possible dangers. One is that any new proposals become the victim of a media 'campaign in defence of A-Levels'. The second is that a set of ill thought out proposals are introduced that please no one and get bogged down in technical details as did the Schools Council proposals in the 1960s and 1970s.

The key reform issues will undoubtedly centre around questions of curriculum breadth and depth or degree of specialization. The first task is therefore to develop alternative models as to how breadth and specialization might be linked as a basis for reform. This was something that the previous attempts to reform A-Levels in the 1960s and 1970s singularly failed to do. They took for granted that anything less specialized than A-Levels was an improvement, without asking why or what might be involved. There are, however, valuable lessons to be learned from these earlier attempts at reform. The next section, following a brief history of previous reform attempts, suggests what they might be.

Lessons from Past Attempts to Reform A-Levels

In considering the history of A-Level reform, I want to begin by making two sets of distinctions. The first is concerned with the dynamics of change and is between *incremental* changes to individual A-Levels and *structural* changes to the A-Level system. Examples of incremental changes are (i) changes in the content of subject syllabi; (ii) the introduction of new subjects; and (iii) new forms of assessment and changes from linear to modular syllabi. Each of these types of incremental change was introduced, at least initially, with little or no political or professional opposition. Structural changes are those that involve the relations between subjects, the size of subjects relative to a student's whole curriculum and changes which appear to shift the balance between what are seen as standard and non-standard approaches to A-Level syllabi and assessment. For A-Levels, the standard syllabus has been linear as opposed to modular in content, it has been associated with the subjects of the traditional Grammar and Public School Sixth Forms and its assessment has been based on an end of course externally marked examination.

Incremental and structural changes are not entirely independent of each other. A good example of the link between them was the development in the early 1980s of modular syllabi and assessment schemes with over 50 per cent coursework assessed by teachers. Initially, these changes were hardly noticed. However, the political opposition to teacher assessed A-Levels became more explicit in the late 1980s and early 1990s and, at the same time, the proportion of modular syllabi with significant amounts of teacher assessment continued to grow. In the new political context of the late 1980s, these syllabi were perceived as a threat to the A-Level *system* and modular syllabi began to be withdrawn. It seems likely that incremental changes are absorbed into the A-Level system so long as they are not seen as affecting its key selective function.

The second set of distinctions involves periodizing past attempts at A-Level reform as a way of linking the fate of different types of reform to the changing political context. Three periods of attempted reform of A-Levels can be distinguished and are discussed in more detail in the next section. The first, between 1951–1979, was a period of expansion of A-Level entries and a long drawn out series of unsuccessful attempts by the Schools Council to reform them. During this period, the debates were largely restricted to the professional education community. The next period (1979–1991) was one of continued expansion of A-Levels and many incremental changes. Only towards the end of the period did the future of the A-Level system become a political issue, partly through opposition by the Right to the incremental changes and partly because the Left began to articulate the possibility of transforming A-Levels into a unified curriculum (Finegold et al., 1990). The final period (1991–1997) began with the 1991 White Paper, includes the Dearing Review (SCAA, 1996) and the new government's consultation paper *Qualifying for Success* (DfEE, 1997). It has been a period when both professional and political conflicts over A-Levels have been more overt, and when the debate about A-Levels has become part of the wider debate about the future of 16–19 education as a whole.

Phase 1 — A-Level Reform 1951–1979 — Proposals but no Reform

The first chance to evaluate A-Levels came in 1959 with the Crowther Report on the Education of 15–18 year olds (MoE, 1959). However, the opportunity was missed; the view of the Crowther Committee was that 'able pupils were subject minded' and that therefore A-Levels were the ideal curriculum for the majority of those 16–19 year olds who stayed on in school. Having accepted that A-Levels did not need to be changed, all Crowther could do was to hope that schools would not allow A-Level teaching to take over the whole Sixth Form curriculum. He recommended that they should not encroach on more than two-thirds of a student's timetable, though he made no suggestions as to how such a limit might be achieved.

Mathieson (1992) traces the sequence of unsuccessful attempts to tackle the question of over-specialization in A-Levels that followed Crowther. The issue was first taken up by the Schools Council in 1966 with a plan to introduce 'major' and 'minor' subjects. Both schools and universities rejected the proposal, doubting that minor subjects would be taken seriously. In the late 1960s, as mentioned in Chapter 1, the Dainton Report on the shortage of scientists (DES, 1968) recommended that broadening the Sixth Form curriculum was the best way to increase the number of students studying science post-16; little notice was taken of it. The Schools Council tried again in 1973 with N (Normal) and F (Further) levels, both to be studied over two years. Reactions were again negative from both teacher associations and universities. They argued that if lower achievers were able to cope with N levels, they would inevitably be devalued as a mechanism for broadening the curriculum of high achievers. In 1979, the new Conservative government announced that A-Levels 'were here to stay', with hardly a murmur of dissent.

There are two lessons from this period. The first is that schools and universities are much more tightly bound to the A-Level system than has often been recognized. The second is that unless it can be shown that breadth enhances specialist study, it will always be seen as being at the price of depth and therefore associated with lower standards.

Phase 2 — Incremental Changes within a Tracked System 1979–1991

The 1980s saw substantial increases in the numbers taking A-Levels and the diversification of the range of subjects offered. Four types of incremental change can be identified, the introduction of new subjects, the idea of half subjects (the AS examinations), modular syllabi and the extension of coursework assessment and core skills. These will now be discussed briefly.

New Subjects

Proposals for changing subject syllabi or introducing new A-Level subjects represent the least radical form of change to A-Levels and leave the A-Level system unchanged. It is not surprising that in the 1980s, when there was TVEI funding to support innovations in the 14+ curriculum, that many new A-Level syllabuses were introduced. Considerable attention was initially given to General Studies as a way of broadening the A-Level curriculum (Smithers and Robinson, 1993). However, although candidate numbers expanded fast, most universities would not accept General Studies A-Level for admissions purposes.

The diversification of A-Level subjects in the 1960s and 1970s took place largely in the social sciences (e.g. economics, business studies, sociology and psychology). However, in the 1980s, under the influence of TVEI, more applied post-16 courses were developed for which there was no accreditation. A-Levels in subjects such as Leisure Studies, Photography and Accounting were introduced in response to this demand. There appear to have been few content criteria for new subjects, provided they complied with the agreed criteria on syllabus design and assessment, although, as with General Studies, this did not mean that the new subjects were necessarily accepted by all universities.

New Half Subjects

Unlike the introduction of new subjects, which arose from a demand from schools and colleges, the introduction of the AS examinations in 1987 was initiated by the government, which hoped it would satisfy the demands for additional breadth and flexibility. However, in a voluntarist system in which students are free to choose what subjects to take, any innovation depends for its success on more than government approval. It depends on the choices and decisions not only of students but of teachers and HE admission tutors. The take up of AS examinations was poor; it never reached above 7 per cent of all A-Level entries. University admission tutors preferred A-Levels and students saw A/AS combinations as more demanding than 3 A-Levels.

The fate of AS examinations is a good example of both the limitations of an incremental change that leaves the system untouched and of how an incremental change can, at least potentially, have structural implications for the A-Level system as a whole. As long as AS examinations remained additional to the A-Level curriculum and taken up by a few students, few were interested in them. As soon as there was a suggestion that the smaller AS exams could replace A-Levels as the main academic qualifications and provide a way of making the system broader and more flexible, there was opposition. In 1991, a Schools Examinations and Assessment Council Committee came up with a proposal to reverse the relationships between AS and A-Levels; they suggested that a student might take five or six AS exams in their first year and continue with two or three of the subjects as A-Levels in the second year. This was perceived by HMC as a way of undermining the A-Level system (Mathieson, 1992); they were influential enough for the proposal to be immediately rejected as a kind of backdoor approach to abolishing A-Levels.

Modular Syllabi and Course Work Assessment

These two changes are taken together, despite the fact that not all course work based assessment schemes were modular. However, both represented efforts on the part of teachers to make A-Levels more relevant and accessible to the wider range of students who were now staying on in school Sixth Forms and colleges.

Three hour written examinations at the end of a course have been one of the defining features of A-Levels since they were launched; it linked them closely to the typical final examination of the single subject honours degree. However, in the 1980s, A-Level syllabuses began to include a proportion of teacher-assessed coursework; the amount varied from 25–100 per cent. It was not, however, until the beginning of the 1990s that these changes in assessment as well as in syllabus design were challenged. In the new and more ideological political climate, criticism of modular courses and teacher-based assessment became part of the government's attack on teachers and what they saw as falling standards. There was no actual evidence that modular syllabuses or course assessment led to lower standards. However it was a time when pass rates in A-Levels (and the number achieving higher grades) were rising steadily. Some members of the right wing think tanks (e.g. Pilkington, 1991) were unwilling to believe that more than a very small number of students could possibly pass an A-Level, let alone achieve high grades and that if they did, it must have been because the assessment system had made it easier for students to get high grades or that the new A-Level subjects were easier than the old. From then on, course work assessment and modularity became political issues, not just technical issues for professional debate among experts.

Core Skills

Core Skills that were not subject-specific were proposed in 1990 as a way of broadening A-Levels and even of unifying academic and vocational qualifications. However, the first attempt to bring core skills into the A-Level curriculum was terminated almost immediately with a change of Secretary of State (Mathieson, 1992). There were clearly technical difficulties that were due partly to confusion about what was meant by core skills and partly to uncertainties as to whether a common system of assessment could be devised for all A-Level subjects. However, over-riding the technical issues was the question of ideology. It was difficult to combine the idea of A-Levels as the Gold Standard with the view, strongly supported by the CBI (1993) that even those with A-Levels could lack core skills. In retrospect, the core skills initiative is best seen as another attempt to make A-Levels more 'relevant' without changing them. Inevitably it was the A-Level system and its selective function which won.

The Higginson Committee's Proposals

The Higginson Report (DES, 1988) stands apart from the other developments during this period in proposing a structural change to the A-Level system. The Committee endorsed the arguments for broadening A-Levels and proposed a five subject examination of 'leaner' A-Levels with smaller syllabi. Despite the radical character of their proposals, they were still a compromise with the A-Level tradition. A five-subject grouped qualification was clearly a break from the 'elective' curriculum represented by A-Levels. However, in keeping with the A-Level tradition, the Committee refused to prescribe which subjects a candidate should take, leaving it to schools and colleges to help students to choose. In another way, also, the Report represented continuity with the past; it assumed a broader curriculum was a good thing and that it involved doing more subjects. The Report did not consider different forms of breadth or how breadth might enhance or subtract from a student's specialist studies. However, the professional climate of opinion towards A-Levels had changed since the 1970s and there was virtually unanimous support for the Higginson proposals. The fact that they were summarily rejected by the government means that we cannot tell whether this support would have been maintained if the proposals had actually been implemented.

This section has reviewed the main examples of incremental A-Level reform in the period 1979–1991. Three conclusions can be drawn. First, content criteria for new A-Level subjects have been flexible; it is the A-Level system that has been so resistant to change. Second, incremental changes, some hardly noticed when they were introduced, built up pressures which were perceived as challenges to the A-Level system itself. The third conclusion from this period is the extent to which, in contrast to the 1970s and early 1980s, A-Level debates from the end of the 1980s became polarized and politicized. This had the effect of minimizing the professional and technical debates and masking differences within the educational community.

Phase 3 (1991–1997) — A-Level Reform within a Framework Approach

The period between 1991 and the publication of the new Labour government's consultation document *Qualifying for Success* in late 1997 (DfEE, 1997) began with the Conservative government's 1991 White Paper which formalized the triple track qualification system of academic, general vocational and work based qualifications. Most of the developments during this period were attempts to establish some kind of *framework* to include all qualifications and thus mitigate the divisiveness of the three-track system without changing the qualifications themselves. Two proposals for Diploma frameworks to include A-Levels were initiated by the Conservative government but were quickly dropped. Other proposals were the Further Education Unit's Credit Framework Initiative (FEU, 1992), the Joint Statement (AfC et al., 1994), the CBI proposals for an over-arching Diploma (1993) and the Dearing Review proposals discussed in the next section.

Dearing's Strategy for A-Levels

The Dearing Report endorsed the familiar features of A-Levels considered ear-lier in this chapter — the collections of insulated subjects, the emphasis on terminal examinations to underline 'rigour' and the preference for linear rather than modular syllabuses. His approach to the reform of A-Levels involved making them more distinctive and establishing an Advanced Diploma frame-work, for those students who wanted a broader curriculum, which would at the same time leave A-Levels unchanged.

The Report asserted that there are 'difficult', 'average' and 'easier' A-Level subjects. It then considered the implications of making 'easier' subjects more 'difficult' and how this would be likely to lead either to fewer candidates or more failures. The Report proposed that students likely to fail A-Level should be guided to follow the GNVQ or the Modern Apprenticeship route — where they would stand a better chance of achieving an equivalent level qualifica-tion. Unable to consider any structural reform of A-Levels, the Report was trapped in the familiar and characteristically English assumption that slower learning students are better suited to vocational courses.

Dearing's second approach to strengthening A-Levels was to consider the overlap of subjects between A-Levels and GNVQs. His argument was that, from the point of view of students making choices and employers assessing the worth of qualifications, there is much to gain by making A-Levels and GNVQs more distinct. Dearing linked the distinctiveness of A-Levels to subject content. He recommended that Examination Boards should reconsider the appropriate type of qualification for subjects such as science, which for him should be an A-Level not a GNVQ, and those like media studies and photo-graphy, which for him are applied and so should be GNVQs and not A-Levels. If taken literally, his proposal would rule out most of the 12 per cent of current entries for 'applied' A-Levels.

Dearing's second strategy was concerned with broadening A-Levels. However, he did so not by asking how A-Levels could be broadened but how A-Level students might broaden their curriculum on the basis of existing A-Levels. His proposals had two parts — a reformulated one year AS (effect-ively a Part 1 of an A-Level) and a four-domain Advanced Diploma. To obtain the Advanced Diploma a candidate would have to take an A-Level in two of the four domains, an AS in the other two and be assessed in core skills. The Diploma would not replace A-Levels; it would, like the AS examinations, be in addition to them. Dearing's proposals leave it up to schools and colleges to decide whether or not to offer the Diploma.

There was a pragmatic advantage in Dearing's proposals for an Advanced Diploma in contrast to earlier attempts like Higginson's 'five lean A-Levels'. He used existing A-Levels for the Diploma but left them unchanged. However, A-Levels were not designed to be part of a broader-based overarching qualification; they are too rigid and inflexible. The four domain proposal based on A-Levels and AS exams appeared impractical for schools and colleges to implement. It seems likely that, if it was implemented on a voluntary basis, it would at best be offered by a few innovative schools and colleges with high A-Level success rates. Such evidence as there is suggests that although schools liked the idea of the Advanced Diploma, they would need a cast iron guarantee from the universities that it would be accepted in preference to three A-Levels. The key issue for university admission tutors is also likely to be whether the Diploma is voluntary; if it is, they will still prefer to select on the basis of good A-Level grades in degree related subjects, regardless of whether a candidate has the Diploma.

Regardless of its possible future, Dearing's Advanced Diploma raised a number of important new issues about advanced level qualifications. First, it does attempt to link breadth to *high* achievement. Second, it is the first official attempt to offer a content-based definition of breadth. Third, it raises the issue, although not explicitly, that a broader qualification than A-Levels will inevitably mean more teaching time and more study time on the part of students. However, if the Diploma is introduced on a voluntary basis, the message to the schools and colleges about valuing breadth is unlikely to be strong enough to balance the risks and the problem of finding the additional resources that would be needed to offer it. Furthermore, it does not take into account the interlocking system that binds schools and colleges, universities and Examination Boards to existing A-Levels, as reliable selectors (for the universities) and as reliable gateways to university (for the schools and colleges).

Qualifying for Success

The 1997 Labour government took over many of the Dearing proposals in launching its Consultation Paper *Qualifying for Success* (DfEE, 1997), although, by the time this was published in Autumn 1997, the Dearing proposals for an AS examination in key skills and for making the vocational and academic tracks more distinctive had been dropped. In relation to A-Levels *Qualifying for Success* remained firmly within Dearing's framework approach, although it showed greater openness on important issues such as the role of coursework assessment, modular syllabuses and grade alignment between A-Levels and vocational qualifications. It presented tentative proposals for an overarching certificate within which A-Levels might be broadened but remained very cautious about phasing them out, even in the longer term. It recognized that such a certificate would need to be 'more than a record of achievement' and that some clear rules of combination would be needed for its components.

However, in the short term, it appeared wedded to retaining A-Levels in their existing form.

Frameworks and the Reform A-Levels: Some Lessons

Both the Dearing proposals for an Advanced Diploma and the *Qualifying for Success* idea of an overarching certificate are examples of a weak framework approach to overarching a strongly track-based system of qualifications (Spours and Young, 1996; IoE, 1997). In both cases existing A-Levels are likely to retain a dominant role in the system as a whole. The crucial barrier to a substantial numbers of students taking the new overarching qualification is that it is likely to be voluntary and up to students and institutions as to whether it is offered or taken up.

Both the Dearing and *Qualifying for Success* proposals for broadening A-Levels highlight the weakness of a framework approach which is voluntary and does not modularize all qualifications and develop common approaches to assessment. They lack both a long term vision of an advanced level curriculum of the future or a 'steps and stages' strategy for getting there.

Conceptualizing an Advanced Level Curriculum for the Future

The previous sections have reviewed track-based and framework-based approaches to A-Level reform. They have also shown how incremental changes are resisted if they are perceived as challenging the A-Level system and how proposals for frameworks have been, at best, ways of collecting A-Levels together and, at worst, ways of avoiding reforming them. To develop a rationale for an advanced level curriculum for the future, it is necessary to go back to first principles and consider what the purposes of advanced level curriculum for the next century might be.

Three such purposes can be suggested, drawing on the analysis in the earlier chapters. First, an Advanced Level Curriculum of the Future must be a way of developing the knowledge and skills that young people are going to need in the next century — in other words, its educational role must be emphasized. This means it will need to include a core programme for all students that relates to the skills and knowledge they will need to become successful citizens, workers and parents. Second, it must enable students to develop specialist areas of knowledge and interest and provide ways of linking a student's specialist studies to the aims of the curriculum as a whole. Third, in realizing these aims, a new advanced level curriculum will need to build on the strengths of existing A-Levels. I referred to the educational role of A-Levels in enabling students to gain access to bodies of specialized knowledge and to the concepts which go with them. Depending on the subjects they choose, A-Level students learn to solve complex and abstract problems in mathematics and the sciences or to process large amounts of text in clear prose in the humanities and social sciences. However, there is a price to pay with existing 'A-Levels through the ideological role that they have. They are socially and intellectually selective and the concepts of learning and knowledge that they give priority to are oriented to the past — what is already known and how knowledge has been produced in the past, rather than to the future — what needs to be known and how knowledge might be produced in the future.

The table below contrasts the socially and intellectually exclusive features of the A-Level curriculum with the socially accessible and intellectually inclusive features of a possible advanced level curriculum of the future.

The A-Level curriculum	An Advanced Level Curriculum of the Future
Socially selective	*Socially accessible*
Linear syllabi	Modular syllabi
Terminal assessment	Continuous assessment
Intellectually exclusive	*Intellectually inclusive*
Academic (knowledge for own sake)	Broadly instrumental (knowledge for specific purposes *as well as* for its own sake)
Purposes implicit (subjects taken as given)	Purposes explicit (and debated) (subjects would be interrogated from the point of view of the learner's short and long term purposes and the goals of a future society)
Prioritizes the reproduction of given knowledge	Emphasizes production of new knowledge as well as reproduction of existing knowledge
Disciplinary concept of knowledge	Interdisciplinary and disciplinary concepts of knowledge
Emphasizes the separateness of subjects	Emphasizes the interdependence of subjects

The two lists in the table represent curriculum models only. They indicate the kind of changes in principle that might be involved in moving from A-Levels to an Advanced Curriculum of the Future. They are not either/or models; any advanced level curriculum will retain some of the selective features of existing A-Levels. Shifts from linear to modular syllabuses and from terminal to continuous assessment that are discussed in Chapter 6 are crucial to an advanced level curriculum becoming more socially accessible than A-Levels. In the final part of this chapter, however, I want to concentrate on the shift from the intellectual exclusiveness of A-Levels to the inclusiveness that would need to be a feature of an advanced level curriculum of the future.

A-Levels represent a highly insulated form of subject specialization which directs learners attention entirely to individual subjects, treated separately. However, as was mentioned in Chapters 5 and 6, new knowledge is more and more being produced at the interface of subjects and disciplines, not only in subjects in isolation from each other (Gibbons et al., 1994). It follows that the A-Level curriculum, which allows students to collect any group of subjects together with only personal preference as a rationale for why one subject is chosen rather than another, is no longer an adequate preparation for working life nor for the new kinds of interdisciplinary degrees being offered at universities. What is needed is an advanced level curriculum that treats the relations between the subjects as being as important as the subject contents themselves. In Chapters 5 and 6, I referred to the principles of such a curriculum as involving *connective specialization*. A curriculum based on connective specialization reverses the relation between subjects and the curriculum as a whole that characterizes the A-Level curriculum. Instead of the subjects, as ends in themselves, defining the purposes of a student's learning programme, as in the A-Level curriculum, curriculum purposes would define the role of subjects. Subjects thus become tools for learning (Holt, 1979). An advanced level curriculum of the future would need to balance specialist studies, both subject-based and applied, with core studies common to all students. Core studies would help lead students from their particular interests and specialization to the wider concerns of becoming a citizen in a future society that would be expressed in the curriculum as a whole.

The basic elements of such an advanced level curriculum would therefore be (a) a set of general and specialist curriculum purposes and outcomes; and (b) two kinds of specialist tools for learning — subjects, disciplines and domains as ways of accessing various kinds of specialist knowledge, and connective skills and knowledge to enable students to make links between subjects, to develop ways of moving from one subject to another and to relate their subject knowledge to practical problems and issues. One attempt to show how a curriculum might be constructed on the basis of the principle of connective specialization is discussed elsewhere (Young and Spours, 1995). It proposes a core/specialization framework as a basis for deciding the balance between the time given to specialist studies and to those core studies which would be common to all students and for subject specialists to define the role of their subjects. The fundamental difference between A-Levels and an Advanced Level Curriculum of the Future would be expressed in the criteria for relating core studies (breadth) and specialist studies (depth) and in the role of subjects. Up until now, broadening the A-Level curriculum has always been seen as involving less study in depth and therefore loss of 'rigour'; furthermore, depth has always been associated with the study of individual subjects. An Advanced Level Curriculum of the Future would go beyond both these assumptions. It would assume that rigour could be expressed in the relationships between subjects and how they may or may not inform solutions to practical problems, as well as in the subjects themselves and that specialist studies can be enhanced by broadening or contextualizing studies.

Conclusions

In this discussion of alternatives to A-Levels, I have stressed the importance of two distinctions; that between their ideological and educational roles and that between two types of specialization — insular and connective. The first distinction reminds us that any reform must involve building on the educational role of existing A-Levels rather than thinking that it is necessary to abolish them — and that, even if the political ideology of A-Levels as the 'Gold Standard' is no longer so dominant, changes from A-Levels to an Advanced Level Curriculum of the Future will not be easy. Professional and parental interests in preserving A-Levels will undoubtedly become more visible, as they were in the 1970s if reform seems likely to be a reality. The second distinction that I have made is between insular and connective specialization as curriculum principles. Connective specialization refers to the way specialist forms of organized knowledge such as subjects need to embody the goals of the whole advanced level curriculum and identify ways of relating to each other. I suggested that it could be the organizing principle for an Advanced Level Curriculum of the Future, and that it does not mean less specialized advanced level programmes but programmes based on a different concept of specialization that is more in tune with the kind of learning demands of the twenty-first century.

A-Level reforms failed in the 1960s and the 1970s because those involved did not have a clear idea of what alternatives to A-Levels might be possible. Reforms have failed since 1979 because successive governments have had both political and ideological interests in preserving A-Levels. Since May 1997, the priorities of a new government are to broaden and enhance rather than merely preserve A-Levels. This provides a new context for a debate about A-Levels and how they might be transformed into an Advanced Level Curriculum of the Future. It is a debate which will need to involve subject specialists, curriculum researchers, university teachers and employers — it has hardly yet begun.

Section 3

Knowledge, Learning and Curriculum in a Learning Society

Chapter 10

Post-compulsory Education in a Learning Society

Post-compulsory Education in England and Wales: A Dual Crisis

In all countries in Western Europe, post-compulsory education is either, as in England and Wales, in crisis or, as in the Nordic countries and Germany, the subject of increasing questioning and critique. This sense of crisis is manifest in a variety of attempts that can be found in almost all countries to introduce greater flexibility within the curriculum and increase the opportunities for students to make choices and bridge the traditional divisions between academic and vocational learning. The pressure for change, while expressed in educational terms, is not primarily educational in origin. It is a consequence of two developments in the global economy and, more specifically, a consequence of the manufacturing and trading success of the new Asian economies[12]. The first is the disappearance of a youth labour market and the consequent increases in the numbers of full-time students in post-compulsory education. The second is the continuing failure of European countries to return to the conditions of full employment of 25 years ago, even when, on conventional indicators, it is claimed that the economic recession is over. Despite the availability of labour as a result of persistent high unemployment and, at least in the UK, the introduction of legislation that restricts the role of trades unions, European production has been slow to compete in terms of the labour costs of mass production with the new Asian economies or even, more recently, with the USA. On the other hand, it has not been able to draw on the familial collectivism and 'firm loyalty' associated with the advanced Asian economies of South Korea and Japan which many see as the reason for their success in high value added markets, such as consumer electronics. Western European cultures, and especially the Anglo-Saxon variant found in the UK, are traditionally associated with individualism and independence, rewards for creativity, a capacity for innovation and a respect for self criticism and debate. However, these capacities have tended to remain part of a relatively insulated middle class culture and not part of mainstream production and services, at least in any systematic way. Making connections between the creativity and innovation associated with European science, humanities and arts and the systematic thinking and practice needed to convert ideas into products and services poses a considerable cultural, intellectual and educational challenge. The challenge is nowhere felt more strongly than in the post-compulsory sector of education with its distinctive features of learner choice and specialization and as the sector with closest links to the labour market. With its traditional links to training and apprenticeships, it is not surprising that post-compulsory education has been seen as providing solutions to problems that are at least in part labour market and production problems.

Post-compulsory education in the UK, however (and for the rest of this paper the UK will refer to England and Wales, as Scotland has more in common with continental Europe), also suffers from a crisis of its own history. The UK faces the economic and cultural challenges shared by all European countries to which I have referred. However, it also inherits a weak system of compulsory education (Green and Steadman, 1993) and low levels of participation and attainment (except among private schools) in a post-compulsory sector with an over-specialized and sharply divided curriculum and fragmented provision for vocational education that carries little credibility (Richardson et al., 1995). Three kinds of reform strategy emerged in the last decade which claimed to tackle these weaknesses; one was part of the educational policies of the 1987–1992 Conservative government and two arose from the professional debate that has developed in response to the inadequacy of the government's proposals. Successive initiatives by governments throughout the 1980s focused on providing an alternative to the over-specialized and highly selective academic track route (A-Levels). These initiatives culminated in the 1991 White Paper, *Education and Training for the 21st Century*, which clarified the two main elements of government strategy. The first was to establish a national tripartite qualifications framework based on an academic track, a full-time general vocational track, and a work-based track. Within this framework, each track was defined in terms of an agreed set of levels; official policy was and remains that the three tracks should have parity of esteem at each level in relation to providing access to higher education. The second element of government strategy was to introduce a performance-related approach to funding that encouraged institutional competition as a way of getting value for money and raising standards.

Two kinds of alternatives to the government proposals have emerged since the 1990s. There are those, first expressed in the IPPR report (Finegold et al., 1990) and discussed in detail in Chapter 5, which have stressed the damaging effects of academic/vocational divisions at 16+, and argued the case for a unified system which links qualifications and curriculum and which guarantees a high level of general education for all students. The other alternative is less easy to define and brings together three groups, those business interests that stress the importance of individual skills as the source of economic growth (CBI, 1989; 1993), those educational professionals associated with the pre-vocational tradition who stress the alienating effects of the academic curriculum especially for disadvantaged learners, and those with a background in adult education who have emphasized the way existing qualifications deny access to so many adults and fail to recognize the skills and knowledge they have developed through experience (FEU, 1992). These latter groups; without necessarily agreeing on everything, have put their faith in promoting greater flexibility of access to learning, modularization of the curriculum, opportunities for credit transfer and unitization of assessment, and played down the powerful effect on opportunities of a divided system of qualifications (FEU, 1993; 1995).

The crisis in post-compulsory education in the UK, however, is not just a product of government policy or the determination of the elite to maintain a narrow and exclusive academic curriculum as the main selective route to higher education. It also reflects the problems of a system which has had to face the doubling of participation in full time education after 16 to over 70 per cent when both its curriculum and one of its main organizational structures — the school Sixth Form — was designed for a minority. The question then becomes whether to diversify the old curriculum and include the new learners (something the French have successfully done with their 'triple' baccalaureate but which has been resisted in the UK) or to leave the old Sixth Form curriculum unchanged and develop an alternative (the recent UK government strategy) or whether to adopt one of the approaches proposed by the reformers and referred to above.

If we bear in mind that the crisis in post-compulsory education, while manifest in educational terms, has its origins in the economy, then any framework for assessing proposals for reconstruction cannot focus only on educational institutions. It has to be a framework that conceptualizes education–economy relationships in the context of changes in the society as a whole. There are a number of options. First, we could start from the view that has dominated economics and sociology of education since the 1970s. This view asserts that, whether we like it or not, economies do determine education systems, whether in terms of their reproductive role (as would be argued by Bowles and Gintis and Althusser in the Marxist tradition) or because people are fundamentally economic actors, as is assumed by human capital theory. The problem with basing a strategy on such analyses is that, while they stress issues of importance, they say little about how specific economy/education relationships work and provide little guide to policy alternatives.

The second possibility is to replace the model of rational 'economic man' with the 'status seeking man' of the Weberian tradition developed by Collins (1979). While Collins provides a useful and probably more accurate account of the expansion of mass education than traditional economic theories, his view of education is limited to a notion of consumer demand as a way groups maintain or promote their relative status; like the economic theories he is able to say little about future education policy options. Furthermore, his argument about credential inflation predates and therefore takes no account of the very changes that have led to the crisis in post-compulsory education in the first place. A third alternative is the one adopted by Ranson (1992), who argues that we should not be taken in by fashionable views that the needs of the economy should be the primary determinant of our educational priorities. He asserts that society is fundamentally about values and therefore óur educational priorities should be moral and political, not economic. This argument is important as a critique of recent government policy in the UK. However, the danger of such an approach is that while correctly characterizing the current focus on the links between education and the economy as instrumental, it provides no basis for a concept of education that integrates personal development and economic life. The fourth possibility is not to separate education and the economy as Ransom does but to explore the idea of a learning-led economy that is reflected in the works of writers such as Reich (1991). Reich stresses the economic importance of providing high quality education and argues that a condition for a successful economy of the future is that it gives priority to learning as a feature of the society as a whole, not just the learning which takes place in specialized learning institutions such as schools and colleges. There are problems with such analyses, especially when related to countries such as the USA and the UK, where an uncritical acceptance of monetarist economics and the role of markets has inhibited the development of any strategic industrial policy. Such approaches can either end up allowing education to take all the blame for our economic ills as Noble (1993) has pointed out, or remain so general that, as Ainley (1994) says, they do little more than restate the obvious point that in some sense all societies are learning societies. However, freed from such over-simplifications, the idea of a learning-led economy or a learning society which links together learning wherever it takes place might provide the criteria for judging different approaches for reforming post-compulsory education. It could also be a framework for reconceptualizing education in the post-compulsory phase that is so uniquely characterized by the interfacing of many different sectors of society.

In this chapter, therefore, I intend to assess recent educational reform strategies and consider the options for reconstructing post-compulsory education from the point of view of the idea of a learning society. In doing so, I have two aims; first, through submitting existing reform proposals to a learning society analysis, I want to identify some criteria for evaluating different reform strategies. Second, I want to develop a concept of a learning society that is an improvement on some of the sloganized and rhetorical ways in which it has been used up to now. A clearer and more grounded concept of a learning society will, I suggest, provide criteria for a post-compulsory curriculum of the future which provides bridges and coherence for learners in a phase of education currently characterized by diversity and fragmentation.

The Idea of a Learning Society as a Contested Concept

There are many definitions of a learning society. Ainley (1994) starts from Hutchins (1970) who defines a learning society as one which in addition to offering part time adult education to every man and woman at every stage of their life, has transformed its values in such a way that learning, fulfilment, becoming human . . . becomes its aim and all its institutions are directed to that end.

At one level this is little more than another idealistic utopia of the kind that educationalists are so fond of. Its generalized view of the future can be celebrated at international conferences when participants are freed from the pressures of implementation and when neither the contradictions embedded in them nor the variety of ways in which they can be used are of great significance. However, as Ainley (1994) points out, it is not by chance that in the 1990s the idea of a learning society began to be used not only by educational theorists but by business and management experts, as well as by governments of the left and right. It is an example, it could be said, of a utopia becoming an ideology.

In linking the idea of a learning society to notions such as skill ownership and educational or training markets, management theory presents a view of society in which social classes no longer exist and divisions are based not, as in the past, on wealth and property but on the distribution of knowledge and skill. According to such a view, the wealth of a society *is* the skills and knowledge of its people. This is a powerful idea and like all ideas it can operate both as a concept and as an ideology. As an ideology it provides a justification for inequalities by masking the extent to which modern societies, as well as depending on the population's knowledge and skills, are also based on growing inequalities of power and wealth (Adonis and Pollard, 1997). As a concept, the idea of a learning society provides a rationale for lifelong learning, for the democratization of education and the broadening of access to learning opportunities. To put the same point in another way, there are material reasons why the utopian visions of Hutchins and others have become appropriated both by progressive educationists and by business and management theorists nearly 20 years after they were first published. The idea of a *learning* society, as well as the associated ideas of an *information* society and a *skills revolution* reflect real economic changes and at least a partial recognition that the mode of production and the conditions for the profitability of European companies have changed. Leading edge companies are no longer those who have displaced and controlled labour with technology but those who have found ways of using technology to enhance the value produced by the labour they employ. In distinguishing the concept from the ideology, the crucial question becomes: what kind of learning society and for whom? I propose, therefore, to view the idea of a learning society as a *contested concept* in which the different meanings given to it not only reflect different interests but imply different visions of the future and different policies for getting there.

The strength of the idea of a learning society as a concept is that in linking learning explicitly to the idea of a future society, it provides the basis for a critique of the minimal learning demands of much work and other activities in our present society, not excluding the sector specializing in education. Its weakness is that in most formulations it neglects the difficult issues of power and, in so far as it provides criteria for a critique of existing provision, these remain very general. Like many terms of contemporary educational discourse, such as partnership and collaboration, the idea of a learning society can take on a variety of conflicting interpretations. The different interpretations of the concept need to be examined in terms of their assumptions and the groups identified with them, as well as their priorities and their limitations for assessing different solutions to the problems that beset post-compulsory education. I shall, initially, describe three models, which I shall distinguish according to the emphasis they place on different educational strategies. Implicit in each are different models of social and economic development, issues discussed at some length by Ainley (1994). In this paper I am primarily concerned with using the models to examine different priorities for educational policy. The three models each represent clearly different foci and priorities. The extent to which they are shared by different groups and found in the policy debates in different countries will reflect the particular circumstances and history of the country concerned. The first model starts from the criterion of high participation in full-time post-compulsory education as a feature of a learning society. I will therefore refer to it as the *schooling model.* The second model takes as the criterion of a learning society the notion that everyone should, if possible, have a qualification that indicates their capabilities. I will refer to this as the *credentialist model.* The third model focuses on individual learners and their opportunities for access to learning. I will refer to this as the *access model* of a learning society. In the next sections I shall analyse these models in relation to current developments in post-compulsory education, drawing largely on UK examples. From this analysis I shall develop a fourth model which I will refer to as the *educative or connective model* of a learning society. This model focuses on the *form of learning* and in particular the relationship between learning and economic life which I shall argue will need to underpin a curriculum of the future. The model will also provide a way of conceptualizing the idea of a learning society that will, I hope, prove useful to curriculum designers and practitioners. It also builds on the concepts of connectivity and connective specialization that were introduced in earlier chapters and links them to the idea of learning as a social process in society as a whole, and not just a feature of specialized educational institutions.

The Schooling Model

The schooling model stresses high participation in post-compulsory schooling as a way of ensuring that the maximum proportion of the population reach as far beyond a minimum level of education as possible. The Nordic countries and some South East Asian countries represent examples of strong versions of the schooling model, although in other ways these societies are very different.

Weak versions of the schooling model are those that retain the ideal of high participation but not the reality; they vary from the UK, in which participation appears to have 'peaked' at 70 per cent (Spours, 1995a), with a steady fall to 35 per cent by the age of 18, to 'third world' countries which lose half of the students of every cohort after two or three years of compulsory schooling. The schooling model has democratic origins in the popular demand for education in Europe in the nineteenth century and in the pressure to expand schooling in the ex-colonies after they gained independence. It has set a standard for virtually all countries and takes one of its most advanced forms in Sweden, where schools have responsibility for the learning and progression of all their pupils up to the age of 20 *even if they are no longer full-time students.*

In recent years, countries with successful schooling models, such as the Nordic countries, have begun to challenge the model as an adequate basis for a learning society of the future (Young, 1993c). This partly reflects economic factors; an extended schooling model is expensive and, as a result of global competition and the liberalization of trade, even the Nordic countries have begun to examine public sector costs. However, the challenges also reflect more fundamental limitations of a model which separates and insulates formal education and, therefore, knowledge and learning from the economy and community life. In the nineteenth century, the fastest expanding sectors of employment were in the heavy industries; the work that was generated was dangerous and demanded much effort but little specialized skill. Much of this work was dehumanizing and there was a powerful case for protecting young people from it as well as assuming that they would learn better if they were not involved in work at all. Two features of the origins of the schooling model are important and reflect the historical circumstances of its origins. First, it was based on a desire to protect young people from the negative features of the early years of industrial production. Second, it drew its concepts of learning and knowledge from the medieval academy. Despite massive changes in production there has been little disenchantment with the academic education that has formed the basis of the schooling model and it has come to dominate educational policy in most countries. Courses in academic or general education have continued to expand and some writers have begun to see this 'academic drift' as a key problem in post-compulsory education (Tanguy, 1991). Academic drift refers to the tendency for students to opt for the 'Royal Road' of the grammar school or gymnasium which they see as leading them to higher education or secure employment. The dilemma for governments is that they are increasingly reluctant to finance the expansion of higher education to satisfy these new demands from below.

However, there are a number of other problems that even the strong versions of schooling models face, especially from the point of view of a learning society. First, they continue to represent a view of education 'as an end in itself' and therefore the curriculum tends to reflect the immediate interests of the producers (teachers and lecturers) rather than the variety of other interests that it claims to serve. It follows that the standards and values of schooling models tend to be internal to the educational system and implicit rather than external and explicit. Second, schooling systems are, as Ivan Illich (1971) pointed out, addictive; they tend to induce a demand for more schooling rather than for opportunities to continue learning after leaving school. Evidence of this is provided by the way students in Nordic countries, who graduate from upper secondary school but do not gain access to university, do not seek employment but re-enter the cycle of upper secondary schooling for a further two or three years in the hope of later entry to university. Third, schooling models are 'front-loaded' rather than continuous development models. In other words they assume that education is predominantly a preparatory activity associated with, at most, the first 20–25 years of a person's life, rather than something that it continues in some form throughout life. Fourthly, the insulation of schooling from other types of learning has two negative consequences. It turns teachers away from thinking about the relationship between school learning and how learning is used and it allows employers (especially in commerce and manufacturing) to avoid responsibility for becoming involved in the transformation of schools and to put the blame for the lack of skills and knowledge of their employees on to the school system.

The strong schooling model does exhibit a number of features of a learning society. There is no doubt that it is an expression of a 'learning culture' (it represents a strong popular commitment to the *public* provision of schools and colleges) and it provides a powerful example to set against weak systems with medium to low participation such as the UK. Whether it offers an appropriate model for developing countries with limited resources and whether its institutionalized concept of learning being linked to the participation of full-time students in schools or colleges is the best way of linking education to their economic reconstruction and development is much more doubtful. These questions are considered briefly in the context of post-apartheid South Africa (Unterhalter and Young, 1995). What the schooling model clearly fails to do is to address the issues of connectivity between different stages and types of learning — in workplaces, in communities and in specialized educational institutions. That is an issue to which I will return in a later section.

The Credentialist Model

The credentialist model has as long a history as the schooling model. It gives priority to ensuring that the vast majority of the population has qualifications or certificated skills and knowledge and that the qualifications people achieve are related to their future employment. Unlike the schooling model, it allows for the possibility that qualifications may be achieved in other ways than through full-time study, although in practice this is rarely possible for qualifications that give entry to high status occupations. The European countries that follow the German tradition are the leading examples of the strong version of a credentialist model. Other countries, including the UK in its efforts in the 1980s to create a Youth Training System have attempted unsuccessfully to copy the German model. The result, at least in the case of the UK, is what at best could be described as a very weak version of a credentialist model. The training schemes for young people only led to qualifications for a minority, links between qualifications and employment were not established and public funding increasingly had to be used as an incentive for achieving qualification targets. In other words, what in the German case has been an employment-led system has, in the UK, become a state-led, qualifications-driven system with few direct links to employment at all. Government agencies have been left with trying to market qualifications to employers that were designed to be employer-led!

Strong versions of the credentialist model give priority to learning that leads to qualifications for occupations and involve legislation that limits recruitment for nearly all occupations to those with the appropriate qualifications. Such models depend on a form of corporatism within which the state, employer organizations and trade unions collaborate. Furthermore, whereas employer organizations 'police' their members with regard to the delivery of training, trade unions undertake a similar task in relation to wages. Such a system worked well in the context of an incrementally growing economy with well-controlled national markets that emerged after the Second World War. However, at just the time when countries such as the UK, with weak education and training systems, are attempting to credentialize their labour forces, the credentialist model is being questioned in countries where it has been most successful in the face of changing economic circumstances. As a result, a number of the more fundamental weaknesses of credentialism as a model for a learning society have become apparent.

Credentialist models are expensive to employers and the state and they are inflexible. There is a parallel with mass production factories in that any change involves the whole system and is an extremely onerous task not undertaken very frequently. In linking qualifications to specific occupations, the credentialist model is based on an increasingly out-of-date concept of the division of labour. Furthermore, it depends on there being clear and relatively specific statements about the skills and knowledge associated with particular occupations — something only feasible when occupations are at least relatively static. A consequence is that credentialist models are prone either to a form of 'vocational inertia' when specific skills are taught long after they have ceased to be used in industry or commerce or to the 'academic drift' that has been discussed as a feature of schooling models. As students opt out of vocational courses for 'the royal road' to higher education, efforts are made to make vocational qualifications more attractive by increasing their academic content. It is only in individual examples, such as the 'learnerrangements' scheme associated with Volkswagen and the development of 'learning and work' assignments that the old and relatively insular relationships between colleges and employers are being challenged (Birke et al., 1998).

The more fundamental problems of credentialist models relate to their view of qualifications and have much in common with those of the schooling model. This is not surprising as both have similar origins in the early phases of nineteenth century European industrialization. Despite the fact that more and more people are gaining certificates even though the jobs associated·with those certificates are diminishing in number, the social function of qualifications has hardly been questioned. In increasingly fluid occupational structures, the role of qualifications, both in occupational selection and in their capacity to be a motivator for learning, is increasingly problematic. The conventional sociological argument (Dore, 1976; Collins, 1979) is that the expansion of qualifications gives rise to a process of credential inflation when a more extended hierarchy of qualifications is developed and older and lower level qualifications are devalued. There was some truth in this view at the time, although it misses the fundamental point about a learning society that is of increasing importance. In a learning society, learning needs to be linked not just to an individual being selected for employment as in the past, but to an individual's capacity to innovate and therefore to having a role in changing work processes. It seems likely that distinct qualifications which are designed as terminal endpoints to programmes of learning and as gateways to jobs will need to be replaced by a qualification framework that encourages *qualifying* as a continuous and lifelong process. Standard setting, which has traditionally been another function of qualifications, will also need to be carried out in new ways if it is to promote qualifying as a learning process rather than as basis for selection. The issue of the role of qualifications in a learning society and how this might change from their traditional credentialist role is returned to in the last section of this chapter.

The Access Model

The *access model* represents a vision of a society of the future in which learning after the phase of compulsory schooling is increasingly freed from its ties with specialized educational institutions such as schools, colleges and universities. It is a vision of a learning society in which people will learn, if free to do so, in any context they find themselves in, by developing skills and knowledge as their needs change at different times of their lives. This model has complex and often contradictory political and cultural origins. It has affinity with the ideas of neo-liberalism, which are suspicious of professional educators who are seen not as sources of expertise but as an interest group concerned to exclude many unqualified people from learning by insisting that they have prior qualifications. Furthermore, the neo-liberal version of the access model extends this critique to all educational institutions unless, like private colleges, they are seen as driven by market demands. The access model elevates the fundamental liberal idea of individual choice to a primary principle, even in relation to learning. However, the access model is also attractive to progressive educators, particularly those associated with adult education, who have spent much of their working lives finding ways round the barriers created by institutional education. Both liberal and progressive versions of the access model link the freeing of learning from institutions to the potential of new technology which, at least in theory, allows everyone to be 'on line' and with access to a learning network. With perhaps a touch of irony the access model is 'seen by some as making institution-based education redundant and leading to the 'virtual college'. More specifically, it casts doubt on the assumption that most learning after compulsory schooling needs specialist teachers and therefore also needs specialized educational institutions.

Despite its emphasis on access and opportunities for learning, the access model represents, if carried through towards its logical conclusion, a reversal of the progressive extension of formal education what has been a feature of every society that has modernized since the nineteenth century. However, it seems unlikely that the access model will be attractive to the growing numbers of wealthy parents who opt for the private sector for their children's education, or for the 20–30 per cent of the middle class parents who can provide the cultural capital to support their children successfully through existing state schools. For the remainder, pressure from cuts in funding, especially for colleges, is leading to more learning centres, distance learning and assessment on demand but fewer opportunities for the interaction and dialogue with teachers and their peers on which real learning depends. In other words, it is difficult to see the access model on its own as other than a way of legitimating reduced spending on public education and therefore becoming a basis for new social divisions and inequalities.

Access model developments such as schemes for the Accreditation of Prior Learning (APL), the setting up of Open Learning Centres based on the Internet, the shift of teaching resources towards expanding careers guidance and the design of 'teacher proof' learning materials all attempt to tackle the question of access to learning by placing the learner at the centre of curriculum policies. Proponents argue that institutions, through their admissions policies, their timetables, their school terms and their academic structures, as well as through the more subtle epistemological processes of the hidden curriculum, exclude rather than include new learners, especially those that are more socially disadvantaged. The access model, on the other hand not only sees people as having a right to choose where and when as well as what to study and when they are ready to be assessed. It assumes that if more and more people are given the opportunity to choose to learn, they will take more responsibility for their own learning and recognize the need to learn throughout their whole life.

The access model promotes learning through its de-institutionalization. Although its supporters would not necessarily endorse the association, it has many features in common with the radical utopianism of Ivan Illich's (1971) deschooling ideas that were popular in the 1970s. In some recent experiments for encouraging work based learning among young trainees, qualifications are marketed by linking them to vouchers for hamburgers; thus a vision is presented of people buying learning in much the same way as they buy any product on a supermarket shelf — it is available on demand 24 hours of every day of a person's life. In aiming to make learning as normal to everyday life as shopping, the access model represents a powerful idea. First, it addresses the reality that many people experience major barriers in trying to gain access to current institutional provision for education. Second, the stress it gives to supporting learners in the management of their own learning is likely to be part of any strategy for achieving a learning society. Third, the access model has some affinity with the fashionable, albeit contentious post modern trend in social theory (Green, 1994) with its stress on cultural diversity and the break up of all institutional structures. Fourth, and unlike the earlier versions of de-institutionalized education of the 1970s, it has powerful forces behind it. These are the software and the communication companies behind the Internet and the National Grid which see the access model as generating a lucrative new market for their products, and governments, for whom the *access model* appears as a way of cutting the costs of public education and of weakening what some see as the sectional power of professional or producer interests.

On the other hand, the *access model* has two kinds of weakness that are exaggerated in the UK context. The focus on learner choice and the recognition of the prior experience of learners makes sense for adults returning to study. However, the extension of such an approach to those between the ages of 16–25 is far more open to question, when many who find themselves on such 'access' courses will have had only negative experiences of learning in their compulsory schooling. It is difficult to see how the problems facing such learners will be solved by making the curriculum more flexible and giving them more choice or indeed what choices would be available to them when they would be excluded from so many programmes by their lack of basic skills.

The second kind of problem applies more generally to the *access model*. I want to briefly consider two of these. As an alternative to institutionalized provision for learning, and one that aims to maximize learner choice and flexibility, the *access model* can be seen as a further step on a road begun by the process of curriculum modularization and was discussed in Chapter 6. However, the international experience of modularization, especially in the USA (Robertson, 1993) where it has become the norm in post-compulsory education, is that if the curriculum is left largely to student choice this leads to the fragmentation of learning and puts limits on the scope for the intellectual development of students. A person's intellectual development does depend on whether they develop responsibility for their own learning. However it also requires agreed curriculum guidelines and strategies for promoting continuity of learning to be established; inevitably, constraints on learner autonomy and choice are involved. The *access model*, of which a modularized curriculum is one expression, is, in effect, placing the major responsibility for the planning and coherence of learning on the learner. However, the learner in question is often one who is least equipped for such a responsibility. It is not surprising, nor does it imply a rejection of the potential of modularization, that an *access model* has found little support elsewhere in Europe.

The second issue for the *access model* involves the question of how learning links to modern forms of production and service work. Researchers such as Reich (1991), Zuboff (1988) and Sparkes (1995), to name a few examples, stress the emergence of new production paradigms in the manufacturing, media and service industries and how the organization of specific work processes is likely to have been planned and designed quite separately from the actual site of production or delivery. The skills needed at work will therefore be increasingly opaque to direct experience, and more and more dependent on the ability of those involved to develop new concepts for understanding the links between specific work processes and the production strategies of companies. These new combinations of skill and knowledge are referred to by a variety of terms such as 'connective', 'conceptual', or 'intellective' skills. Despite the fact that their operational meaning is far from clear, it is increasingly argued that they will be at the centre of any improvements in European production processes. Indeed, it is likely that it is partly an awareness that their employees are going to need new types of skill that has triggered the business interest in the idea of learning organizations and a learning society. It is, however, difficult to see how the new skills and knowledge that are needed for advanced forms of production and services will be developed on the basis of an *access model* which tends to separate work based learning from the sources of conceptual innovation developed in universities and other specialized educational institutions. Combining conceptualization and execution will need planning and the design of innovative learning assignments will depend upon close collaboration between production supervisors and learning specialists in colleges, universities and companies. The *access model's* focus on learner choice, access to IT and credit transfer can, on its own, only lead to the development of low level routine skills which all the trend data suggests, are less and less relevant to production in leading edge companies. Furthermore, if, as is likely, the qualifications achieved through such learner-centred methods do not gain currency value in terms of job opportunities, this could foster disillusion and scepticism about the value of any kind of learning for just those groups who have been traditionally excluded from any learning culture.

Summary: Three Models of a Learning Society

In the previous sections, I have distinguished between three models of a learning society and related them to three strategies for reforming post-compulsory education. I have discussed the strengths and the fundamental weaknesses of these models both as strategies for improving post-compulsory education in general and as ways of addressing the specific weaknesses of post-compulsory education in England and Wales with its characteristic social divisions and voluntarist concept of the role of the state. In the final section of the paper, I shall draw on these criticisms and develop a fourth model of a learning society — what I refer to as an educative or *connective* model — and suggest some of its implications for reforming post-compulsory education.

Post-compulsory Education for a Learning Society: Towards a Connective Model

Implicit in all definitions of a learning society is the idea of giving priority to individuals developing *learning relationships* throughout their lives in any work, study or other activity in any institution or community in which they are involved. However, in the three models of a learning society discussed so far, the focus has not been directly on learning relationships nor on learning processes but on participation in institutions, gaining qualifications and on access to learning opportunities for individuals. In each model, the assumption is made that another process, participation, gaining a qualification and choosing among and having access to learning opportunities represents the process of learning. Unlike the schooling model, the educative or connective model does not assume that increases in the proportion of the population engaged in full-time study or expanding the educational provision offered by specialized educational institutions, such as schools and colleges, necessarily leads to a learning society. Nor, as in the case of the access and credentialist models does the connective model reduce learning to individuals choosing courses or gaining a qualification. The model points to a diversification and interconnection of sites of learning and a shift in the location and role of educational specialists; their relationship with other specialists and productive work of all kinds becomes based on learning relationships; it is in that sense that I refer to a connective model. In the last part of this chapter the educational implications of the idea of a connective model of a learning society are discussed, albeit in a preliminary way. I consider four themes in beginning to conceptualize a connective model of a learning society and suggest some of their implications for the reform of post-compulsory education. The first three follow from my critique of the previous models and focus on the need for (a) new concepts of institutional and curricular specialization to replace the divisions between school and non-school learning and academic and vocational curricula; (b) a new concept of the process of qualification to replace the traditional credentialist and screening models; (c) a re-conceptualization of the relationship between learning and production that takes into account the changing nature of work at the end of the twentieth century. In the final section, I will discuss the need to re-conceptualize the concept of learning itself by drawing on Engestrom's idea of expansive learning (Engestrom, 1991; 1994).

Institutional and Curricular Specialization in a Learning Society:
Beyond the Schooling Model

The concept of a learning society points to the transformation of all institutions into 'learning organizations' and thus challenges the idea that learning is primarily associated with specialist educational institutions, such as schools or colleges. Such 'learning organizations' would be characterized by having a research capacity which would enable them to develop a learning relationship with their environment (Morgan, 1988), and a human resource development strategy that linked the 'continuing re-professionalization' of all staff to the primary goals of the organization. The fact that such a development would involve more and more organizations in different sectors taking on an *educational* role does not imply a diminution of the educational role of schools and colleges as specialist teaching and learning organizations or of the role of universities as specializing in research and the teaching of advanced courses. That would be a reversal of the achievements of specialization of the last century. Rather it implies a change in the internal relationships of organizations so that schools and colleges themselves begin to develop their research and human resource strategies, and in the external relationships between educational and other institutions as they identify shared purposes and explore new forms of partnership. This change is what I have referred to in Chapter 5 as a shift from *insulated* (and in many cases *divisive*) *specialization* to *connective specialization* based on negotiated understandings between organizations about common purposes and futures. Examples of possible future concepts that might underpin partnerships between schools and colleges and other organizations in the private and public sectors would be ideas of sustainable growth and new forms of international collaboration which individual organizations might be unable to realize on their own. These shared future concepts would not only shape the external relations between schools/colleges/universities and the industrial and service sectors of the economy but the internal relationships between the different specialist teachers in different fields and lines of study. The concept of connective specialization, therefore, is a basis for new relationships between institutions and for a new model of the curriculum.

The curricular possibilities arising from a shift from insulated to connective specialization are profound and only beginning to become apparent. One example is the way the new programme for the Swedish upper secondary schools distinguishes between 16 lines of study. Each 'line' makes links between discipline-based knowledge and some aspect of productive life and includes core and specialist areas of study, many of which need to be based on new kinds of relationships between schools and organizations involved in commercial, community or manufacturing activities. Breadth of learning and new combinations of study are possible in such a model both through a core entitlement for all students and through the design of the specialist areas. Inevitably, the old divisions between academic and vocational learning do not suddenly disappear, and those going to university will tend to cluster in a small number of more 'academic' lines of study. However, the possibility is there for students to develop conceptual skills in the food, construction or business administration lines as much as it is through lines of study in the natural or social sciences or humanities. Whether these possibilities become a reality in Sweden will depend in part on the extent to which the society as a whole has taken on the implications of becoming a learning society. A possible model applied to the UK of the Swedish version of connective specialization is outlined in Spours and Young (1995).

Qualifications in a Learning Society: Beyond the Credentialist Model

Qualifications in the credentialist model remain gateways to employment or future study as they have been since the nineteenth century. They function primarily, therefore, as mechanisms of selection, and secondarily, through such a selection process, as guarantors of standards. Such a concept of qualifications is based on a static model of society in which it is assumed that the occupational division of labour only evolves slowly. It bears little relationship to a society of the future when people are likely to have to change their jobs and re-qualify several times in their lives. With a relatively static economy it is not surprising that sudden increases in opportunities to gain qualifications, as when a developing country gains independence from a colonial power, can lead to credential inflation and the devaluing of qualifications.

The current tension in the credentialist model is between the selective role of qualifications which originated in a division of labour based upon a minority of the population being qualified and the demands in a learning society for the majority to be qualified in new and flexible ways. The shift needed would be from (a) *a qualification* terminating the qualifying process to *qualifying as a continuous process*; and (b) from a concept of a qualification certifying that certain standards have been achieved to the idea that the process of qualification is concerned with raising and enhancing standards and developing new skills and understandings over time. Such a shift would involve new relationships between those involved in course design and the moderation of assessment and the different groups involved in the use of qualifications — employees, employers and their respective organizations. It would also involve new approaches to quality assurance. The crucial change would be in the new kinds of relationships between various kinds of qualification users and providers and the new kinds of assessment that would need to be developed to guarantee standards and underpin the focus on their development.

Learning and Production in a Learning Society

Most attempts to conceptualize a learning society have one striking weakness. They invariably refer to skills for employment and it is largely business rather than educational interests that have argued for the emphasis on skill ownership. However, the typical concept of the learner buying her/his skills in a training market and selling them in the labour market (CBI, 1991; 1993) is a highly individualized one. It follows that, learning is detached from the specific production or work processes where the employee 'as learner' might be involved in innovation and therefore be productive in the sense likely to be needed in the future. There is no explicit connection between learning and production in a skill ownership model of learning. How production processes are changing and the implications these changes may have for how knowledge about production is made available to students are important in shaping the knowledge and skills that may be needed by those involved in production. Hales (1978) writes about the 'pre-conceptualization of production' independently of production sites which is a consequence of the increasing sophistication of electronic control engineering. However, changes in work organization are not just about the impact of new technologies. The more general point is that as processes of production change faster and become less accessible to direct experience, the need increases to replace traditional apprenticeship models of work-based learning by developing new ways of linking learning based on the experience of work and conceptual learning (Young and Guile, 1994; Guile and Young, 1997b). Possible examples of new relationships between learning and production are suggested in some of the newer European Union Programmes which aim to support employees in finding ways of transforming declining industries and in the Ford (UK) EDAP scheme which provides workers with learning credits to follow any course of study they choose. Such examples of *connective* relationships between education and production are still rare and largely restricted to those already in full-time employment.

Linking learning with production can pose a threat for many managers, especially those brought up in the Anglo Saxon 'command' tradition. This is well described in Zuboff's study of paper mills in the USA (Zuboff, 1988). Zuboff describes how managers oppose demands by employees to develop their conceptual understanding of production processes. Such perceptions of threat arising from employees learning about company processes are probably the core of the contradiction in the business enthusiasm for the idea of learning society. The tension in the possibilities of new relationships between learning and work is also at the heart of the crisis in the post-compulsory curriculum and the difficulty even the most egalitarian societies have in overcoming divisions between academic and vocational learning (see Chapters 5 and 6). The educational literature of the last decade is strewn with attempts to conceptualize forms of learning that go beyond such divisions — connective skills and knowledge, intellective skills, cultural practice, critical vocationalism, technological literacy, symbolic analysis and cognitive apprenticeship are but some of the attempts. As I suggested in Chapter 5, the French and the Germans are in a better position to take the debate further with their concepts of 'bildung' and 'formation' for which we have no translation in English. Creating new links between learning and production remains one of the crucial unresolved issues for the learning society of the future. It is an educational problem, in that it requires educationalists to go beyond their traditional distinction between instrumental rationality and the development of the whole person that has dominated liberal educational discourse. On the other hand, it is not just a problem of curriculum design that can be solved by educationists alone. It is also a production issue concerning the meaning and viability of what is becoming known as 'intelligent production' and the new kinds of relationships between work and learning that such models of production necessitate. The globalization trends that are reflected in the location of Japanese and Korean factories in the UK have not been based on new ways of linking learning and production. They have relied largely on the vulnerability (to unemployment) of many workers in Wales and the North East of England as well as the restrictive trade union legislation introduced in the last 15 years. However, unless the question of links between learning and production are addressed, there is little chance of developing the more autonomous possibilities of globalization which will be the basis for production in the future.

Re-conceptualizing Learning

None of the models of a learning society examined in the previous sections problematizes the central concept of learning itself. In the schooling model learning is equated with participation, in the credentialist model with gaining qualifications and in the access model with individual choice. Only the last of the three challenges the conventional notions of learning being dependent on teaching as the transmission of knowledge. However, the *access model* ends up by replacing a teacher dominated model by one which has no place for teaching at all; furthermore, it individualizes learning in a way that misrepresents the process of learning itself. The *connective model* of a learning society starts with two assumptions. The first is that the main function of any society is educative; in other words it is through being a member of a society that individuals learn and shape that society. It follows that all social life involves learning, whether conscious and planned or not, and equally all learning is social, whether explicitly so or not. The second assumption is that from the point of view of a learning society it is crucial to distinguish between different types of learning and that it is the particular form of learning that is dominant that distinguishes learning societies from other societies all of which have an educative role. Engestrom (1994) makes a useful distinction between adaptive, investigative and expanded learning. Pre-industrial societies were characterized by adaptive learning — for survival; the earlier phases of industrialization were dominated by investigative learning — the application of science to an increasing range of problems. Expanded learning which refers to when the learner questions the origins of the problem that has given rise to the need for learning in the first place is at the heart of a learning society. The criterion for a learning society therefore becomes how far, in schools and colleges and other learning contexts, is the object or focus of learning is *expanded*, in Engestrom's sense. Engestrom's proposed strategy for expanding learning consists of three steps in a cycle of learning contexts; each develops different kinds of higher level skills as follows:

- the *context of criticism* in which the teaching and learning practices of the school are challenged and the tensions between a school view of the world as expressed in textbooks and views expressed in the media and elsewhere are explored
- the *context of discovery* in which new concepts are developed and used

- the *context of practical application* in which new ideas are tried out in the real world

This is not another top/down strategy for creating a learning society; that would be a contradiction in terms. As a learning strategy, it can only start with teachers and learners, whether in schools or colleges or in workplaces or communities. If they follow through its implications, Engestrom (1994) argues, teachers in schools and colleges or trainers on training programmes can enable their students and trainees to 'design and implement their own futures, as their prevailing practices show symptoms of crisis'.

The strength of the model is the extent to which it is, as Engestrom claims, built on the contradictions of current practice, rather than on some utopian ideal; its weakness is that it still remains abstract in conception, despite its claim to be located in real contradictions. What is undoubtedly true is that teachers involved in projects based on such ideas 'will be working at the edge of (their) competence'. The implications of the approach raise quite new questions for the professional development of teachers and the links between teachers, employers and educational researchers.

A Concluding Note

In this chapter I began with a critique of the UK system of post-compulsory education which, it is widely acknowledged, is urgently in need of reform. I used an analysis of different models of a learning society in order to develop some reform criteria. My preferred model of a learning society I termed *connective* and I suggested that it would involve four sets of re-conceptualizations — the form of specialization, the nature of qualifications, the relations between learning and production and the concept of learning itself. My hope is that these concepts will be of use in giving practical reality to three important ideas. The first is that a society of the future will embody an education-led economy rather than an economy-led education system. The second is that a curriculum of the future will need to be defined by the kind of learning needs we envisage that young people preparing to be adults in the twenty-first century will need. The third idea is that instead of protecting young people from the dangers of work, work in a learning society could become, as Gramsci once hoped, an educational principle.

Chapter 11

Towards a New Curriculum for Teacher Education

Introduction

Two trends in the 1980s and 1990s influenced educational policy in almost every country in the world. The first was the emergence of a new set of economic conditions associated with significant increases in the global competition faced by previously relatively well protected national economies. The educational outcomes of this trend varied and were of course partly political. In many countries, they were expressed in the adoption of neo-liberal economic policies devoted to trying to cut public expenditure and maximize the economic benefits of educational spending by increasing its efficiency and directing its goals to economic rather than social or cultural ends. Led by the USA, such policies were taken far further in the UK, Australia and New Zealand and in some Latin American countries than in Asia and other European countries. Nevertheless, no country has been completely immune from policies associated with Reaganomics and Thatcherism.

The second trend was expressed in a series of fundamental educational reforms, of which changes in the structure and content of teacher education formed a part. A common theme underlying these educational reforms that linked them to the first trend was that they treated public education as an instrument of *economic* policy. The assumption was that the reforms would lead to a more highly skilled workforce qualified at a lower cost per person, and that this would improve national productivity and make the country better able to perform in the global marketplace. My argument in this chapter will be that, although there was a great need to reform teacher education in the UK, the policies developed and increasingly copied in other countries were less a response to global economic changes and more a reflection of an emerging right wing ideology. Becoming globally competitive does not just involve delivering existing education at a lower cost; it requires a fundamentally new approach to learning and to relationships between education and the economy. However, the outcomes of the new policies have often been in conflict with the needs of a country responding constructively to the new economic circumstances. This is partly because of a misunderstanding of the significance of the changes represented by globalization and partly because, for ideological reasons, governments in the UK have used an inappropriate model for modernizing teacher education.

The remainder of this chapter is divided into four parts. First, I make some cautionary observations about the emerging global context and the extent to which it accounts for developments in educational policy; second, I suggest that it is useful to see the links between global economic change and changes in teacher education policy in terms of different approaches to modernization. I therefore make a distinction between three types or phases of modernization as a framework for interpreting recent changes in teacher education policy; third, I outline a number of changes in teacher education in the UK which reflect what I refer to as moves towards *technocratic modernization*; fourth, and arising from a critique of technocratic modernization, I suggest that if teacher education is to prepare teachers for the likely future demands that will be made upon them, reforms will need to be based on the principles of *reflexive* not *technocratic* modernization (Beck et al., 1994). Reflexive modernization starts with a critique of the process of modernization itself and is expressed in the idea of educational reform being a process of *public learning* (Stewart, 1996). Such an approach, I suggest, will involve the re-thinking of four core issues that lie at the heart of any teacher education programme — its approach to learning, the role of knowledge in the teacher education curriculum, the role of schools and higher education in teacher education and the question of accountability and standards.

The Global Context

Two views of globalization can be contrasted. The first is fashionable but, I argue, misconceived. The second highlights certain new realities that transcend national boundaries and which all countries are having to face (Hirst and Thompson, 1996). The first view of globalization sees it as an inexorable set of economic forces impinging on every country in the world. These forces, it is argued, diminish the potential role of national governments and privilege the interests of multi-national corporations which only have loyalties to themselves. Globalization, from this perspective, is about the power of the global market which no individual country and no policy can avoid. In this view, the only policy option for a national government is to facilitate the entry of their country into global markets in as many sectors of the economy as possible. This, it is argued, will be achieved through the wholesale de-regulation of markets, the cutting of public expenditure, the extending of private enterprise into fields such as transport that in many countries were previously public and subjecting the remaining areas of public provision such as education to the rigours of markets (albeit quasi-markets). This view has been powerful and pervasive and has been adhered to by the major international organizations such as the World Bank and the IMF and to varying degrees by the governments of the major industrial countries.

However, as Hirst and Thompson (1996) show clearly, this view of globalization, although plausible and much promoted, is at odds with much of the evidence; most key investment and other decisions are still national. Most countries share certain common circumstances and even a common interpretation of these circumstances; however, this does not make such circumstances into independent forces of history. Such a view of globalization is best seen as an ideology used by governments, usually of the Right, to justify taking certain decisions. Global reality is much more complex and is reflected in the increasingly wide differences, even among economists, about what changes can really be said to be global and what this means. These new circumstances, which have emerged since the 1970s, include the increasingly global markets for manufactured goods, the expansion and diversification of consumer demand, the emergence of the new communication technologies and the expansion of air transport (Castells, 1996), and the end of the Cold War ideological divide. All these changes are part of the new context within which national governments find themselves; how they are responded to and their implications for educational policy will depend on decisions made by governments and others which will reflect (a) the position of a country in the world economic order; (b) the national tradition of the country in question; and (c) the policy choices of specific governments.

Modernization and Teacher Education

How governments respond to global economic change will in part reflect the view they have of how their institutions need to be modernized. I therefore interpret teacher education policy choices made in the UK as attempts to modernize a system which was proving increasingly inadequate. However modernization is a highly contested idea with a variety of meanings. For the purposes of this chapter I treat it as a generic term which in the broadest sense refers to changes designed to replace traditional institutions and modes of practice such as family, kinship and inheritance by more rational, democratic institutions and modes of decision making. In recent years the concept of modernization has been much criticized by social scientists as masking ideologies and inequalities in the distribution of power. Some have rejected it altogether. Here I wish to retain both the conceptual power of the idea of modernization as well as its progressive assumptions, while at the same time recognizing the problems to which mainstream versions have given rise. For this purpose I draw on the analyses developed by Beck, Giddens and Lash (1994) and distinguish between three types of modernization — evolutionary, technocratic and reflexive. I use this typology as a framework for discussing recent teacher education policies in the UK and to draw some more general conclusions. For these writers, reflexive modernization is both a new approach to interpreting the history of industrialization and an attempt to identify certain social conditions of the late twentieth century. The next sections provide a brief account of each type.

Evolutionary Modernization

Evolutionary modernization refers to the social, political and economic changes that began in the early nineteenth century in Europe. It was at the heart of the processes of industrialization and democratization of Western Europe, and later of America, Japan and other Asian countries. Among its features were:

- an uncritical belief in the link between science and progress
- the extension of rational and scientific methods from technological issues to decisions about education, health etc.
- the expansion of specialist formal education institutions
- the structural differentiation of occupations and the increasingly specialized production of knowledge

Technocratic Modernization

Technocratic modernization refers to how western and other countries responded to the global economic crises of the 1970s and 1980s and the awareness that allowing the process of modernization to evolve as it had in the previous decades was no longer adequate. The shift involved the extended application of scientific methods, the replacement and/or control of growing areas of routinized work by computer systems, the self conscious introduction of business efficiency models into the public sector including education and the extension of evaluation, monitoring and the testing of skills.

Reflexive Modernization

For Beck and Giddens and Lash (1994), reflexive modernization is an expression of the growing recognition that technocratic approaches to modernization create problems that they cannot solve. They argue that the critique that science applies to traditional forms of knowledge and social organization needs to be applied to the application of the scientific method itself. Unlike post-modernists, they do not reject modernization or science, but see the need for a critique of science as a further development of science itself. They argue that it is only through reflexivity, or exploring the grounds of its own practice and legitimacy, that modernization can realize the emancipatory possibilities to which it has always laid claim. It is an approach to social organization best expressed as a form of public learning and is found where the crises in technocratic modernization have become most public and most explicit. One example is the response to the risks associated with genetically engineered crops and the new models of risk management that have been developed; these have begun to challenge the authority of expert knowledge and to establish new forms of dialogue between experts and lay stakeholders.

Teacher Education Reforms in England and Wales Since the 1980s

Teacher education policy in the UK since 1980 can be seen in terms of the shift from evolutionary to technocratic modernization as successive Conservative governments tried to make the system more efficient and cost effective at the same time as attempting to solve such problems as pupil drop out and the low levels of achievement associated with urban schools. However, with its priority of greater control, technocratic modernization has created new problems such as teacher demoralization which may account for the drop in the recruitment of new teachers, especially in shortage subject areas such as physics and technology. The contradictions which arise from the technocratic modernization of teacher education are most evident in the tension between the attempt to specify teacher competencies more closely on the one hand and the parallel demand for teachers to take on new and broader responsibilities that are not specifiable in competence terms. In this section, I discuss four more specific examples. All are drawn from the UK experience.

From Discipline-based to Classroom Problem-based Curricula

From the 1960s until the 1980s teacher education curricula in the UK were dominated by the educational disciplines, especially philosophy, psychology and sociology. The assumption was that these disciplines would provide conceptual frameworks which would enable professional teachers to understand their roles and would be a basis on which they could build in their studies for higher degrees. Under pressure from new demands for raising standards in schools, this disciplinary basis of the teacher education curriculum collapsed in the 1980s for two reasons. The first was practical. Educational disciplines are inevitably abstracted from any real life teaching situations. They cannot, therefore, provide an adequate basis for student teachers to understand the problems that they face in the classroom. In the 1960s and 1970s, when the educational disciplines dominated teacher education and were taught as separate courses, student teachers were somehow expected to bring together the ideas from the various disciplines and make them relevant to their practice. The second reason was political. The disciplines, especially sociology, were seen by the governments of the time as critical rather than constructive; they identified systemic problems, but did not point to pedagogic solutions (see Chapter 3).

In response to the widely perceived inadequacy of its disciplinary framework, the curriculum of teacher education was reconstructed in the 1980s on the basis of the typical classroom-based problems and issues faced by student teachers. Examples of such problems were pupil discipline and class control, dealing with pupils with learning difficulties and coping with classes with pupils from different cultural and linguistic backgrounds. Despite the changes in teacher education curricula, student-teachers still came back from teaching practice with problems they could not solve. With their focus on 'problems', the university-based courses tended to confirm a 'social pathology' view of schooling; in other words, student teachers learned that schools failed either because pupils lacked motivation or ability or because they had bad teachers. Though student teachers are likely to experience the problems of school failure as classroom-based, a teacher education curriculum that treats the problems as if their origins lie solely within the classroom will inevitably be inadequate. The new problem-based curricula denied students access to concepts which, by linking their practical experience to the wider context which shaped it, might have helped them understand the problems they faced and enabled them to improve their practice.

Giving Schools More Control Over Teacher Education

In the 1990s the government in the UK attempted to weaken the link between teacher education and the universities. The most extreme example of this policy was SCITT (School Centred Initial Teacher Training) which allowed schools, on their own, to certificate students as qualified teachers. However, such schemes, despite their initial attraction to right wing politicians, have not been successful and have remained very much in a minority. More common expressions of the outcome of the new government policies have been forms of partnership in which the university and the schools shared programmes of teacher education.

Teacher education has always had an uneasy location in the universities in the UK, and probably in most countries. Mostly delivered through one year post-graduate programmes, it has traditionally been a loose combination of 'learning by doing' in school, practical pedagogic advice for teaching specialist subjects and multi-disciplinary educational theory. Policies designed to reduce the role of universities in teacher education aimed to give a greater role to practising teachers and require universities to concentrate more on specialist pedagogic advice and less on 'theory'.

University departments of education were seen by government in the 1980s as representing the vested interest of a 'liberal' educational establishment opposed to modernization in principle. This view of the universities was of course partly true; it is arguable that they are almost inherently 'conservative'. However, minimizing a role for 'theory' and replacing it by a focus on teachers becoming technically competent practitioners through a form of school-based apprenticeship creates its own problems. An apprenticeship model assumes that the core of any teacher education programme should be the experience of learning to teach in school under the guidance of experienced teachers. An element of apprenticeship has always been at the core of teacher education programmes. However since the 1980s a view has developed that (a) the experience of teaching in a single school could be an adequate model for being prepared to become a teacher; and (b) the knowledge needed by future teachers could be largely based on the experience of trying to teach, watching other teachers and learning from their experience. In other words, learning to teach was seen as a largely practical and experiential process, and in so far as any theory was involved, it would arise from student teachers reflecting on their practice. A further assumption made by policies to reduce the role of universities in teacher education is the devaluing of the importance of student teachers, and teachers more generally, having access to university-based research. The arguments for weakening the links between universities and schools have recently been taken a step further by two educationists, David Hargreaves, a Professor of Education at the University of Cambridge and Chris Woodhead, the Chief Inspector for Schools. Both dismiss most educational research undertaken by universities as largely worthless and propose that funds for educational research which currently go to the universities should be transferred directly to the schools. However, the relatively small budget devoted to university-based educational research would hardly be noticed if it was split up between every school in the country. Furthermore weakening university/school links rather than finding ways of extending them is more likely to make university-based educational research less rather than more able to play a role in improving educational practice.

Shifting the Responsibility for Assessing Teacher Competence

Throughout the period up to the 1980s which I have described as evolutionary modernization, certifying the competence of teachers was delegated to the universities. The formal expression of this was that Qualified Teacher Status (QTS) was confirmed when a student achieved a university awarded Certificate. However, governments of the time increasingly questioned this reliance on academic expertise, especially in the context of public anxiety about levels of literacy and numeracy among young people. Progressively greater controls over university departments of education were introduced. These began with the Council for the Accreditation of Teacher Education (CATE) and the requirement that all initial teacher training courses be inspected by HMI (later OFSTED) and was extended by establishing the Teacher Training Agency (TTA) which has responsibility for the supply and quality of teachers. In other words, the original 'trust' associated with the delegation of the award of QTS to universities has been displaced by new forms of testing and bureaucratic control.

Decentralizing Decisions about the Continuing Professional Development of Teachers

In the 1960s and 1970s there was a considerable expansion of the opportunities for teachers to continue their studies for diplomas and higher degrees during their working life. This expansion of opportunities for the continuing education of teachers was based on a typical 'professional' model. Individual teachers applied to the university to take a course; if their application was accepted by the university, supported by the Headteacher and approved by the Local Education Authority responsible for the school, the course fees and the salary for their replacement was largely paid for by central government. In this process, the possible human resource needs of schools were hardly considered; the focus of further professional development was almost entirely on individual teachers. Towards the end of the 1980s, this 'professional' model was replaced by what might be called an 'institutional' model. Most funds previously allocated to further professional development of teachers became incorporated into individual school budgets which also covered teacher salaries, textbooks and building and maintenance costs. The result has been (a) the virtual disappearance of opportunities for teachers to be released for significant periods of full-time study; (b) a drop in the number of teachers studying for part-time degrees; (c) a shift in the Diploma and Masters courses offered from those based on the educational disciplines towards applied fields such as management and administration; and (d) a substantial increase in the number of short courses organized by individual schools for their own staff.

This shift in the provision of further professional development for teachers from a *professional* model to an *institutional* model has a number of features that relate to the general argument about technological modernization. First, it provides at least a framework, for the first time, for linking teachers professional development to the human resource needs of schools. Second, it can be seen as an extension of the arguments for privatization and deregulation of training provision for the private sector of industry. In other words, schools like businesses are assumed to be in the best position to decide on their own training needs. Third, it assumes that Headteachers and senior managers of schools have the expertise to identify the human resource needs of their schools and see that as part of their role. Fourth, it relies on schools allocating funds for the further professional development of their staff when they are under pressure of short term needs like the replacement of staff and new textbooks. Inevitably, the continuing professional education of their staff is experienced by schools as a longer term and less urgent need and so, in practice, is easily neglected.

To summarize this chapter so far: I have suggested that the reforms of teacher education in the UK since the 1980s which were designed to overcome the weaknesses of the older system can be understood as an example of technocratic modernization. As such they have created as many problems as they have solved. When seen in relation to the far greater regulation of standards and the curriculum that schools now experience, the reforms are in danger of preparing teachers to be technicians, rather than professionals of the future (Young and Guile, 1996). The next section discusses the ways that the concept of reflexive modernization might provide the basis of an alternative.

Towards the Reflexive Modernization of Teacher Education

Earlier in this chapter, I suggested that the distinction between technocratic and reflexive modernization could be expressed in terms of a policy shift from prioritizing *increased control* through more specific evaluation criteria, skill tests and more frequent inspections, to a policy of extending the process of *public learning* both internally amongst those involved professionally in education and in the relations between educational professionals and others with an interest in education, whether voters, employers or parents. It would involve the development of new types of feedback learning between teachers and students, between staff at different levels in a school hierarchy, between schools and their user communities, including parents and local employers, between schools and universities and between the education profession as a whole and the government.

This model of modernization has a number of advantages. First, it would lead to an increase in the 'collective intelligence' of the educational system at every level; this is something that is not achievable through a policy that focuses only on control. Second, it would be part of a policy of making learning a priority for all young people and all citizens, including teachers, throughout their lives; thus it would be a way for the educational community to become part of a learning society and schools becoming learning organizations (see Chapter 10). Third, it points to the importance of bringing together the three elements of teacher education — initial education and training, in-service updating and research and postgraduate study — into a single system rather than seeing them as largely separate. Such a change in approach to teacher education would require the re-thinking of the four issues at the heart of any programme of teacher education referred to earlier in this chapter — the concept of learning, the organization of knowledge in the teacher education curriculum, relationships between schools and universities and the responsibility for accountability and accrediting teacher competence. Each of these issues is now dealt with briefly.

The Concept of Learning in Teacher Education

The reflexive modernization of teacher education would involve rethinking the prevailing concept of learning in teacher education in at least three ways. The first is in relation to what teachers need to learn and how their initial training can prepare them for seeing the promotion of lifelong learning as being at the centre of their future role as teachers. If teachers are to be required to introduce ideas about lifelong learning to their pupils, they too will have to see that lifelong learning will be at the heart of any future teacher professionalism. The second way is in relation to the form and content of learning in teacher education and its location. This would involve identifying those learning objectives achievable through school-based apprenticeship and reflection on experience and those requiring student teachers to have access to systematic bodies of theory and research. Schools generate practical knowledge in their everyday activities which can be the basis for both student and career teachers to learn; however, both groups also need theoretical knowledge in order to be able to conceptualize how to change their practice in response to new demands. Except in exceptional circumstances, this kind of knowledge is unlikely to be produced in the schools. In other words, a new approach to professional learning requires new kinds of relationships between schools and universities. The role of government would be to provide a framework and incentives within which these types of learning and knowledge could be connected by linking initial training and the continuing professional development of teachers. Third, one of the lessons from the critique of technocratic modernization is that while individual teachers and students learn, learning is always a social process. It follows that a major aim of any teacher education reform must be to enhance and extend those 'communities of practice' (Lave and Wenger, 1994) within and between schools, between schools and the communities which they serve and between them and the universities (Guile and Young, 1997a). Another way of expressing this is in the argument that if teachers are to learn from the experience of being in schools, schools themselves have to prioritize learning, not only among their pupils but among their staff; in other words schools must become learning organizations. Furthermore, not only do schools have to become learning organizations; they need to develop new kinds of learning relationships with other organizations, both other specialist learning organizations like other schools and universities and organizations within the local service, retail and productive sectors of the economy.

Knowledge and the Teacher Education Curriculum

The teacher education curriculum associated with evolutionary modernization was based on guided apprenticeship together with a dual system of disciplinarity — the educational disciplines and the subject disciplines of the school curriculum. This dual form of disciplinarity was abolished by the reforms I described earlier and the educational disciplines were replaced by a focus on techniques of transmission and assessment. As a result, teachers have become more effective at raising the level of pupil achievements in specific subjects, as indicated by the steady improvement in public examination results at 16+ and 18+ over the last 10–15 years. However, this narrowing of the teacher education curriculum has limited the opportunities for teachers to develop the intellectual resources to respond to wider economic changes which are giving less emphasis to *subject content* and more to *relations between* subject contents. What is needed is a parallel shift within the teacher education curriculum from insular to connective specialization that I argued for in relation to the post-compulsory curriculum for schools and colleges in Chapter 9. Just as the Advanced Level Curriculum of the Future needs to develop new relationships between school subjects and between them and the world outside of school, so a teacher education curriculum based on connective specialization has to develop a new relationship between the educational disciplines and between them and the practical problems facing teachers. It is through a critical relationship with disciplinary knowledge that teachers will be able to explore their aims and develop the concepts for relating their specialist subjects to other subjects, the curriculum as a whole and its broader educational purposes.

School/University Relationships

Evolutionary modernization replaced the informal school-based apprenticeship that characterized early forms of teacher training with specialist institutions such as teacher training colleges and university departments of education. Technocratic modernization policies attempted to give a bigger role to schools on the grounds of efficiency and greater control. However, this latter shift is occurring at a time when new pressures on schools such as target-setting are insulating them from universities and the wider society, thus making them less appropriate learning contexts for student teachers and for career teachers to develop new skills and knowledge. The logic of reflexive modernization would be that the new demands being made on teachers and the new types of learning needed would need to reverse this trend and be reflected in new forms of partnership between schools and universities (Guile and Young, 1997a).

Accountability and the Responsibility for the Accreditation of Teacher Competence

University-based assessment of the competence of teachers is increasingly likely to be replaced by the external assessment of their teaching skills through national tests. In the search for greater control, the new model removes the element of trust associated with the older 'professional' model which recognized that teachers have to make judgments and be held responsible for them like members of other professions. Reflexive modernization recognizes the weakness of both models. The old model of professional trust was always flawed because it lacked accountability and was liable to become a basis for protecting vested interests and be a barrier to change; furthermore, it did not take account of the ambivalent attitude of the universities to assessing teaching practice. More emphasis was invariably placed on written work than on teaching skills in the process of certification. The new competence model is flawed for quite different reasons. In trying to exclude the element of trust in improving teacher quality, it plays down the extent to which the work of both teacher educators and professional teachers involves making judgments. The alternative is for teams of professional teachers and university-based teacher educators to (a) develop general rather than specific criteria of teaching capabilities as guides to judgments about teacher competence and (b) find ways of extending the 'communities of practice' which underwrite the certification of teachers by including both employers of teachers and users of education — in particular, the business community and parents. Such a policy would lead to a strengthening of the social basis on which teacher educators and professional teachers made their judgments by involving lay as well as professional interests. It would parallel new approaches to involving users in assessing risk management in areas such as genetic engineering and environmental pollution that were referred to earlier in the paper.

Conclusions

The technocratic modernization of teacher education in the UK since the late 1980s has been part of the wider neo-liberal project of successive Conservative governments which has parallels throughout the world. It has demoralized teachers and teacher educators in universities and produced only limited gains in terms of improved teacher effectiveness. It is as yet unclear whether the changes being introduced by the new Labour government are a step further along the road of technocratic modernization or the beginnings of the conditions for a shift to reflexive modernization. The responsibility of those based in universities is not just to critique the bureaucratic character of recent reforms. It is also to articulate real alternatives and how they can raise standards and support a new teacher professionalism which puts learning at the centre of the curriculum of teacher education.

Chapter 12

From the 'New Sociology of Education' to a Critical Theory of Learning

Introduction

Both social and natural scientists face pre-shaped realities in their research, although the forms that the pre-shaping takes are fundamentally different. For the natural scientist, the pre-shaping consists of the conceptualizations of their peers and earlier scientists set against the material nature of the physical and natural world itself. For the social or educational scientist, social and educational realities are doubly pre-shaped, by fellow researchers and more fundamentally by the policy makers and practitioners whose activities constitute the realities being studied. It follows that although the production of new knowledge in both the natural and social sciences involves a dialogue amongst researchers about a reality external to them, the production of new knowledge in the social and educational sciences cannot avoid also being a dialogue with those involved in educational policy and practice and who may or may not be influenced by educational research. Debates within the educational sciences, therefore, are always expressions both of professional differences amongst peers and of real conflicts and dilemmas faced by others practically involved in education, however disconnected the two may in practice appear to be. It is somewhat ironic that we hear so much of the irrelevance of educational research for practice, when that practice cannot avoid being central to the empirical basis of educational research.

Although these differences between the natural and social sciences are often seen as undermining of the status and authority of educational research, they can equally be seen as a strength. There are three reasons for this. First, in attempting to improve their explanations and in exploring alternatives to existing practice and policy, educational researchers do not need to and, indeed, cannot rely only on a dialogue and debate with fellow researchers, as is the case with their colleagues in the natural sciences. They also have recourse, both as data on which to base their theories and as alternative theories, to the understandings of policy makers and practitioners themselves. Second, social and educational researchers have the advantage of their own experience of educational institutions, such as schools, which they share with those who work and study in them. Third, social or education scientists cannot limit the testing of their ideas to refuting the alternative theories of their colleagues. No less important is whether those ideas make sense of dilemmas in policy and practice faced by those involved. In so far as they are involved in changing policy or practice, the ideas of researchers become a part of the reality that they study.

It is this inescapable relationship with practice and policy that makes all educational research a critical inquiry involved in the transformation of practice as well as understanding it (whether this is recognized by those who undertake the research or not). Sociology of education is no exception to this argument. However, perhaps more than other sub-fields, sociology of education has faced difficulties with its relationship to the specific institutional context — schools — which has been its central topic and site for research. It is, I shall suggest, these difficulties which have, at least in part, led to its current state of crisis of role and identity. In the 1990s sociologists of education have appeared split between those concerned to expose the contradictory attempts of successive Conservative governments to marketize public education and those with a more pragmatic involvement in various kinds of policy analysis and evaluation. The relatively coherent theoretical concerns of the 1970s and 1980s have largely disappeared; except in the fragmenting and ultimately incoherent form of post-modernism (Green, 1994). This crisis is best understood, I suggest, in terms of the institutional context within which sociology of education as a sub-discipline arose. In the UK this was in direct response to the expansion of state schooling after World War 2 and to its failure to develop as a democratic public system of education for all. However, sociology of education and mass education have both been part of the same process of modernization and although the former has frequently pointed to the anti-egalitarian outcomes of mass schooling, this has been from a perspective that has broadly supported its continued expansion.

It is this relationship between sociology of education and mass schooling as part of an uncritical acceptance of modernization that I want to focus on through the concept of 'reflexive modernization' developed by Ulrich Beck (1992) and others. He makes a distinction between reflection and reflexivity as two ways in which a critical theory can confront 'the bases of modernization . . . with its consequences'. Whereas for Beck *reflection* describes the 'increases in knowledge (and their impact) on modernization', *reflexivity* refers to self-confrontation with the effects of risk society (Beck's description of modern industrial society) and in particular with its 'autonomous modernization processes which are blind and deaf to their own effects and threats'.

Applying Beck's distinction to the sociology of education, reflection would describe the support that it was assumed sociology of education would provide for the improvement of mass schooling. Reflexivity, on the other hand, means 'self confrontation with the effects of risk society that cannot be dealt with and assimilated in the system of industrial society'. It follows that from the point of view of both sociology of education and mass schooling, a reflexive approach has to start by recognizing that the problems associated with mass schooling cannot, as is sometimes assumed, for example, by the 'school effectiveness movement', be dealt with by improvements in schooling alone. The failure of schools to give a high priority to the conditions for learning is not just a problem of school improvement. It can only be overcome in a learning *society* which privileges learning relationships in *all* spheres and sectors of society (see Chapter 10).

The institutional boundedness of the sociology of education is a product of its location in the context which has been its topic — formal education. Although initially and still, in some senses, a strength, this location has also been a weakness. It has been a strength because it has led to detailed knowledge about 'how educational institutions work'. It has also been a weakness, because its critique of this boundedness has offered little more than the political polemics of Marxist sociologies of education which argue that schools in a capitalist society must inevitably produce alienation, the educational polemics associated with the deschooling arguments of the 1970s, or the theoretical pessimism of the 1990s. The latter view is exemplified by Moore (1996) who argues that it is important to distinguish between sociologies *of* education 'which create knowledge about how education works' and what he calls sociologies *for* education. He sees the latter as having been a feature of many approaches claiming to be critical or radical in the past which, because they took on educators' problems, did little more than 'reproduce them within the theory . . . of sociology of education'.

Moore goes on to argue that 'it is better for (sociology of education) to support schools in doing most effectively *the things they can do best*' (my emphasis). Moore's argument that some sociology of education has tended to over-estimate the capacity of schools to contribute to social transformation is sound. However, by the late 1990s, in a period of accelerating social and economic change in every sphere of life, it is increasingly difficult to be sure what the things are 'that the schools can do best'. In other words, his prescription for schools appears peculiarly a historical and conservative and is tantamount to admitting that sociology of education has very little to offer either to educational practitioners or to policy-makers.

In suggesting that Beck's concepts of reflexivity might offer an alternative and more constructive approach, I want to develop two lines of argument. The first is to go back to the conditions of the emergence of sociology of education as a critical response to the contradictions of mass schooling. I shall suggest that by the late 1990s the crisis in mass schooling has shifted from the problem of selection at 11 or 14 or 16, which to some extent can be solved (as it has in the Nordic countries) by expanding provision, to the problems of knowledge and learning. What I mean is that although schools claim something of a monopoly over young people's learning, they remain far from being effective learning organizations themselves. Similarly, universities have had a similar near monopoly over knowledge production and yet they find it increasingly difficult to respond to the knowledge demands of modern societies. My argument will be that it is in relation to how we promote learning and the production of new knowledge, which are far from limited to a focus on schools and other formal institutions of education, that the future of sociology of education as part of a critical theory must be established. My second line of argument, in disagreement with Moore, is that a sociology *for* education — in the sense that it provides concepts for teachers and other educational practitioners which may enable them to transform their practice — must be the basis for developing a sociology *of* education — one that will produce reliable accounts of 'how education works' and not just elaborated versions of educators' problems.

I shall explore these arguments, first, through commenting briefly on a number of recent trends in educational policy in the UK and the deeper social changes that may underlie them and, second, by suggesting that these new circumstances and the crisis they have generated is both a danger *and an opportunity* for the sociology of education. I shall attempt to show that responding to the roots of this crisis is a sound basis for going beyond the distinction between a sociology of education that claims to explain 'how education works' but has little relation to teachers' practice and one that becomes trapped in their day-to-day professional concerns.

The Differentiation and De-differentiation of Learning

The sociology of education was a response to the process of structural differentiation that led to the massive expansion of specialist educational institutions such as schools and colleges (Halsey, 1958) and to a number of distinct but related tensions. Typical examples of these tensions were the competing demands for resources of different sectors (e.g. schools, colleges and universities) within increasingly differentiated education systems, and the conflicts between the needs of education systems as seen by those who work in them and the demands made on them by economic pressures and various social groups. It is in analysing these tensions that sociology of education as a subdiscipline developed. It formulated analyses of the instrumental and largely reproductive role of educational institutions in industrial societies, the ideological role of state education, the socially selective and divisive role of many assessment, pedagogic and curricula strategies and of the biases in how schools have responded to the diversity of non-school cultures. However, sociology of education has remained a creature of the formal education system and has to a large extent accepted as inevitable the expansion and structural differentiation of education into more specialist institutions, a process which was the condition for its emergence.

However, it is just this process of progressive expansion and structural differentiation of learning into specialist educational institutions and the consequent devaluing of the *informal learning* that goes on inside and outside them that is beginning to be challenged by policy developments of the last decade. The most direct illustration is the way that fears about the costs of the ever increasing proportions of the population involved in post-compulsory education are leading governments to search for ways of shifting those costs and limiting the demand for more schooling. One strategy being adopted in the UK has been to make it easier for people to use their experience to obtain qualifications and not be dependent on the provision of formal education or training. This interest in non-school learning is often associated with the claim, illusory or not, that information technology can improve access to learning as well as reduce costs. However there are deeper changes at work in the global processes of production which bring out the limitations of a policy of continued expansion of specialized learning and knowledge-producing institutions. They point to the need to encourage learning and knowledge production in a much wider range of sites not normally associated with either learning or knowledge production (Gibbons et al., 1994; Young and Guile, 1996) (see Chapter 10).

Evidence of these processes of de-differentiation away from specialist educational institutions takes a number of forms; I shall mention three. The first is the growing enthusiasm for removing the distinctiveness of educational institutions by a variety of attempts to either privatize them or force on them some kind of 'market' or 'business' principles. This is found in some strands of the 'school effectiveness movement' which accept that schools can be accountable in the same way as businesses and that some parallel can be drawn between the ideas of 'core business' and 'core technologies of teaching and learning'. There are two problems with such approaches. First, even in business circles, the 'core business' argument is a matter of debate. There is evidence that what is distinctive about successful, long-surviving companies is not that they retain their same core business but that they retain a distinctive approach to any business. Second, the idea of core technologies implies that teaching and learning are like other technologies, relatively well understood and agreed. Nothing, of course, could be further from the truth.

This de-differentiating trend is also expressed in the succession of educational policies such as the Technical and Vocational Education Initiative, Business Compacts, Education-Business Partnerships and Enterprise in Higher Education, which have been designed to bring education and employment closer together. In some ways, these developments can be seen as examples of the way the UK is catching up, in its own peculiar way, with the way that business ideas were long ago brought into the public schools in the USA (Callaghan, 1972).

A further trend is the increasing emphasis in educational policies on lifelong, work based and experiential learning — all forms of learning which take place *outside* institutions of formal education. The most successful private companies are seen to be becoming 'learning organizations'; schools and colleges are encouraged to copy them, educational policy documents stress learner-centredness and lifelong learning and research programmes are publicized as promoting a learning society.

All these developments can be seen as reflecting a shift from a policy of expanding the provision of formal education that began in the nineteenth century and took off as a worldwide phenomenon in many countries after World War 2. More recent policies have involved limiting the expansion of specialist educational organizations and trying to make existing ones 'more efficient' according to outcome-based performance indicators. Linked to the drive to make schools and colleges more efficient has been the promotion of the educational potential of 'non formal' contexts where if learning takes place, it is at no extra cost to government.

These 'de-differentiation processes' are not unique to formal education — clear parallels can be seen in the closing of psychiatric hospitals and their replacement by 'community care' policies in the health sector. However, there is not the space here to pursue these parallels further. One response might be to challenge the new policies in relation to their claimed outcomes which are more likely to lead to new inequalities, and argue that they need to be reversed and an expansionist approach to schooling continued. However, this would be to accept without question the progressive potential of mass schooling and the continuation of the process of institutional specialization more generally. In keeping with what I referred to earlier as a reflexive approach to modernization and its links with mass schooling, I shall suggest that these 'de-differentiation processes' can be treated as an opportunity, in Beck's terms, to 'confront' the role of mass schooling and its future. Before exploring this point further, I want to consider the impact of one of these de-differentiating trends on the sociology of education — the moves to give a bigger role to schools in the initial and further education of teachers that was discussed in Chapter 11.

The Rise and Fall of Sociology of Education in Educational Studies

The expansion and transformation of educational studies in universities has been critical to the development of the sociology of education at least in the UK (Young, 1990). Educational Studies began as a largely prescriptive and philosophical foundation for preparing future teachers. However, the 1960s saw a period of expansion of education at all levels and a belief that this expansion would be facilitated by an extension of the role of the social sciences in professional education. It followed that a more research-oriented agenda formed the basis for programmes of teacher education from the late 1960s and the growth of sociology of education in educational studies was part of this development. As Karabel and Haley (1977) argued, it was the link with the professional education of teachers that shaped sociology of education in the UK and gave it its particular curricular and pedagogic concerns.

If one takes the view that sociology is able to develop relatively 'objective' knowledge about 'how education works' within a disciplinary mode of knowledge production, then this professional location would appear as a limitation and be likely to distract rather than support research. If, on the other hand, it is recognized that the perspectives of teachers are a major factor in 'how education works' then the relationship between the knowledge generated in sociology of education and the knowledge and attitudes of teachers becomes critical and a link with professional contexts becomes not merely an advantage but a necessity. The involvement of the sociology of education with educational practice in the schools and colleges — both within teacher training programmes and through teachers bringing their professional experiences to their higher degree studies — meant that sociology had a unique opportunity to relate theory and practice. In some cases, it is true, sociologists may have over-identified with the professional and political concerns of teachers, but it would be a mistake to see this as an inevitable outcome of either the location of sociologists of education within institutions involved in teacher training or their involvement with practical pedagogic issues.

From the later half of the 1960s to the early 1980s, sociology of education challenged many of the dominant conceptions of education of the time (see Chapter 3). A retrospective assessment would suggest that, given its links with professional practice, the conditions for sociology of education to play a role in transforming practice were promising but that the theories which were developed were weak. A failure to grasp the contradiction that sociology needed to be both critical *and* supportive of mass education meant that the trans-formative possibilities for the sociology of education collapsed into forms of political pessimism, cultural oppositionism and relativism (depending on the different intellectual roots of the theory). Sociology of education failed to develop the concept of future possibilities that might have been the intellectual basis for genuine educational transformation (Young, 1994).

From the beginning of the 1980s, opportunities for the sociology of education within university Education Departments began to decline. This process reflected overt government prejudice ('there is no such thing as society', said Mrs Thatcher famously and therefore, of course, there was no need for sociology or sociology of education), and the emergence of more practical and skills-oriented approaches to teacher education as well as the increasingly inward-looking theoretical approaches of the sub-discipline itself. The consequence has been that by the end of the 1980s sociology of education had virtually disappeared from the initial training and further professional development of teachers. In the 1990s, some sociologists of education have kept open the idea of a critical dialogue with government policy, especially that concerned with 'marketization', while others have become involved in school effectiveness studies or become trapped in a theoretical pessimism which, as suggested earlier, leads to similar consequences to giving up sociology of education altogether.

This argument about the fate of the sociology of education in the 1980s is parallel to that made earlier in this chapter about the more general process of structural differentiation of education. The twin conditions of an expanding system of mass education and public confidence in the supportive role of the social sciences no longer existed. I want therefore to argue that, if sociology of education is to make a contribution to a critical theory of education, it needs to take as its starting point the new crisis in mass schooling as well as the greater scepticism about the social sciences and to see both as features of a more general crisis in the process of modernization itself. Before suggesting what this might involve, it is useful to consider a division within the sub-discipline that emerged in the conditions of the 1970s. It was in part a product of the specific location of sociology of education in the UK in university Education Departments and the tension between the theoretical demands of the discipline and the practical demands of relating theories and findings to the problems facing teachers in schools and classrooms. The division took the form of differences in theoretical 'focus' and in political 'stance' and the tendency for 'focus' to become separated from 'stance'.

Differences of Focus and Differences of Stance in the Sociology of Education

It was the rapid expansion of the social sciences in an education system uniquely dominated by social class relations that provided the conditions for the sociology of education to 'take off' in the 1960s and 1970s in the UK, both as a research agenda and as a formative part of the curriculum of initial and further professional development of teachers. Two broad theoretical foci at the time can be distinguished; a **contextual** *focus* on classroom practice that was represented in the 'new sociology of education' discussed in Chapter 3 which saw teachers as the main agents of educational transformation, and a **societal** *focus* as in the Marxist analyses of Bowles and Gintis (1976) and others which emphasized the priority of class struggles in the wider society. With hindsight, it is easy to see the theoretical weaknesses of each approach. For example, the 'new sociology of education' over-emphasized the emancipatory role of teachers and neglected other powerful intermediary actors, such as advisers, administrators and head teachers, who might have provided the links between classroom teachers and wider political forces. The major weakness of the Marxist sociology of education, on the other hand, was its concentration on the contradictions of capitalism and the assumptions that they would lead to its collapse; this led Marxists to neglect how capitalism was changing and how these changes were transforming the terms of educational policy debates and struggles.

The location of most sociologists of education not only shaped their theoretical focus, it also shaped their view of the political role of their work — what I refer to here as their political stance. The distinction between 'intellectualist' and 'politicist' stances used by Horton (1968) to describe differences among social anthropologists is also useful in distinguishing between the different stances of sociologists of education. In the 1970s they tended to adopt an *intellectualist* rather than a *politicist* stance to their research. In other words, the priority was on winning battles within the sociology of eduction as a sub-discipline rather than on the broader political implications of their analyses. This *intellectualist* stance that privileged *sociological* questions was important at the time, especially for those working in the Education Departments of universities, where the intellectual culture was often highly prescriptive and framed by unquestioned assumptions about education as a 'good'. There is little doubt, however, that such debates limited the broader role of sociology of education in contributing to debates about policy and practice. Furthermore, it was also an example of taking for granted an intellectual division of labour, in this case the one which separated sociology of education from the other educational disciplines. The questions this account leads to is whether and how, in the new circumstances of the 1990s, these divided foci and stances can be brought together in a more integrated critical education theory. In the next section of this chapter I suggest how the new circumstances are expressed in current policy trends away from a focus on specialized learning organizations such as schools, colleges and universities.

The New Crisis in Mass Schooling: Conditions for Reconstructing a Critical Education Theory for the Twenty-first Century

Two current developments in educational policy have been referred to in this chapter: the recent emphasis on boosting non-formal learning contexts, as exemplified in the growing popularity of ideas such as 'the learning organization', a learning society and lifelong learning discussed in Chapter 10, and the steps to give a bigger role to schools in the preparation of teachers (Chapter 11). In the next two sections, I shall consider these trends in educational policy away from a focus on the specialization of education.

Earlier in this chapter, I pointed to the origins of the sociology of education in the process of modernization and, in particular, its links with the contradictions associated with growth of mass schooling. This link was exemplified in its concern, in the UK, with the social class basis of the selection of students and (later) of curriculum knowledge, and how these processes of selection were extended from social class to other sources of inequality such as gender and race. Although these contradictions still remain as features of public schooling, the circumstances within which they are located have changed. The role of public education itself is under challenge, as is the set of values that have, since the nineteenth century, linked science, modernization, progress and mass schooling. Investment in public education is being reduced and, within a rhetoric of promoting individual choice, anything beyond a minimum of provision of education is not seen as a 'public good' but as something people should be encouraged to buy (or not) if they so wish. Expanding state funded education is no longer seen as an unquestioned part of the democratic political agenda, even for a Labour government.

If sociology of education is to play a role in developing a critical theory in the next decade, it has to relocate itself in this new crisis facing public education and more generally in the crisis facing the process of modernization itself.

The trends that I have referred to as 'de-differentiaton' could have two outcomes. One possibility is that they could be a basis for new forms of stratification as those with wealth and influence ensure the future of their own children through private or quasi-private schools and the remainder have to make do with inferior public provision. This is the educational version of what Hutton (1995) has called the 30:30:40 society. Before elaborating on the possible implications of an alternative to this scenario I shall consider briefly the processes of 'de-differentiation' of learning and knowledge production and the broader trends that underlie them.

Beyond Specialized Learning Organizations

The recent interest in experiential and work-based learning and in the educational role of non-specialist learning organizations such as businesses reflects deep changes in industrial societies. In the short term, it reflects attempts to find ways of reducing the growing costs of public education as the proportion of the population participating in education expands. In the longer term, it highlights two problems for the older industrialized societies as they face increasing global economic competition. The first problem is what Muller (1996) refers to as the 'increasing saliency of knowledge'. This arises from the progressive shift away from natural to human resources as the main determinant of a nation's economic prosperity and from the increasingly short life of new knowledge as it becomes more and more a part of the process of continuous innovation. Formal education, as it has expanded from its nineteenth century beginnings, is not well suited to this new 'saliency' of knowledge. Its modes of knowledge production which are based on the separation of the production of knowledge from its use and symbolized by the academic disciplines, are slow, exclusive and not easily related to quickly changing external demands. The 'knowledge' issue then is concerned with the future of disciplines as the dominant form of knowledge organization which has been the bedrock of the growth of science since the nineteenth century and one of the distinguishing features of both the university and the upper secondary school curriculum in every country in the world.

Gibbons and his colleagues (Gibbons et al., 1994) point to the recent emergence of what they refer to as Mode 2 (or transdisciplinary knowledge) where discipline-based scientists form partnerships with business and community groups to produce knowledge related to specific problems. The demise of the university's monopoly on the production of knowledge, which is indicated by this emergence of transdisciplinary knowledge, created a new set of conflicts. For example, there are conflicts between the 'conservative' academics who want to preserve the disciplinary mode of knowledge production and their autonomy which they see as depending on it (Gibbons et al.'s Mode 1), and the industrial modernizers in governments and business who want to steer knowledge production to commercial, industrial or at least policy-oriented ends (Gibbons et al.'s Mode 2). Should the move towards Mode 2 knowledge production be resisted or encouraged? It is in addressing this question that a critical sociology of education could play an important role. Instead of opting for the position of the industrial modernizers or their opponents, the weaknesses of both positions need to be analysed. Whereas the industrial modernizers appear willing to allow all intellectual activity supported by public funds to be accountable to the demands of commerce and industry, their opponents treat the disciplines — a particular historical mode of knowledge production — as an almost universal condition for the creation of new knowledge. The alternative is to consider the principles that might inform new relationships between disciplinary, transdisciplinary and non disciplinary knowledge, and their links with the broader educational role of the university in public debates about educational priorities.

Just as one of the primary purposes of universities is the production of new knowledge, they also have, together with schools and colleges, a key pedagogic function; they are, of course, organizations which specialize in systematic teaching and learning. However, most university teaching programmes have changed little in form in the last century and still rely on the assumption that learning is a largely individualized process of transmission. More fundamentally, in their failure to treat their mode of teaching as a major research issue, universities have neglected the new research on learning that has demonstrated that it is fundamentally a social process. This has led to a number of problems underlying the crisis in mass education more generally.

First, because the *social* conditions for learning are neglected, more and more educational institutions get trapped in the logic of selection — in other words, they try to choose the students that they think will succeed. As the French sociologist, Pierre Bourdieu has argued so cogently, schools are most successful with those whom they do not have to teach how to learn — such students develop their learning skills and habits elsewhere, usually in the home. The crisis in mass schooling is that schools cannot *on their own* tackle the problem of learning for *all* learners, despite the fact that governments expect them to and modern societies need all their citizens to be learners. The second problem, which is also related to the neglect of the *social* conditions of learning is that, although schools and universities specialize in the learning of their students, they are invariably not learning organizations themselves in the sense of maximizing the opportunities for their staff, teachers and non-teachers, to learn. The third problem facing schools and other specialist learning organizations in trying to promote learning arises from their insular relationship with their environment. One consequence of this insularity is that although most students leave school with improved knowledge and, with some additional skills, they rarely have the skills and motivation to continue learning after they have left school or college. Fourth, in that, both schools and universities lack an explicit theory of learning, teaching and research have become seen as distinct activities with research largely confined to universities. This separation has two consequences; the first is that only when something is designated 'research' is it seen as leading to the production of new knowledge and the second is that universities (and, less surprisingly, schools) invest virtually no resources in research into one of their two main activities, teaching and learning. Whereas universities bring all their considerable critical and intellectual resources to bear on the production of new knowledge, teaching and learning are treated as unproblematic routine activities that are left to be investigated by a few specialists.

Learning has traditionally been neglected by sociologists of education, except by those in the symbolic interactionist tradition, on the mistaken assumption that it is a psychological or at best social psychological issue. However, this assumption has been turned on its head by the American social anthropologist, Jean Lave and others who have developed an approach to learning as *participation in a 'community of practice'* (Lave and Wengler, 1994). The advantage of starting from such a basic definition drawn from anthropological studies is that it is not 'school-centric' and avoids associating learning automatically with teaching. It does not, however, deny that planned pedagogy and systematically organized curricula can assist learning; it merely points out that there is a fundamental social process underlying any successful learning. Another advantage of such a perspective on learning is that it gives priority to learning as a form of *social participation* not, as in school-centric approaches, as a form of *social selection*. Its weakness is that it can play down the importance of *what* is learned, the question that lies at the heart of curriculum debates and the justification of formal schooling. The issue therefore is not to polarize formal/informal or school/non-school centric learning as good or bad, as was a feature of some of the debates in the 1970s inspired by the de-schooling literature. It is to explore and enhance the diverse forms of 'community of practice' both within and external to schools, colleges and universities and the extent to which they create or inhibit opportunities for what Yrjo Engestrom, calls 'expanded learning' (Engestrom, 1994) (see Chapter 10).

Having argued that knowledge and learning are the major issues in the current crisis in schooling, the next section of the chapter returns to the role of the university and of disciplinary knowledge such as the sociology of education, as a basis of a critical theory of education.

Critical Theory and the Re-professionalization of Teachers

The 1960s and the 1970s saw the progressive upgrading and expansion of teacher education in the UK — from two to three and four year courses. An increasingly graduate profession and the growing number of teachers obtaining Masters degrees in Education were also signs of the same trend. Student teachers were encouraged to be critical of educational institutions as well as to become competent practitioners. Why did this integration come to a halt? Two developments, I suggest, were important. First, teachers and university education departments in particular became victims of a more general government attack on the professions as vested interests, and, second, there was a growing awareness that student teachers were not developing the knowledge and skills that they needed to deal with the increasingly complex problems that they faced in the classroom. In other words, universities showed themselves better at enabling teachers to develop critiques of current policy than at helping them develop their pedagogic competence. Any possible integration of the two elements of professional development was impossible in the political climate of the time as teaching competence became increasingly narrowly defined.

The demise of disciplinary knowledge in teacher education was part of a more general demand discussed earlier for more immediate and relevant knowledge; in this case the demand related specifically to classroom practice. However, the attempt to replace knowledge with skills failed to recognize that the problem of relevance is not just one of content or about skills rather than knowledge. It is a question of the relationships between universities and the schools and between the different kinds of knowledge generated in the two contexts. University-based research generates knowledge *about education* that relates to general principles and trends but not to specific contexts, even when it arises from research that takes place in classrooms. Educational knowledge generated from professional experience relates to individual pupils and aspects of the curriculum as it is experienced in specific schools, although it may have wider relevance. The solution to the problem of relevance is not, as in the policies of the 1980s and the 1990s, to reject the disciplinary knowledge but to create opportunities for interrogating it from the point of view of teachers' professional knowledge and vice versa. Educational research and the professional education of teachers are both dialogues between theory and practice, albeit with different but complementary purposes.

The wider demands being made on teachers as a result of the greater delegation of responsibility to schools means that their initial professional education will need to be broader rather than narrower and schools will have to give more emphasis to the further professional development of their teachers. This does not suggest a return to specialist higher degrees in the educational disciplines that flourished in the 1970s. However, it is difficult to see schools, on their own, responding to the issues of knowledge and learning raised earlier. Whether sociology of education plays a role in these developments will in part depend on the extent to which it is willing to drop its previous insular definition of its specialist role. Some indications of what might be involved are suggested in the final section of the chapter.

Conclusion — Towards a Critical Theory of Learning

Sociology of education began as a form of critical theory — raising questions about one of the major institutions of modern societies — mass education. In the UK, it considered the extent to which as mass education developed, selection and social control took precedence over democratic participation.

Sociology of education has been in decline since the 1980s in the UK, largely a result of an increasingly unfavourable political climate. However, its own internal tensions have played a part as has its largely uncritical acceptance of the structural differentiation of educational knowledge into a range of insular educational disciplines.

I have argued that, in the 1990s, global social changes and the beginning of a process of de-differentiation of institutions to which they have led have given rise to a number of quite new problems to which neither formal education institutions, in practical terms, nor the existing educational disciplines as sources of theory, have been equipped to respond. I have identified these issues as the promotion of learning in the society as a whole and the production of new knowledge that is not bounded by traditional modes of knowledge production. Both pose dilemmas for specialist learning organizations such as schools, colleges and universities, as both imply the end of what has been their near monopoly of planned learning and new knowledge production. Specialist learning organizations have no alternative but to develop new relationships with other types of organization.

By conceptualizing learning as linked to rather than separate from the production of knowledge and by recognizing that, although learning is a social process not bounded by specific institutional contexts, there are some forms of learning that require specialist learning institutions, the principle of connective specialization developed in earlier chapters points to new possibilities for schools and colleges in establishing relationships with non-specialist learning organizations in an increasingly learning-oriented society. It follows that a focus on learning rather than on institutions such as schools, subjects or curricula, must be at the centre of a critical education theory of the future. The main elements of such a theory would need to be that:

- it has a concept of the future and of education in relation to a vision of a society of the future;
- it connects rather than insulates the concepts and approaches developed by the different educational disciplines;
- it gives primacy to the issues of learning and the production of new knowledge;
- it has an educational purpose associated with realizing the emancipatory potential of learning for all people throughout their lives;
- it is critical in relation to the expansion of mass schooling and formal education generally as well as of the limits of learning in workplaces and communities.

The challenges facing education in the UK, which such a theory has to take up are far more complex than the contradictions of mass schooling that faced the early sociology of education and it is for this reason that the insular disciplinarity which developed in the 1960s and 1970s has no place in the future of educational studies. Some of these challenges are:

- developing criteria for bringing together the insights of different disciplinary approaches to learning;
- identifying the possible consequences of policy shifts away from expanding opportunities for formal learning and the new forms of stratification that they may give rise to;
- incorporating the concepts of 'learning as social participation' and 'community of practice' into schools, colleges and universities and their relationships with other types of organizations where learning takes place;
- exploring the different ways that school and non-school learning and disciplinary and non-disciplinary knowledge can be related to and enhance each other.

This is a considerable research agenda and depends on a quite new meaning being given to making education the highest political priority. However the educational issues facing all societies at the end of the twentieth century are no less considerable.

Notes

1 It is a paradox of the English educational system that those who would appear to be most in need of education get least of it.

2 In comparing university curricula in the USA, USSR and UK, among other countries, shows wide variations in the criteria on which knowledge is stratified in different countries.

3 There are problems in the use of the term 'abstract' because it can presuppose some kind of absolute notion of what is 'abstract', and can neglect the way in which one can have different 'kinds of abstraction', some of which may be 'labelled' concrete by others using different 'abstraction' criteria (Horton, 1968).

4 English Literature, English Language, Mathematics, French, German, Latin, History, Geography, Physics, Chemistry, Biology.

5 The concept of 'New Vocationalism' as 'behavioural occupationalism' is explored by Moore (1988).

6 Moore (1988).

7 A detailed analysis of the process of division and reform of qualifications in the UK can be found in Spours (1988).

8 Some of the most innovative developments across the social and natural sciences and engineering have taken place in higher education. Not only are the pressures to be selective so much less than in schools, but the tradition of academic freedom has limited the scope of direct government involvement.

9 Using different terminology, Raffe (1992) describes any use of modules that does not change the relationship between qualifications as an *integrative* strategy in which modules are regarded as:

> a convenient unit within which to develop alternative pedagogic approaches.
> For example, a module might be based on an activity or project designed
> to develop specific skills or capabilities.

10 A well known example of an organizational view of ethos is that adopted by the authors of *15,000 Hours* (Rutter et al., 1979).

11 An important research question is the extent to which the autonomy of Examining and Validating Bodies will be reduced or extended by the recent merging NCVQ and SCAA to form the QCA. This question and the issue of qualification change more generally is being explored in the ESRC funded 'Unified Learning Project', which is co-directed by David Raffe, Centre for Educational Sociology, University of Edinburgh, and the author. [ESRC (L1235 1039)]

12 At the time of revising this chapter, the extent of the crisis in Asian financial institutions is unclear and its wider implications are far from certain.

References

ACKER, S. (1981) 'No-woman's land: British sociology of education 1960–1979', *Sociological Review*, **29**, 1.

ADONIS, A. and POLLARD, S. (1997) *A Class Act*, London: Hamish Hamilton.

AINLEY, P. (1994) 'Two roads to modernisation: Two versions of a learning society', (unpublished mimeo; Post-16 Education Centre, Institute of Education).

ANDERSON, P. (1969) 'Patterns of national culture', in COCKBURN, A and ANDERSON, P. (eds.) *Student Power*, Harmondsworth: Penguin.

ANTIKAINEN, A., HOUTSEN, J., KAUPPILA, J. and HUOTELIN, H. (1996) *Living in a Learning Society*, London and Washington DC: Falmer Press.

APPLE, M. (1979) *Ideology and Curriculum*, London: Routledge and Kegan Paul.

ASSOCIATION FOR COLLEGES, THE GIRL'S SCHOOL ASSOCIATION, THE HEADMASTERS' CONFERENCE, THE SECONDARY HEADS ASSOCIATION, THE SIXTH FORM COLLEGES' ASSOCIATION, THE SOCIETY FOR HEADMASTERS AND HEADMISTRESSES IN INDEPENDENT SCHOOLS (1994) *Post-compulsory Education and Training: A Joint Statement*, London: Association of Colleges.

BARNETT, C. (1987) *The Audit of War*, London: Macmillian.

BARTHOLOMEW, J. (1977) 'The schooling of teachers: The myth of the liberal college', in WHITTY, G. and YOUNG, M. (eds.) *Explorations in the Politics of School Knowledge*, Driffield: Nafferton Books.

BECK, U. (1972) *Risk Society*, London: Sage.

BECK, U., GIDDENS, A. and LASH, S. (1994) *Reflexive Modernisation*, Cambridge: Polity Press.

BERNSTEIN, B. (1971) *Class, Codes and Control* Vol 1, London: Routledge.

BERNSTEIN, B. (1973) 'On the curriculum', in *Class, Codes and Control* Vol 3, London: Routledge.

BIRKE, B., BLUMBERGER, W., BREMER, R. and HEIDEGGER, G. (1998) 'Enhancing vocational programmes in Austria and Germany', in LASONEN, J. and YOUNG, M. (eds.) *Strategies for Achieving Parity of Esteem in European Secondary Education*, University of Jyväskylä, Finland: Institute for Educational Research.

BLAUG, M. and GANNICOTT, K. (1969) 'Manpower forecasting since Robbins: A science lobby in action', *Higher Education Review*, Autumn, **2**, 1.

BLOOR, D. (1973) 'Wittgenstein and Mannheim on the sociology of mathematics', *Studies in the History and Philosophy of Science*, **4**.

BOWLES, S. and GINTIS, H. (1976) *Schooling for Capitalist America*, New York: Basic Books.

BRITISH TELECOM (1993) *Matching Skills: Report of a Collaborative Project*, London: British Telecom.

BROWN, P. and LAUDER, H. (1991) (eds.) *Education and Economic Survival: From Fordism to Post-Fordism*, London: Routledge.

BROWN, P. and LAUDER, H. (1995) 'Post Fordist possibilities: Education, training and national development', in BASH, L. and GREEN, A. (eds.) *Youth, Education and Work, World Yearbook of Education*, London: Kogan Page.

BURCHELL, H. (1992) 'Reforming the advanced level curriculum', *Educational Studies*, **18**, 1.

BURKE, J. (ed.) (1994) *Outcomes and the Curriculum*, London: Falmer Press.

CALLAHAN, R. (1972) *Education and the Cult of Efficiency*, Palo Alto: Stanford University Press.

CARR, W. (1995) *For Education: Towards Critical Education Enquiry*, Buckingham: Open University Press.

CASTELLS, M. (1989) *The Informational City*, Oxford: Blackwell.

CASTELLS, M. (1996) *The Rise of the Networked Society*, Oxford: Blackwell.

CBI (1989) *Towards a Skills Revolution*, London: Confederation of British Industry.

CBI (1993) *Routes for Success-Careerships: A strategy for All 16–19 Learning*, London: Confederation of British Industry.

COHEN, P. (1984) *The New Vocationalism*, Occasional Paper 2, Centre for Vocational Studies, London: Institute of Education, University of London.

COLLINS, R. (1979) *The Credential Society*, New York: Academic Press.

COX, C.B. and DYSON, A.E. (1969a) *The Fight for Education*, Black Paper 1, Critical Quarterly.

COX, C.B. and DYSON, A.E. (1969b) *The Crisis in Education*, Black Paper 2, Critical Quarterly.

CROMBIE WHITE, R., PRING, R. and BROCKINGTON, D. (1995) *Education and Training: Implementing a Unified System of Learning*, London: Royal Society of Arts.

DEPARTMENT FOR EDUCATION AND EMPLOYMENT (1997) *Qualifying for Success*, London: HMSO.

DEPARTMENT FOR EDUCATION AND SCIENCE (1968) *The Dainton Report*, London: HMSO.

DEPARTMENT FOR EDUCATION AND SCIENCE (1988) *Advancing A Levels: Report of the Committee Chaired by Professor Higginson*, London: HMSO.

DEPARTMENT FOR EDUCATION/DEPARTMENT FOR EMPLOYMENT/WELSH OFFICE (1991) *Education and Training for the 21st Century*, London: HMSO.

DEPARTMENT OF TRADE AND INDUSTRY (1995) *Competitiveness White Paper: Forging Ahead*, London: HMSO.

DONALD, J. (1992) *Sentimental Education*, London: Verso.

DORE, R. (1976) *The Diploma Disease*, London: Allen and Unwin.

ENGESTROM, Y. (1991) 'Non scolae sed vitae discimus: Towards overcoming the encapsulation of school learning', *Learning and Instruction*, **1**, p. 243.

ENGESTROM, Y. (1994) *Training for Change: A New Approach to Instruction and Learning in Working Life*, Geneva: ILO.

ENTWHISTLE, H. (1979) *Antonio Gramsci: Conservative Schooling for Radical Politics*, London: Routledge and Kegan Paul.

FINEGOLD, D. and SOSKICE, D. (1988) 'The failure of training in Britain: Analysis and prescription', *Oxford Review of Economic Policy*, **4**, 3.

FINEGOLD, D., KEEP, E., MILIBAND, D., RAFFE, D., SPOURS, K. and YOUNG, M. (1990) *A British Baccalaureate: Overcoming Divisions Between Education and Training*, London: Institute for Public Policy Research.

FLOUD, J., HALSEY, A.H. and MARTIN, F. (1957) *Social Class and Educational Opportunity*, London: Heinemann.

FORQUIN, J.C. (1983) 'La Nouvelle Sociologie d'education en Grand Bretagne: Orientations, apports theoriques, evolution (1970–1980)', *Rev. Fr.de Pedagogique*, Avril-Juin.

FRIERE, P. (1971) *Pedagogy of the Oppressed*, Harmondsworth: Penguin.

FURTHER EDUCATION DEVELOPMENT AGENCY, INSTITUTE OF EDUCATION AND THE NUFFIELD FOUNDATION (1997) *GNVQs (1993–1997) Final Report of a National Survey*, London: FEDA.

FURTHER EDUCATION UNIT (1992) *A Basis for Credit? Developing a Post-16 Credit Accumulation Transfer Framework*, London: FEU.

FURTHER EDUCATION UNIT (1993) *Discussing Credit: A Collection of Occasional Papers*, London: FEU.

FURTHER EDUCATION UNIT (1995) *A Framework for Credit Framework Guidelines: Levels, Credit Value and the Award of Credit*, London: FEU.

GIBBONS, M., LIMOGES, C., NOWOTNY, H., SCHWARTZMAN, S., SCOTT, P. and TROW, M. (1994) *The New Production of Knowledge*, London: Sage.

GIDDENS, A. (1994) *Beyond Left and Right*, Cambridge: Polity Press.

GLASS, D. (1954) *Social Mobility in Britain*, London: Routledge and Kegan Paul.

GLEESON, P. (1991) (ed.) *Training and Its Alternatives*, Buckingham: Open University Press.

GOODMAN, P. (1969) 'The present moment in education', *New York Review of Books*, April.

GOODSON, I. (1987) *School Subjects and Curriculum Change*, Lewes: Falmer Press.

GOODY, J. and WATT, I. (1962) 'The consequences of literacy', *Comparative Studies in History and Society*, **V**, 3.

GORBUTT, D. (1970) Subject choice and the 'swing from science' a sociological critique, MA Thesis, University of London.

GORBUTT, D. (1972) 'The "New sociology of education"', *Education for Teaching*, **89**.

GRAMSCI, A. (1971) *Selections from the Prison Notebooks* (Edited and Translated by Quentin Hoare and Geoffrey Nowell Smith), London: Lawrence and Wishart.

GREEN, A. (1984) 'Education and training: Under new masters', in DONALD, J. and WOLPE, A.M. (eds.) *Is Anyone Here From Education?* London: Pluto.

GREEN, A. (1990) *Education and State Formation*, Basingstoke: Macmillian.

GREEN, A. (1991) *The Reform of Post-16 Education and Training*, Post-16 Education Centre, Working Paper II, Post-16 Education Centre London: Institute of Education, University of London.

GREEN, A. (1993) *Educational Achievement in Britain, France, Germany and Japan: A Comparative Analysis*, Post-16 Education Working Paper 14, Post-16 Education Centre London: Institute of Education, University of London.

GREEN, A. (1994) 'Post modernism and state education', *Journal of Education Policy*, **9**, 1 pp. 67–83.

GREEN, A. and STEADMAN, H. (1993) *Educational Provision, Educational Attainment, and the Needs of Industry*, Report No. 5. National Institute for Economic and Social Research.

GREENE, M. (1971) 'Curriculum and consciousness', *The Record*, **F3**, 2.

GUILE, D. (1995) *Work Related Learning and A Level Science*, Post-16 Education Centre, London: Institute of Education, University of London.

GUILE, D. and YOUNG, M. (1997a) Reflexivity, knowledge and learning: The challenge for specialist and non-specialist learning organisations (forthcoming).

GUILE, D. and YOUNG, M. (1997b) 'The question of learning and learning organisations', in KELLEHER, M. (ed.) *Understanding Organisations*, Oak Tree Press.

HALES, M. (1978) *Living Thinkwork*, London: Conference of Socialist Economists Books.

HALL, S. (1983) 'Education in crisis', in DONALD, J. and WOLPE, A. (eds.) *Is There Anyone Here From Education?* London: Pluto.

HALSEY, A.H., RIDGE, I.M. and HEATH, A.F. (1980) *Origins and Destinations*, London: Clarendon.

HALSEY, A.H. (1958) 'Trend Report: Sociology of Education', *Current Sociology*, **6**.

HANDY, C. (1994) *The Empty Raincoat*, London: Hutchinson.

HICKOX, M. and MOORE, R. (1991) 'Post Fordism and education', in BROWN, P. and LAUDER, H. (eds.) *Education and Economic Survival: From Fordism to Post-Fordism*, London: Routledge.

HIRST, P. (1969) 'The logic of the curriculum', *Journal of Curriculum Studies*, **1**, 2, May.

HIRST, P. and THOMPSON, K. (1996) 'Globalisation: Ten frequently asked questions and some surprising answers', *Soundings*, **4**, pp. 47–67.

HODGSON, A. (1997) 'Building institutional capability for the national reform: The case of the formative value-added system', in HODGSON, A. and SPOURS, K. (eds.) *Dearing and Beyond*, London: Kogan Page.

HODGSON, A. and SPOURS, K. (eds.) (1997) *Dearing and Beyond*, London: Kogan Page.

HOLT, M. (1979) 'Why N and F had to die', *Education*, 6 July.

HORTON, R. (1968) 'Neo-Tylorianism: Sound sense or sinister nonsense?' *MAN(NS)* **3**.

HURD, G. and CONNELL, I. (1988) Media studies and the cultural industries, unpublished manuscript.

HUTCHINS, R. (1970) *The Learning Society*, Harmondsworth: Penguin.

HUTTON, W. (1995) *The State We are IN*, London: Vintage Books.

ILLICH, I. (1971) *Deschooling Society*, Harmondsworth: Penguin.

INMAN, S. and BUCK, M. (1995) (eds.) *Adding Value? Schools Responsibility for Personal and Social Development*, Stoke on Trent: Trentham Books.

INSTITUTE OF DIRECTORS (1991) *Performance and Potential, Education and Training for a Market Economy*, London: Institute of Directors.

INSTITUTE OF EDUCATION (1997) *Response to Qualifying for Success*, London: Institute of Education, University of London.

JAMIESON, I., MILLER, A. and WATTS, T. (1988) *Mirrors of Work: Workplace Simulations in Schools*, Lewes: Falmer Press.

JESSUP, G. (1991) *Outcomes: NVQs and the Emerging Model of Vocational Education and Training*, London: Falmer Press.

JOHNSON, R. (1980) 'Really useful knowledge', in CLARKE, J. et al. (eds.) *Working Class Culture*, London: Hutchison.

KARABEL, J. and HALSEY, A.H. (1977) *Power and Ideology and Education*, Oxford: Oxford University Press.

KEDDIE, N. (1971) 'Classroom knowledge', in YOUNG, M. (ed.) *Knowledge and Control*, London: Collier-Macmillan.

KEDDIE, N. (1973) *Tinker . . . Tailor: The Myth of Cultural Deprivation*, Harmondsworth: Penguin.

KIVINEN, O. and RINNE, R. (1992) *Educational Strategies in Finland in the 1990's*, University of Turku, Finland: Research Unit for the Sociology of Education.

KRESS, G. (1995) *Writing the Future: English and the Making of a Culture of Innovation*, Sheffield: NATE.

LABOUR PARTY (1995) *Aiming Higher: Labour's Plans for Reform of the 14–19+ Curriculum*, London: Labour Party.

LADWIG, J. (1996) *Academic Distinctions*, London: Routledge.

LASONEN, J. (ed.) (1996) *Surveys of Strategies for Post-16 Education to Improve Parity of Esteem for Initial Vocational Education in Eight European Countries*, University of Jyväskylä, Finland: Institute for Educational Research.

LASONEN, J. and YOUNG, M. (1998) *Strategies for Achieving Parity of Esteem in European Secondary Education*, University of Jyväskylä, Finland: Institute for Educational Research.

LAVE, J. (1993) 'The practice of learning', in CHAIKLEN, S. and LAVE, J. (eds.) *Understanding Practice*, Cambridge: Cambridge University Press.

LAVE, J. and WENGLER, E. (1994) *Situated Learning: Legitimate Peropheral Participation*, Cambridge: Cambridge University Press.

LAYTON, D. (1973) *Science for the People*, London: Allen and Unwin.

LENEY, T. and SPOURS, K. (1996) *A Comparative Analysis of the Submissions and Responses of the Educational Professional Associations to the Dearing Review*, Mimeo, Post-16 Education Centre, London: Institute of Education, University of London.

LISTER, I. (1974) *Deschooling: A Reader*, Cambridge: Cambridge University Press.

LYNCH, G. (1974) Ideology and the social organisation of educational knowledge in England and Scotland 1840–1920, MA Dissertation, Institute of Education, University of London.

MARSHALL, R. and TUCKER, M. (1993) *Thinking for a Living: Education and the Wealth of Nations*, New York: Basic Books.

MATHEWS, J. (1989) *Tools for Change: New Technology and the Democratisation of Work*, Sydney, Australia: Pluto Press.

MATHEWS, J., HALL, G. and SMITH, H. (1988) 'Towards flexible skill formation and technological literacy: Challenges facing the education system', *Economic and Industrial Democracy*, **9**, 4.

MATHIESON, M. (1992) 'From Crowther to core skills', *Oxford Education Review*, **18**, 3.

McCULLOCH, G. (1995) 'From education to work: The case of technical schools', in BASH, L. and GREEN, A. (eds.) *Youth, Education and Work*, World Yearbook of Education, London: Kogan Page.

McPHERSON, A. (1969) ' "Swing from science" retreat from reason?', *Universities Quarterly*, Winter.

MEAD, M. (1938) 'Our educational emphases in primitive perspective', *American Journal of Sociology*, **43**.

MILLS, C.W. (1939) 'On the methodological consequences of the sociology of knowledge', *American Journal of Sociology*, **XLVI**, 3.

MINISTRY OF EDUCATION (1959) *15 to 18: Report of the Central Advisory Council for Education*, (Vol. 1), London: HMSO.

MOORE, R. (1988) 'The correspondence principle and the radical sociology of education', in COLE, M. (ed.) *Bowles and Gintis Revisited*, London: Falmer Press.

MOORE, R. (1996) 'Back to the future: The problem of change and the possibilities of advance in the sociology of education', *British Journal of the Sociology of Education*, **17**, 2, pp. 145–61.

MORGAN, G. (1988) *Images of Organisation*, London: Sage.

MULLER, J. (1996) 'The making of knowledge', Paper presented at a conference on the future of higher education in South Africa, Capetown, February.

MURRAY, R. (1988) 'Life after Henry (Ford)', *Marxism Today*, 3 October.

NATIONAL EDUCATION COMMISSION (1992) *Towards a Well Qualified Workforce*, London: NCE.

NOBLE, D. (1979) 'Social choice in machine design: The case of numerically controlled machine tools', in ZIMBALIST, A. (ed.) *Case Studies in the Labour Process*, Monthly Review Press.

NOBLE, D. (1993) Let them eat skills: Essay review of Marshall and Tucker's Thinking for Living. (Unpublished mimeo, University of Rochester, New York).

OFSTED/AUDIT COMMISSION (1993) *Unfinished Business*, London: OFSTED/Audit Commission.

PATEMAN, T. (1971) *Countercourse*, Harmondsworth: Penguin.

PILKINGTON, P. (1991) *End Egalitarian Delusion*, London: Centre for Policy Studies.

PIORE and SABEL, C. (1984) *The Second Industrial Divide: Possibilities for Prosperity*, New York: Basic Books.

POWER, S. (1991) 'Pastoral care as curricular discourse: A study in the reformulation of "academic" schooling', *ISSE*, **1**, pp. 193–208.

PRING, R. (1972) 'Knowledge out of control', *Education for Teaching*, Autumn, 89.

PROSPECT CENTRE (1991) *Growing an Innovative Workforce*, Kingston: Prospect Centre.

RAFFE, D. (1984) 'Education and training policy initiatives (14–18) content and context' in WATTS, A.G. (ed.) *Education and Training; Policy and Practice*, Cambridge, CRAC.

RAFFE, D. (1992a) *Modular Strategies for Overcoming Academic/Vocational Divisions*, University of Jyvaskyla, Finland: Institute for Educational Research.

RAFFE, D. (1992b) *The New Flexibility in Vocational Education*, Netherlands: University of Twente.

RAFFE, D. et al. (1992) *Modularisation in Initial Vocational Training: Recent Developments in Six European Countries*, University of Edinburgh: Centre for Educational Sociology.

RAFFE, D., HOWIESON, C., SPOURS, K. and YOUNG, M. (1997) 'Unifying academic and vocational learning: English and Scottish Approaches', *British Journal of Education and Work*, **10**, 1.

RAINBOW, R. (1993) 'Post-compulsory education and a national certificate and diploma framework', in TAIT, T. (ed.) *Discussing Credit*, London: FEU.

RANSON, S. (1984) 'Towards a new tertiary tripartism', in BROADFOOT, P. (ed.) *Selection, Certification and Control*, London: Falmer Press.

RANSON, S. (1992) 'Towards the learning society', *Educational Management and Administration*, **20**, 2.

REEDER, D. (1979) 'A recurring debate: Education and industry', in BERNBAUM, G. (ed.) *Schooling in Decline*, London: Methuen.

REICH, R. (1991) *The Work of Nations: Preparing for 21st Century Capitalism*, London: Simon and Schuster.

RICHARDSON, W., SPOURS, K., WOOLHOUSE, J. and YOUNG, M. (1995) *Current Developments in Modularity and Credit*, Learning for The Future Working Paper 5, Post-16 Education Centre, London and Warwick: Institute of Education, University of London, and Centre for Education and Industry, University of Warwick.

ROBERTSON, D. (1993) 'Credit frameworks: An international comparison', in FURTHER EDUCATION UNIT *Discussing Credit: A Collection of Occasional Papers*, London: FEU.

ROBERTSON, D. (1994) *Choosing to Change: Extending Access Choice and Mobility in Higher Education*, London: HEQC.

ROWE, G. and WHITTY, G. (1993) 'Five themes remain in the shadows', *Times Educational Supplement*, 9 April.

ROYAL SOCIETY (1991) *Beyond GCSE*, A Report by a Working Group of the Royal Society's Education Committee, London: The Royal Society.

RUTTER, M. (1979) *15000 Hours*, London. Open Books.

SASSOON, A. (1988) *Gramsci's Politics*, London: Hutchinson.

SCAA (1996) *Review of Qualifications for 16–19 Year Olds*, Sir Ron Dearing, London: School Curriculum and Assessment Authority.

SCOTTISH OFFICE EDUCATION DEPARTMENT (1994) *Higher Still: Opportunity for All*, Edinburgh: HMSO.

SEAC/SCAA (1993) *SEAC Sets the Standard for Modular A-Levels*, DFE Press Notice.

SHACKLETON, J. (1988) 'The professional role of the lecturer', in FEU. *Planning the FE Curriculum: Implications of the 1988 Education Reform Act*, London: FEU.

SHARP, R. (1975) *Knowledge, Ideology and the Politics of Schooling*, London: Routledge and Kegan Paul.

SILVER, H. and BRENNAN, J. (1988) *A Liberal Vocationalism*, London: Methuen.

SIMON, J. (1975) 'New direction sociology and comprehensive schooling', *Forum*, **7**, 1.

SMITHERS, A. (1994) 'The paradox of A-Levels', *The Curriculum Journal*, **5**, 3.

SMITHERS, A. and ROBINSON, P. (1993) *General Studies: Breadth at A-Level?* London: Engineering Council.

SPARKES, J. (1994) *The Education of Young People Aged 14–18 Years: Learning for Success*, London: Royal Academy of Engineering/National Commission on Education.

SPOURS, K. (1992) *Recent Developments in Qualifications at 14+ Post-16 Education Centre Working Paper*, London: Institute of Education, University of London, London.

SPOURS, K. (1995a) *Post 16 Participation, Attainment and Progression, Post Education Centre Working Paper 17*, London: Institute of Education, University of London.

SPOURS, K. (1995b) *Post-Compulsory Education and Training: Statistical Trends*, Learning for the Future Working Paper 7, Post-16 Education Centre, London and Warwick: Institute of Education, University of London and Centre for Education and Industry, University of Warwick.

SPOURS, K. (1997) 'GNVQs and the future of broad vocational qualifications', in HODGSON, A. and SPOURS, K. (eds.) *Dearing and Beyond*, London: Kogan Page.

SPOURS, K. and YOUNG, M. (1988) 'Beyond vocationalism: A new perspective on the relationship between education and work', *British Journal of Education and Work*, January, **2**, 2.

SPOURS, K. and YOUNG, M. (1994) *Enhancing the Post 16 Curriculum: Value-Added Perspectives*, Centre Report 10, Post-16 Education Centre, London: Institute of Education, University of London, London.

SPOURS, K. and YOUNG, M. (1996) *Institutional Responses to the Dearing Report* (unpublished), Post-16 Education Centre, Institute of Education, University of London.

SPRADBERRY, J. (1976) 'Pupil resistance to curriculum change: The case of the mathematics for majority project', in WHITTY, G. and YOUNG, M. (eds.) *Explorations in the Politics of School Knowledge*, Driffield: Nafferton Books.

STEWART, J. (1996) 'Thinking collectively in the public domain', *Soundings*, **4**, pp. 213–23.

STRAIN, M. and FIELD, J. (1997) 'On the myth of the learning society', *British Journal of Educational Studies*, **45**, 2.

TAIT, T. (ed.) (1993) *Discussing Credit*, London: Further Education Unit.

TANGUY, L. (1991) *Quelle formation pour les Ouvriers et les Employeés en France*, Paris: La Documentation Francais.

TROTTIER, C. (1987) 'La "nouvelle" sociologie de l'education en Grande-Brettagne: Un movement de pensee en voie de dissolution?' *Rev. Fr de Pedagogie*, 78.·

UNTERHALTER, E. and YOUNG, M. (1995) 'Human resource development in post apartheid South Africa', in BASH, L. and GREEN, A. (eds.) *Youth, Education and Work* World Year Book of Education, London: Kogan Page.

VULLIAMY, G. (1976) What counts as school music? in WHITTY, G. and YOUNG, M. *Explorations in the Politics of School, Knowledge*, Driffield: Nafferton Books.

WALDEN, G. (1996) *We Should Know Better*, Fourth Estate.

WATSON, J. (1991) *The French Baccalaureate Professionale*, Working Paper 9, Post 16 Education Centre, London and Warwick: University of London and the Centre for Education and Industry, University of Warwick.

WEBER, M. (1952) *Essays in Sociology*, Translated and edited by H. Gerth and C.W. Mills, London: Routledge.

WEINER, M. (1980) *English Culture and the Decline of the Industrial Spirit, 1850–1980*, Cambridge: Cambridge University Press.

WEXLER, P. (1983) *Beyond Equality*, New York: Bobbs Merril.

WEXLER, P. (1988) unpublished paper presented at AERA Annual Meeting, New Orleans, USA, April.

WHITE, J. and YOUNG, M. (1975) 'The sociology of knowledge (Part 1)', *Education for Teaching*, 98.

WHITE, J. and YOUNG, M. (1976) 'The sociology of knowledge (Part 2)', *Education for Teaching*, 99.

WHITTY, G. (1974) 'Sociology and the problem of radical educational change', in FLUDE, M. and AHIER, J. *Educability, Schools and Ideology*, London: Croom Helm.

WHITTY, G. (1986) *Sociology and School Knowledge*, London: Methuen.

WHITTY, G., ROWE, G. and AGGLETON, P. (1994) 'Subjects and themes in the secondary school curriculum', *Research Papers in Education*, 9, 2 pp. 159–81.

WHITTY, G. and YOUNG, M. (1976) *Explorations in the Politics of School Knowledge*, Driffield: Nafferton Books.

WILLIAMS, R. (1961) *The Long Revolution*, London: Chatto and Windus.

WILMOTT, J. (1983) 'The post-16 CAT framework and modular developments post-14', in FEU *Discussing Credit*, FEU Occasional Paper, London: FEU.

WITTGENSTEIN, L. (1967) *Remarks on the Foundations of Mathematics*, Oxford: Basil Blackwell.

WOLF, A. (1992) *An Assessment-Driven System: Education and Training in England and Wales*, ICRA Working Paper 3, London: Institute of Education, University of London.

WOOD, D. (1993) *The Classroom of 2015*, National Commission Briefing Paper No: 20.

YOUNG, M. (1971) (ed.) *Knowledge and Control: New Directions for the Sociology of Education*, London: Collier Macmillan.

YOUNG, M. (1972) 'On the politics of educational knowledge', *Economy and Society*, 1.

YOUNG, M. (1973) 'Taking sides against the probable; Problems of relativism and commitment in teaching and the sociology of knowledge', *Educational Review*, 25.

YOUNG, M. (1976) 'The schooling of science', in WHITTY, G. and YOUNG, M. (eds.) *Explorations in the Politics of School Knowledge*, Driffield: Nafferton Books.

YOUNG, M. (1986) 'A proposito de uma sociologia critica de educacao', *Rev Bras. de Estus. Pedagogicos*, 67, 157.

YOUNG, M. (1987) 'Education', in WORSLEY, P. (ed.) *The New Introducing Sociology*, Harmondsworth: Penguin.

YOUNG, M. (1990) 'Bridging the theory/practice divide: An old problem in a new context', *Educational and Child Psychology*, **7**, 3.

YOUNG, M. (1991) *The Post-16 Core: Issues and Possibilities*, Centre Report 6, Post-16 Education Centre, London: Institute of Education, University of London.

YOUNG, M. (1993a) 'A curriculum for the 21st century: Towards a new basis for overcoming academic/vocational divisions', *British Journal of Educational Studies*, **41**, 3.

YOUNG, M. (1993b) *Recording and Recognising Achievement in a Unified System*, Working Paper 13, Post-16 Education Centre, London: Institute of Education, University of London.

YOUNG, M. (1993c) 'Bridging the academic/vocational divide: Two Nordic case studies', *European Journal of Education*, **28**, 2.

YOUNG, M. (1994) 'Modularisation and the outcomes approach: Towards a strategy for a curriculum of the future', in BURKE, J. (ed.) *Outcomes and the Curriculum*, London: Falmer Press.

YOUNG, M. (1995) 'Post-compulsory education for a learning society', *Australian and New Zealand Journal for Vocational Education Research*, **3**, 1.

YOUNG, M. and BARNETT, M. (1992) *The Technological Baccalaureate; Interim Evaluation Report of the Pilot Project*, Post-16 Education Centre, London: Institute of Education, University of London.

YOUNG, M. and GUILE, D. (1994) *Work-based Learning and the Teacher/Trainer of the Future*, Report of a National Development Project, Post 16 Education Centre, London: Institute of Education, University of London.

YOUNG, M. and GUILE, D. (1996) Knowledge and learning in specialist and non-specialist learning organisations, Paper presented to the ECLOS (European Conference of Learning Organisations) held in Copenhagen, May.

YOUNG, M., HAYTON, A., HODGSON, A. and MORRIS, A. (1994) 'An interim approach to unifying the post-16 curriculum' in TOMLINSON, S. (ed.) *Educational Reform and its Consequences*, Rivers Oram Press.

YOUNG, M., HAYTON, A. and LENEY, T. (1997) *Key Skills and the ASDAN Award Scheme*, Post-16 Education Centre, London: Institute of Education, University of London, London.

YOUNG, M. and LENEY, T. (1995) *A-Levels and the Post Compulsory Curriculum: Past, Present and Future*, Working Paper 2, Post-16 Education Centre, London and Warwick University of London and the Centre for Education and Industry, University of Warwick.

YOUNG, M., LENEY, T. and HODGSON, A. (1995) *Unifying the Post-compulsory Curriculum: Lessons from France and Scotland*, Post-16 Education Centre, London: University of London.

YOUNG, M. and McDONALD, J. (1997) *CILNTEC/SRB GNVQ Innovation and Development Project: Evaluation Report*, Post-16 Education Centre, London: Institute of Education, University of London, London.

YOUNG, M. and SPOURS, K. (1992) *A Curriculum of the Future*, Post-16 Education Centre, Discussion Paper.

YOUNG, M. and SPOURS, K. (1995) *Post-compulsory Curriculum and Qualifications: Options for Change*, Learning for the Future Working Paper 6, Post-16 Education Centre, London and Warwick: University of London and the Centre for Education and Industry, University of Warwick.

Young, M. and Watson, J. (1992) *Beyond the White Paper: The Case for a Unified System at 16+*, Post-16 Education Centre, Centre Report No 8, London: Institute of Education, University of London.

Young, M. and Whitty, G. (1977) *Society, State and Schooling*, Lewes: Falmer Press.

Young, M. with Arnman, G. and Kutshka, G. (1995) *Evaluation Report on the Experiments in Upper Secondary Education in Finland*, Helsinki: Ministry of Education.

Young, M. et al. (1994) 'An interim approach to unifying the post-16 curriculum', in Tomlinson, S. (ed.) *Educational Reform and its Consequences*, IPPR/Rivers Oram Press.

Zuboff, S. (1988) *In the Age of the Smart Machine*, London: Heinemann.

Chronology of Original Papers

All the chapters in this book are based on papers originally written for conferences or previously published. The sources are listed below for readers who may be interested.

1. Chapter 1 is based on a paper presented to the Annual Conference of the British Sociological Association held in 1970. It was later published as *An approach to the curriculum as socially organised knowledge* as Chapter 1 of Young (1971).

2. Chapter 2 is based on my Doris Lee memorial lecture *Curriculum Change; Limits and Possibilities* which was published in *The Curriculum, Studies in Education*, Institute of Education 1975.

3. Chapter 3 is based on an invited address to the 1988 Annual Conference of American Educational Research Association, held in New Orleans. It was published as an Occasional Paper by the Post 16 Education Centre, Institute of Education, University of London with the title *Curriculum and Democracy* and later translated into Portuguese, French, Spanish and Finnish, in Brazil, Canada, Spain and Finland.

4. Chapter 4 is based on a paper co-authored with Ken Spours. It was originally written for Clio, the London History Teachers' journal and was later published in the British Journal of Education and Work, 1988, Vol 2, No. 2 as *Beyond vocationalism: A new approach to linking education and work.*

5. Chapter 5 is based on a paper presented to an international seminar at the University of Jyvaskyla, Finland and later published with the title *Towards a curriculum of the 21st century; A new basis for overcoming academic/vocational divisions* in the British Journal of Educational Studies, Vol 41, No. 3.

6. Chapter 6 is based on a paper given to a seminar organized by NCVQ and later published in *Outcomes and the Curriculum* edited by John Burke (Burke, J. 1994).

7. Chapter 7 is based on a paper *The future basis for 14–19 entitlement?* written for a book titled *Added Value: Schools' Responsibility for Pupils' Personal Development*, edited by Sally Inman and Martin Buck (Trentham Books 1995).

8. Chapter 8 is based on a paper titled *The Dearing Review of 16–19 qualifications* and originally written for the book *Dearing and Beyond* (Hodgson and Spours 1997).

9. Chapter 9 is based on a paper written with Tom Leney and titled *A-levels and an advanced level curriculum of the future* and originally written for the book *Dearing and Beyond* (Hodgson and Spours).

10. Chapter 10 is based on a paper titled *Post compulsory education for a learning society* which was originally published in the Australian and New Zealand Journal of Vocational Education Research, Vol 3, No. 1 1995.

11. Chapter 11 is based on a paper *Globalisation and teacher education: Lessons from the English experience.* It was originally presented to an international conference in Santiago, Chile, where it was published in Spanish. In its earlier form the paper appeared as Rethinking Teacher Education for a global future: lessons from the English Experience — in the Journal of Education for Teaching, Vol 24, No. 1 1998.

12. Chapter 12 is based on a paper titled *Towards a critical sociology of education* that was written for *Education and Sociology* (ed.) David Levinson, Alan Sadvovnik and Peter Cookson (Taylor and Francis 1997).

Index